PELICAN BOOKS

A230

RED BRICK UNIVERSITY

BRUCE TRUSCOT

BRUCE TRUSCOT

RED BRICK
UNIVERSITY

PENGUIN BOOKS

HARMONDSWORTH · MIDDLESEX

THE FIRST PART OF THIS BOOK WAS PUBLISHED
IN 1943; THE SECOND PART IN 1945;
THE WHOLE PUBLISHED IN
PELICAN BOOKS 1951

MADE AND PRINTED IN GREAT BRITAIN
FOR PENGUIN BOOKS LTD
BY C. NICHOLLS AND COMPANY LTD

CONTENTS

PART I: RED BRICK UNIVERSITY

Chapter One

I. *The standpoint of the student:* At Oxbridge the student has social advantages, amenities and the advantages of both a high and a low standard in work. At Redbrick he has longer terms, is better looked after and has fewer expenses.

II. *The standpoint of the teacher:* At Oxbridge the teacher is slightly better paid, has far greater opportunities and deals with a superior type of student. At Redbrick his students are more interested in their work and more industrious; and in addition he can do the work of a pioneer.

III. *The rise of the modern university.* At first it took most of the products of secondary schools; then Oxbridge began to drain these of their best pupils. The present position: Redbrick is looked upon as a poor second-best.

IV. *The ideal of the future: decentralization.* How to attain it: (i) Larger Treasury grants for the modern universities: with these they could (*a*) increase their residential facilities; (*b*) found more open scholarships and thus attract better pupils; (*c*) develop individual Schools. (ii) A modification in the attitude of secondary and public schools towards sending their pupils to universities. (iii) Interchanges of students and staff between universities.

Chapter Two

I. *What is a University?* A corporation or society which devotes itself to a search after knowledge for the sake of its intrinsic value.

II. *Both in ancient and in modern universities this idea is in danger of being lost.* The undergraduate's view of a university – before and after his experience of it.

III. *But particularly it is in danger at the modern university:* (i) Economic pressure severer; (ii) Superficial resemblance between university and school; (iii) Influence of the city.

Chapter Three

Chapter Four

Chapter Five

Chapter Six

Chapter Seven

PART II: REDBRICK AND THE FUTURE

Chapter One

Chapter Two

Chapter Three

Chapter Four

Chapter Five

WORKS REFERRED TO IN THE TEXT
BY ABBREVIATIONS ONLY

A.U.T. – Association of University Teachers: *Report on Salaries and Grading* (May 1938).

A.U.T., April 1943. – Association of University Teachers: *Report on University Developments*. Draft dated April 1943.[1]

A.U.T., May 1944. – 'Report on University Developments, 1944. Adopted by the Council of the Association of University Teachers on 16th December 1943.' In *The Universities Review*, May 1944, pp. 52–65.

A.U.T. (Research). – Association of University Teachers: *Report on University Developments*. Reports from the Science and Arts Sub-Committee on Research. Draft, undated and unpaged.[1]

B.A.C. – British Association for the Advancement of Science: *Report of Committee on post-war University Education*. London, 1944.

Communication. – The Journal of the Association of University Professors and Lecturers of the Allied Countries in Great Britain.

Dobrée. – Bonamy Dobrée: *The Universities and regional life*. Newcastle-upon-Tyne, 1943.

Flexner – Abraham Flexner: *Universities: American, English, German* (Oxford, 1930).

Herklots – H. G. G. Herklots: *The New Universities* (London, 1928).

L.M.U. – *The Life of a Modern University*. Edited by Hugh Martin (London, 1930).

Newman – John Henry, Cardinal Newman: *The Idea of a University* (London, 1927).

N.U.S. 1937. – *Graduate Employment*. A Report of the 1937 Congress of the National Union of Students, etc.

N.U.S. 1939. – National Union of Students of the Universities and University Colleges of England and Wales: *Report of the Annual Congress*, 1939.

N.U.S. 1940. – *Students in Congress* (Report of the Annual Congress, 1940).

1. These draft reports have been circulated to members of the Association and I am allowed to quote from them by courtesy of the Council, but it should be made clear that, though the Council has approved them in principle, they are subject to re-arrangement and verbal alteration: nothing said in the text of this book should be taken as implying the contrary. – B.T.

N.U.S. 1941. – *Students Face the Future* (Report of the Annual Congress, 1941).

Simon. – Sir Ernest (*now* Lord) Simon: *The Development of British Universities*. London, undated (1944).

T.E.S. – *The Times Educational Supplement*.

U.G.C. 1930. – University Grants Committee: *Report including Returns from the Universities and University Colleges in receipt of Treasury Grant, 1928–9* (London, 1930).

U.G.C. 1936. – University Grants Committee: *Report for the Period 1929–30 to 1934–5, etc.* (London, 1936).

PREFACE

Red Brick University first appeared, in the summer of 1943, at a time when the future of the modern universities was being widely discussed all over the country, and was followed in 1945 by *Redbrick and these Vital Days*, which was less concerned with general principles than with particular problems. The present volume contains the whole of the first book, together with those chapters of the second which the author judges to be most closely connected with it and of permanent interest. These latter chapters will be found under the heading 'Redbrick and the Future'.

Red Brick University was published under a pseudonym, and had no preface. That was not because there was no room for one, or no need for one, but because of the author's desire to sink his own personality and focus attention on his theme.

The policy, however, was not entirely successful. Most Redbrick readers were less moved by the book to a healthy introspection than to excited speculation on the identity of the author. Frenzied fingerings of *Who's Who* and the *Oxbridge University Calendar* failed to reveal any mention of Bruce Truscot – which was not entirely surprising, as that gentleman had carefully examined the same volumes a few months earlier in order to ascertain that he did not exist. Then began a search through the book itself for what is known in academic groves as internal evidence – again with no great success, as the author had also anticipated these activities and had taken some little trouble to cover his tracks. The book appeared to establish, for example, that Truscot's particular Oxbridge was situated on the Cam – but actually the passages in it about both the Oxford and the Cambridge of to-day had been either supplied or approved by members of those universities still in residence. It seemed, again, to suggest that the author was a graduate in Modern History: what he certainly could not be, wrote one appreciative reviewer, was a graduate in English Literature, since a remark made on that subject was at least thirty years out of date. Which conclusion was among the few that extracted a reply from the author, who had, in fact, taken First Class Honours in English some forty years before.

Further investigations were even wider of the mark. Poor Truscot was unmasked as 'True Scot' – an alumnus not only of Oxbridge but previously of Glasburgh, who, balked of a career in his *alma stepmater* (one distinguished critic quite mistakenly described his first chapter as 'bitter'), spent a few disillusioned years in a Redbrick not a hundred miles from Redditch, and then returned to the land of his birth in order to vent his hypothetical spleen upon a system of which he had been the victim. Another story was that Truscot had emigrated, shortly before the War, to one of the Dominions; a third, that he was writing from a well-earned retirement. The general impression was certainly that he had, either temporarily or permanently, taken leave of the scenes of which he wrote, and was discoursing reminiscently – perhaps, as one benevolent reviewer surmised, of conditions that in some respects had passed away. Another general impression seemed to be that he was a crusted bachelor: apparently his *saeva indignatio* might have been tempered had a woman's gentle hand been applied to his fevered brow – though one of his acquaintances, from whom the invisible cap that he habitually wears concealed his identity, went so far as to assert, with some confidence, not to say emphasis, that he was in fact a woman.

All but one of these guesses were completely incorrect – and I must say, considering that most of them have been made by people skilled in handling literary evidence, that they have considerably shaken my faith in the reliability of present-day criticism. The author of *Red Brick University* is wholly in the busy world, not quite beyond it. He speaks of what he knows; and the eminent professor who wrote to him expressing a fear that he might 'bob up at his elbow at some Faculty or Senate meeting' had ample cause for alarm. Though shortly afterwards Truscot did have the grace to feel slightly ashamed when he heard that his correspondent had himself been credited with the authorship in question.

And now let the somewhat oppressive third person be discarded in a brief apology for the pseudonymity of the book and an attempt to justify it. Though the critics of *Red Brick University* failed to discover much about its author, some of them very effectively penetrated to the most serious purpose which lay beneath its calm and sometimes even flippant surface. And they at least will understand why it could only have been published under a pseudonym.

In the first place, being not unknown as a writer already, I knew that, if my criticisms were read as coming from me, many readers would give them an added weight which I did not covet for them, while others would discount them in a way no more to my liking. I wanted my view of the modern university, whatever it might be worth, to be considered solely on its merits.

Secondly, I was anxious to put across a body of views with which I need not necessarily be associated professionally. The commonest remark I have heard about *Red Brick University*, even from those who have spoken most kindly about it, has been: 'Of course, I don't agree with all of it, by a long way.' To which remark I have invariably replied: 'No, neither do I.' And with perfect truth. I wrote throughout with a deep sense of responsibility, and I advanced no view which did not seem to me worthy of serious consideration. But among them were some which I put into Truscot's head solely because I thought they badly needed discussion, and, in order to provoke that discussion, I incited him to enunciate them in a challenging and provocative form. Had I written over my own name, I should have had, in fairness to myself, to state both sides of the case; and this, instead of startling the already over-complacent Redbrickian into serious thought, and perhaps even into some form of action, would merely have lulled him into a more deplorable complacency than before.

Thirdly, I had to consider my colleagues. If I was to say anything of value, I must speak out. The very heart and root of my criticisms is the deep conviction that in certain respects the modern universities are not pulling their weight, and that the responsibility for this lies at more doors than anyone has yet realized. The Treasury has starved Redbrick of money, making its grants so minute that it cannot do a tithe of the things of which it is capable. The schools have starved it of talent, sending all their brilliant pupils to Oxbridge and encouraging even the average ones to go there if they can. Professors and lecturers, though admittedly underpaid, have been content to spend only a modicum of time on research and to regard themselves as fulfilling their duty by doing a bare eight or ten hours a week of teaching. Laymen with little understanding of academic problems have done untold harm by their activities on university Councils. Undergraduates have pursued a narrow course of study, thought too little of the world beyond Redbrick's unlovely quadrangles, and rejected all kinds of opportunities of widening their vision. And these are only a few items of the diagnosis. Fortunately the book was published at an auspicious moment: its criticisms were the first slow drops of what has already become a heavy shower and is likely before long to develop into a thoroughly wet day. The worst offenders, of course, have put up large-sized umbrellas and run no danger at all of getting their clothes wet – I mean, for example, the most unenlightened members of Council, the most snobbish schools, the professors who have never done a stroke of original work since their appointment and never will. But there are signs that others are at least feeling the wind, if not the rain, and my hope, when I first sat down to write, was that they would feel it a good deal more.

Therefore I felt it essential to be able to refer, in support and illustration of my various theses, to situations, to institutions, and to individuals, and this in language which should be direct and incisive, without, I hoped, being offensive. For practically all such references as are made here I can personally vouch; only now and then is a trivial detail altered to avoid causing unmerited distress or emphasizing the personal aspect of some allusion. Once my own identity was known, the identity of those of whom I had written would immediately have been recognized; and not only so, but a good many identities would have been discovered which I had never put there. No good that I could see would be done, and considerable resentment might well be caused, if my colleagues went hunting for each other in the more trenchant of my pages. It seemed a much more healthy and harmless pursuit that they should go hunting for me.

The somewhat considerable precautions which I took to preserve my anonymity were planned in a none too hopeful spirit. Having myself indulged, among other things, in historical investigation and literary criticism, I believed that those of my acquaintances with like experience would unmask my identity with comparative ease. The solution seems so simple – when you know it. After all, I have been in the thick of things for a generation and on almost every page of the book there must be remarks I have made, illustrations I have used, anecdotes I have related, in conferences, at Senate meetings, and in casual or convivial conversation. Only one or two of these needed to be recalled and the secret would be out; and once it was out in one University it would spread. My great hope was that the existence of a real Bruce Truscot would be taken for granted and at each of the modern universities it would be assumed that he came from one of the others.

That hope had no substance, but the thing which I had not dared to envisage came off with a success that I should have considered impossible. The book was published at a time of the year when professors and lecturers have just settled down to a three-months' vacation during which they can meditate to their hearts' content on their sad lack of leisure. In my own mind I gave the secret a life of three months exactly. On the first day in October when I walked into the University refectory, some facetious colleague at the High Table would greet me with a 'Hullo, Truscot, how are you?'

Parenthetically, I may say here that if he had I should have asked him what in the world he meant, and I should have no hesitation whatever, if asked point-blank whether or no I was the author of *Red Brick University,* in answering 'No'. I hold that, while it is a social and a moral duty to give a true answer to any question which may properly be put to one, there is no kind of obligation either to answer, or to answer truly, a question which no-one has the right to ask. The author of *Red Brick University* is a personality created by me and given the name of Bruce Truscot, and he is no-one else. Let us assume that my legal name is Robert England. In writing my second book I referred from time to time to its predecessor to see if the two were consistent. But I did not consult Robert England's opinions for the same purpose: in fact, as I have said, Robert England does not share all the opinions of Bruce Truscot, nor does he always approve of his provocative manner or of his unacademic picturesqueness. Some years ago, our popular seaside resorts used to be visited on Saturdays in the season by a gentleman rejoicing in the pseudonym of Bobby Bud, an emissary of the *Daily Tale,* which published his photograph beforehand and was prepared to pay out a substantial sum of money to the first person who recognized him and challenged him correctly. To win the money, however, you had to use an exact form of words, such as: 'You are Mr Bobby Bud and I claim the *Daily Tale's* prize.' If you so much as omitted the Mr, I understand, the individual would ask you what you meant by it, since he was merely John Jones, who was looking for Bobby Bud himself. A similar experience would have been the lot of anyone who had inquired of me after the health of Bruce Truscot. The freedom of the individual must include freedom to evacuate his personality and to assume another if he so wishes, provided the purpose is legally and morally unexceptionable.

However, I need not have troubled. None of my colleagues even once challenged me. Rather, they invited me, as a knowledgeable person who sits on various inter-university committees, to swell the pool of guesses as to Truscot's identity with a few of my own. I did my best – and at least it was as good a best as anyone else's: once or twice I even ventured suggestions which were distinctly warm. There was one curious fact which I noticed in going from one

University to another: a psychologist, perhaps, could explain it. At no University was it ever considered possible that the author could come from there. At Bristol the Common Room debated if he was from Leeds or Liverpool. At Leeds they gave perfectly good reasons why he must come from Birmingham. At Sheffield or Manchester some allusion had been found which made it clear that he was writing of conditions at Bristol. It was not simply that Truscot had carefully gathered his material from all sources instead of confining himself to one or two. There was a kind of wishful belief that the place where lectures are so uninspiring, where the lay element in the Council is so reactionary and where in twenty-two weeks of vacation a professor produces a single article and three-twentieths of a book must be somewhere other than here.

It seems likely, then, that Truscot will remain Truscot until the whole of his work is done. So let the last word in this preface be, not his, but mine. During the closing months of the War I had a long letter from a young officer in Burma who had been one of my 'students' (as we call undergraduates at Redbrick) a few years previously. He had just been reading a book which had made him feel quite homesick, so vividly did it recall the old days at the University. 'I should like you to read it too,' he went on. 'I expect you can get hold of it somewhere. But I ought to warn you that it draws a very unflattering picture of a professor, and I shouldn't like you to think that was why I wanted you to read it. Don't worry: none of your old students would ever think that the author was drawing *you*.'

Which is certainly the most curious, probably the most un-expected and perhaps the most charming compliment I have ever received.

PART ONE

Red Brick University

INTRODUCTION

ON the banks of two picturesque but undistinguished streams, the Isis and the Cam, stand the two universities of Old England.

While in so diminutive a country as ours no single town or village can be said to know the meaning of isolation, Oxford and Cambridge, even geographically, enjoy a measure of genteel aloofness. Their situation, in fact, by contrast with the situations of such other places of learning as (in Dickens' phrase) 'there may happen to be', is an ideal one. Like all really well-bred institutions, they are within easy reach of London, yet they lie just far enough from the main railway lines running west and north from the capital to enjoy a certain degree of inaccessibility. A still more fortunate circumstance is that, although as the plane flies they are little more than sixty miles apart, the rail journey from the one to the other normally involves a slow train to the junction of Bletchley, a change, a wait, and another train which seems even slower – a matter of from three to four hours in all. This providential disposition has not merely made it more difficult for the one university to meddle in the affairs of the other but has contributed to that sense of detachment, both from its ancient English rival and from all the remaining universities in the world, which each would recognize as an important element in its tradition.

Neither university, presumably, would choose to be located where it is if without loss of amenities and prestige it could miraculously transport itself elsewhere. The country around Cambridge is flat and bare and all but the very young find the east winds which sweep through it anything

but pleasant. The surroundings of Oxford are more attractive – in places they might even be called beautiful – but the
city itself is low-lying, damp, relaxing, and unhealthy. It is
the medieval courts and quadrangles, the storied windows,
the congenial, cultured society that attract, at the one extreme, the untravelled schoolboy about to be transformed
into an undergraduate, and, at the other, the venerable
scholar from without the pale seeking a sheltered haven for
his retirement. And, apart from these, there is something,
it appears, in the academic atmosphere of an ancient university which makes up for any defects in climate. Or so we
should gather from the pages of *Oxford*, the organ of a
society of alumni founded in 1932 to effect, in somewhat
American fashion, a realization of potential assets the existence of which was for long politely ignored.

There is no 'Cambridge Society' – no doubt Cambridge
wishes there were, but unfortunately Oxford had the idea
first and to create one now would be to copy Oxford! And
that reflection brings us within measurable distance of com-
paring the two. The temptation to do this in any detail must
be firmly thrust aside. Just as, when discussing Oxford
politics at the High Table of an Oxford college hall, one has
a feeling that Cambridge exists only in legend, which persists until, ensconced in the arm-chair of a Cambridge don,
one realizes that only now has the escape been made from
myth to reality, so, in the more bracing if dust-laden air of
the modern university, both Oxford and Cambridge seem
to belong to a medieval past. Let it suffice to inform any
foreigners who may read these lines that Oxford, dating
from the late twelfth century, must always be mentioned
before Cambridge, which resignedly accepts an origin in
the early thirteenth, and that each of the two has not only
its distinctive architectural glories and academic treasures
but also its highly individual conceptions, traditions and
methods of education. These last an outsider may find it
hard to detect and impossible to define; and it is true that,
of recent years, with increased and still increasing inter-
migration, with the invasion of State influence by way of the

Treasury Grant and with the introduction of new subjects of instruction, they have been growing much more blurred. Nevertheless, to Oxford and Cambridge men they are still very real, and the use in this book, to indicate either or both of the two universities in respects in which they are similar, of the barbarous but convenient term 'Oxbridge' must not be taken as an attempt to minimize their importance. The author himself, educated at one of the two and a frequent visitor to the other, has, during a somewhat long professional life at a number of other universities, consciously aimed at inculcating certain of the main ideals of education formed in his youth and to this day would strenuously maintain that those of 'the other place' (referred to in public more court-eously as 'the sister university') are notably inferior to them.

Until the beginning of the nineteenth century, Oxford and Cambridge were the only two universities in England, and university education was a prerogative of the more or less well-to-do and a discreetly respected preserve of the Church of England. It was a decade or so after the Battle of Waterloo had been won on the playing-fields of Eton that the principle of the Modern University materialized in the most natural and appropriate place – the capital city of the British Empire. The foundation, in 1828-9, first of University College and then of King's College, led to the creation, in 1836, of the University of London, in which were subsequently in-corporated over sixty more colleges, institutes, hospitals and schools. So unique has the University of London become, and so essentially its own are the problems which it has to solve, that in this book very little specific mention will be made of it. These problems are due partly to the numbers of its internal students, which considerably exceed those of Oxford and Cambridge combined; partly to its location in a city of seven millions, to the nature of its constituent insti-tutions, to the difficulty of communication between them and to the character of their relations with the central body; and partly – perhaps principally – to the admission, long ago, into the University of the 'external' system, which

has brought a university degree within the reach of thousands to whom it would otherwise have been inaccessible but
has also involved the University in periodical opprobrium.

'I confess myself,' remarks that benevolent though
astringent American critic of our universities, Professor
Abraham Flexner, 'unable to understand in what sense the
University of London is a university at all.'[1] The confession,
which one gathers did not necessitate any great searching
of heart, is quite understandable. On the one hand, while
his book was in the making, he had resided as an honoured
guest in Oxford, and had thus been 'enabled to feel something of Oxford's charm'[2] – as well, no doubt, as of her
prejudices; on the other, he was a native of a country in
which, through overinclusiveness, university education has
to a great extent become degraded. So, while granting that
it 'avoids the excesses and absurdities of Columbia and
Chicago',[3] which elsewhere in his book he castigates with
enormous gusto, he sees, in the incorporation in it of such
an institution as the King's College of Household and Social
Science, something remarkably like the thin end of a wedge.
'Could anything,' he inquires, 'be more absurd? ... What
does such a school gain by being a School of the University?
And what does "University" mean when such a school is
included?'[4]

Reasonable Englishmen, unacquainted with the puerili-
ties of American university 'home study' courses, might
find no difficulty in answering this question and feel complete confidence that the soundness of the English educational tradition would save its universities from overinclusiveness, or at least from the worst excesses of that vice.
There is a greater disposition in this country to criticize
London's practice of granting external degrees, which have
won a popularity that can never originally have been contemplated, and which is the more surprising when we
remember that there are now not four universities in England and Wales as there were when the external system was

1. Flexner, p. 231.   3. Op. cit., p. 231.
2. Op. cit., p. vii.   4. Op. cit., p. 232 n.

introduced, but twelve. To those who believe that the letters 'B.A.' ought invariably to denote something more than the passing of examinations, and indeed something wider and deeper than purely academic proficiency at all, there is no more that can usefully be said. To others, however, who hold as firmly as they that residence or close association with fellow-students is a valuable part of university education but who also feel that a person should not be refused the other part because through no fault of his own he is debarred from attaining the whole, the question is a more open one. They think it suitable, desirable, and even symbolic, that a practical expression of the belief that education is the right of all who can profit by it should come, not from some commercial institution constituting itself an examining body, but from the great university of the capital of the British Empire. They recognize the excellence of the work done by that University's external system in enabling 'internal' graduates of other universities to continue their studies though compelled to earn their living under conditions in which no other form of university study is open to them. They appreciate that the creation, as it were, of little cells of learning all over the country may become as conducive to the growth of educational ideals as the concentration of learning in a few large centres. They realize that the conferring of external research degrees, an important feature of London University's extra-mural activities, promotes original investigation as well as the acquisition of knowledge. And all this is only the beginning of an argument the full presentation of which would demand a separate volume.

Though little will be said, then, of the University of London, it should be understood that the author is among the most ardent of its apologists and would be proud if he could claim it for his Alma Mater. 'Mother of orphans', 'mother of them that have no "advantages"', it has 'provided a way of escape for thousands of imprisoned souls'[1] – what finer testimony, from one of such souls, could any university desire?

1. L. P. Jacks, *The Confession of an Octogenarian*, London, 1942, p. 64.

In 1832, three years after the foundation of the first London colleges, the North of England gave birth to the first of its Universities, Durham. The connection of that University with the Church of England has given it, in the popular mind, a place apart, such as King's College, London, also an Anglican foundation, might have had but for its incorporation in a larger and an undenominational body. Its adoption, in a modern form, of the collegiate system (Durham has eight colleges) and the association of two of its Chairs with canonries in Durham Cathedral enhance its prestige still further. Among cultured people in general, then, the University of Durham is vaguely felt to be more respectable than any other English university save Oxford and Cambridge, and its seniority of about half a century over the 'modern universities' has given it a prestige in no way diminished by its later incorporation of the College of Medicine and Armstrong College (since renamed King's College), Newcastle-on-Tyne. At the same time, it is not Oxford, and it is not Cambridge, though it enrols numerous undergraduates who, even in the old exclusive days, might quite well have gone to either. Only its Newcastle college, perhaps, can properly find a place in this survey.

Once North and South had their universities, the existence of neither of which sensibly diminished the completeness of the monopoly held by Oxford and Cambridge, the craze for further centres of higher education seemed for a time to have subsided. The next step forward was the foundation of colleges for women: Bedford College, London (1849)[1]; Girton (1869) and Newnham (1871) at Cambridge; and at Oxford; Lady Margaret Hall (1879), Somerville (1879), St Hugh's (1886), and St Hilda's (1893). Only with the widespread development of secondary education and the rapid growth of the great cities, particularly in the North of England, did university expansion enter upon a

1. The University of London, however, did not allow women to take its degrees on the same footing as men until 1878.

new chapter, and this must be considered as having begun
in the 'seventies and 'eighties, when almost every one of the
colleges which developed into the universities to be dealt
with in these pages had its modest rise.

The oldest of the group was Owens College, Manchester,
founded in 1851. Then, with a rush, after more than twenty
years, came Yorkshire College, Leeds (1874), University
College, Bristol (1876), Mason College, Birmingham (1880),
University College, Liverpool (1881), University College,
Reading (1892), and University College, Sheffield (1897).
The seniority of Manchester was recognized in 1880 by the
incorporation of Owens College in the Victoria University,
to which were affiliated first the Liverpool college and then
the college at Leeds. In 1903-4 these three were separated
and became respectively the Universities of Manchester,
Liverpool, and Leeds. Meanwhile, in 1900, Mason College
had been transformed into the University of Birmingham;
Sheffield obtained its Royal Charter in 1905; and Bristol in
1909. The University of Reading was founded much later,
in 1926, and Nottingham University in 1948. Parallel developments had been taking place in Wales, where the three
colleges of Aberystwyth, Cardiff and Bangor, established in
that order, were merged, in 1893, into the federal University
of Wales, to which was added University College, Swansea,
in 1920. Finally there are four English University Colleges,
situated at Southampton, Exeter, Hull and Leicester, which
provide teaching to degree standard but grant no degrees,
presenting their students for the very convenient external
examinations of the University of London. A fifth University College, of a somewhat different type, opened its
doors in 1950 at Stoke-on-Trent.

It is primarily with eight of the twelve English universities
that this book is concerned: Birmingham, Bristol, Leeds,
Liverpool, Manchester, Nottingham, Reading and Sheffield.
With the exception of Reading, a small university,
very largely residential, they are all very much of the same
type — a type which, if it can be modified in ways shortly

to be suggested, will probably dominate English university education in centuries to come. Their foundation is due to local effort; their endowments come largely from local pockets; they are aided by grants from local municipal authorities; and their students, though to a slowly decreasing extent, are drawn from local areas. It is impossible to speak too warmly of the men chiefly instrumental in their foundation – members, for the most part, of wealthy and influential families, engaged in business, and often themselves graduates of Oxford and Cambridge, who could so easily have satisfied any zeal they might have felt for education by endowing scholarships to one of those universities to be competed for solely by students of their own city or area. Had they been content to do this, not only would students in perpetuity have benefited from their generosity, but the names of the donors would have been assured of a perpetual place on the roll of benefactors of their college or university. But their generosity and (a more significant thing) their insight, initiative and faith went far beyond this. They foresaw that, as the tide of prosperity in the country continued to rise, educational ideals and standards would rise with it and the four universities already in existence would soon be no longer sufficient for the national needs. They believed that a university established with noble, worthy and disinterested aims in the twentieth century would in time do as much for education as one that dated from the twelfth. They foresaw, again, that such a foundation could from the very first exercise a powerful moral and cultural influence upon the life of a large and rapidly growing community which was necessarily to a great extent preoccupied with material values. And foreseeing and believing these things, they were prepared to throw into the task of making a new foundation, not only their money, but their interest, their influence and their personal service, risking failure, and the contumely which would follow upon failure, in the strength of the faith which they had in their ideal and in the generations which, after they themselves had passed away, would work for its fuller realization. It is difficult to measure the immense indebtedness to these founders of a posterity which is even now beginning to justify them.

At the same time, it must be confessed that superficially (and to some extent, as we shall see, in more important respects as well) these new universities were not prepossessing. Those who came to them from Oxford and Cambridge thought them at first positively sepulchral in their gloom. To begin with, since undergraduates, living at home, would stream daily into the busy city from all four points of the compass, the buildings had either to be dingily central or, for a large proportion of their staff and students, inconveniently remote. As a university requires numerous buildings, costly equipment and large-scale endowments, and as, even in the prosperous Victorian era, financial resources were not inexhaustible, it was impracticable to purchase expensive city sites and pull down large areas of valuable property for building upon. So more than one of our modern universities stands in the midst of the humblest dwellings – not far removed, to put it bluntly, from slums. Nor were the buildings erected during the late Victorian and Edwardian epochs either imaginative or appealing. For the most part the material used in them was a light stone which the coal-dust of the city quickly turned to a dismal and depressing grey, or a hideously cheerful red brick suggestive of something between a super council-school and a holiday home for children. Within, harsh and ugly blue or yellow tiles lined halls and passages which led up interminable staircases to corridor upon corridor out of which opened lecture-rooms, all of precisely similar pattern. Of amenities, in those early days, there were few. Each block of the university buildings was like a glorified technical school, with a common-room perhaps for the staff, but certainly none for the undergraduates. If they wanted to dance they had to clear some lecture-room of tables or desks and foot it featly under the auspices of statues of the ancient gods or in an atmosphere perfumed with sulphuretted hydrogen When some University Council or Senate organized a social event

for any large number of people there was often no single
hall or lecture-room large enough to take more than a
quarter of them at the same time; so the University's guests
would have the choice of sitting down to tea in the physics
laboratory, the gymnasium or the library.

To-day, though the grinning red brick, the dirty grey
stone and the unspeakable blue and yellow tiles still remain,
Treasury grants, a multiplicity of benefactions and an
improvement in our architectural notions have added a
number of really striking and beautiful buildings, surpassed
neither by Oxford or Cambridge nor even by the more
materially prosperous universities of the United States. The
Edgbaston buildings at Birmingham, the new libraries at
Leeds and Liverpool, the hostels most recently erected at
Bristol and Liverpool and the fine blocks at Bristol and
Nottingham are typical examples. And what is true of the
buildings is equally applicable to the personnel. An Oxford
don who half a century ago made the necessary sacrifices
and came as a professor to Mason or Owens College must
have found the circle of his academic acquaintances all too
limited in size (for staffs were small) and in capacity (for
almost from the first these modern foundations have been
overmuch given to inbreeding). Now, with fifteen hundred
or two thousand undergraduates, they can have larger
staffs and go farther afield to look for them. And they do:
the range of interests represented in a Redbrick staff common-room at coffee-time is as extensive as that of a Corpus
or Trinity high table at dinner. Drawbacks and defects, as
will be seen, still remain, but the worst of them, at least
have vanished.

Such is the English university system: two ancient collegi
ate universities, no longer exclusive but still to a very larg
extent metropolitical; two more modern collegiate uni
versities, one northern and one southern, one large and
overgrown, one small and retiring; eight modern universi
ties, mainly non-residential, none as much as fifty years ol
and all founded within a period of just over twenty-five; an

five university colleges, the future histories of which will probably be widely varied. If we concentrate our attention mainly on the eight, some part of what is to be said will no doubt be applicable to the rest, and even to the University of Wales, the four ancient universities of Scotland and the one ancient and two modern foundations in Ireland. None of these, however, is specifically envisaged in these pages save where it is mentioned by name. It should be added that, while a great part of the book is no doubt applicable to many of the varied Faculties of a modern university, it has been written, from beginning to end, exclusively from the point of view of the Arts Faculty of such a university and of the Arts subjects studied at Oxford and Cambridge. Though red brick, rather than dingy grey stone, has been chosen as the symbol of the new foundations, it must be categorically stated that no one university alone has been in the author's mind: he has preferred to draw upon his personal experience of several and upon information or documents, kindly sent him by correspondents, regarding them all.

CHAPTER ONE

The Battle of the Ancients and the Moderns

IT is over twenty years since an able young critic of the British university system, fresh from the presidency of the Cambridge Union and the editorship of the *Granta*, expressed 'a very sincere distress that so great a gulf has been fixed' between the old universities and the new.[1] To bridge that gulf too little has since been done; and one of the most pressing of post-war problems will be to ensure that our modern universities shall have greater opportunities to develop and grow, instead of being half-strangled, as they are to-day, by Oxford and Cambridge.

I

At present, practically every boy or girl leaving school for a university who can possibly do so elects to go to Oxford or Cambridge, and a considerable proportion of university teachers – though a smaller and probably a diminishing one – looks upon appointment to one of those foundations as the giddy height of an academic career. Let us see what grounds there are for that attitude.

If a boy has grown up in a preparatory and a public school, to go on to Oxford or Cambridge seems to him merely a natural stage of evolution. However poor the tuition might be in the subjects necessary for his future profession, not one Etonian or Harrovian in a thousand would consider entering a shabby modern university, unlovely in appearance, unmellowed by tradition and attended by men who actually live with their families and probably have only the faintest idea of the respective significance of a dinner jacket and a white waistcoat. To pass from Eton to Redbrick would be as much a crime against society as to have gone from an expensive preparatory school in Surrey

1. Herklots, p. xii.

or Hampshire to a municipal secondary school in Bradford
or Leeds. As to the boy who has passed through the secondary school from the Council School in the next street to
which stands the council house where he was born, it may
be natural enough for him to go on to Redbrick, but to win
a scholarship and enter Oxbridge is something infinitely
more exciting – a marvellous adventure to occupy the
golden years of adolescence, a leap out of the atmosphere of
the council house, up the coveted social ladder, an opportunity of escaping from his environment which he feels to
be unique, in the literal sense that, if he misses it, it is almost
certain never to present itself again.

At Oxbridge, the university of his dreams, if he can get
there, he will find himself on a plane of something like
equality with young men, not only of a higher average
social class, but of a much greater variety of experience
than any group he could possibly meet at home. There will
be aristocrats – though he may never know them except by
name; men from the greater and the smaller public schools;
men from schools whose headmaster has to exhort them
periodically never to forget that 'you *are* a public school';
men who have achieved education by unusual processes –
through private tutors, for example, or by foreign travel –
and are both deliriously more experienced and yet astonish-
ingly more naïve than the average freshman; colonials and
foreigners – Rhodes scholars, perhaps – who have only
just set foot in England; older men, who have entered the
university after years spent in business. And all these will
not only sit in the same lecture-room as our hypothetical
freshman: they will live with him, entertaining him in their
rooms on a neighbouring staircase, eating with him in
the same dining-hall, attending the same societies, playing
games on the same playing-fields. Instead of going home
every day at tea-time, to listen to Dad on the political situation and Mum on current market prices or the iniquities of
the neighbours, he will be free, from the hour of Hall on-
wards, to live in one of a dozen new worlds, each more
thrilling than the last. At Drabtown, he can never entertain

a friend without admitting him to the family board and the family circle, and subjecting him to the family scrutiny, and, in some measure, to the family discipline. At Oxbridge, if he lives in college, he can entertain whom he pleases, with perfect freedom; and instead of being packed grumblingly off to bed every night at ten or eleven he can invent political utopias or discuss the eternal verities until the small hours of the morning.[1]

All this he knows, not only from books, but from old boys of his school – his contemporaries and immediate seniors, who left school in July, boys like himself, and came back to see the old place in December, heroes. From their own lips he learns of the thrilling people to be met at Oxbridge; of tutors and dons, Masters and Deans; of the undergraduate's room, of which he can sport the oak, so as to work with complete freedom from distractions; of the famous men who come to address meetings or to speak at the Union; of the glories of Christ Church and Magdalen or of King's Chapel and the Backs – of the deeper, wider and fuller education, in short, which may be his own, if he can find the money – i.e., win the scholarships – that will give it him. And with the story told by Jack Smith after his first term at Jesus or Trinity, which loses nothing in the telling, he contrasts what he has seen of the academic life of Bill Jones, who, incapable of winning a State or a County scholarship plus an open Entrance scholarship awarded by an Oxford college, has had to make do with a miserable thirty-pound-a-year City Exhibition which will take him no farther than the university of his native town. Poor Bill Jones! No Hall and Chapel and oak-sporting for him; no invitations to breakfast at the Master's Lodgings; no hilarious

1. It is not implied, of course, that all Redbrick undergraduates come from these particular varieties of Drabtown school and home. Many (especially the women, who are in the main of a better type than the men) are educated at schools as good as any in the country (though seldom at the 'best') and many (again especially the women) have ample facilities at home for undisturbed study and even for privately entertaining their friends. But the average school and home would probably be much nearer to those described in the text than to these.

bump suppers or moonlight strolls in romantic quadrangles;
no all-night sittings with a congenial group round his own
– his very own – fireplace. No: Bill goes off five mornings a
week to Redbrick University exactly as he went to Back
Street Council School and Drabtown Municipal Secondary
School for Boys – and he goes on his bicycle, to save the
twopenny tram-fare. Exactly as at those earlier institutions,
he climbs the similar flights of dirty, sordid stairs (only there
are more of them), sits in a rather larger classroom of the
same type and with the same grimy outlook and answers to
his name called from very much the same kind of register.
His lunch consists, according to the state of his finances, of
a shilling made-up meat-dish, or of a roll and a cup of
coffee, taken hurriedly at the University Union and followed
by the meeting of some society sandwiched between lunch
and afternoon lectures because no society that meets in the
late afternoon can hope for more than the most diminutive
attendance. Between four and five o'clock he goes home to
the same sort of high tea as he has had all his life and then
attempts to settle down to an evening's work, either alone
in an unused sitting-room, in his unheated bedroom or,
more probably, in the living-room, where Lizzie, at the same
table, is wrestling with her algebra, Bertie is continually
appealing to him for help with his French, and at all too
frequent intervals the wireless is turned on for the entertainment or edification of the rest of the family.

Who can blame a boy if, while still at school, he decides
that only at Oxford and Cambridge is there such a thing
as true university education? And, should he succeed in
realizing his dream of 'going up' there, he will soon find his
opinion not only borne out by facts, but confirmed by new
advantages which he had never thought of. He may be
fortunate enough, for example, to be reading a subject in
which his university has made a name for itself and to be
attending lectures by some of its acknowledged authorities.
If he is an attractive or a brilliant youth, he will find favour
with the dons – not myopic and scholarly dreamers, as
novelists mistakenly suppose, but men of the world with

wide experience and numerous social contacts – or establish relations with influential parents of fellow-undergraduates which will be useful to him all his life. Here and there he will discern opportunities for specialized preparation of various kinds which the newer universities have not yet been in a position to establish. If he has come up to work, he will find how much more stimulating it is to compete with intellectual equals whose background and education have been quite different from his own than with the 'chaps' at Redbrick, all of whom come from schools exactly like Drabtown, have used exactly the same text-books and passed exactly the same examinations. If, on the other hand, he has no intention of doing more than the minimum of work, and aims at making his reputation through games, organization or public speaking, he is consoled to discover that, though the standards of the highest classes in Honours at Oxford or Cambridge are as high as, or even higher than, anywhere else, the lowest classes certainly descend to a depth reached nowhere else in the whole country. If he is at Oxford, indeed, he need not even suffer from the disadvantage of the statesman who said he only travelled third class because there was no fourth; for our most ancient University can display the unique phenomenon of a Fourth Class in Honours; and, whereas most modern universities demand for admission to an Honours School a standard equal at least to that of a pass in the Higher Certificate for a subject studied in schools, an undergraduate at Oxford or Cambridge may gaily enter for Honours in such a subject knowing nothing whatever about it, and attend the same lectures as men who have done it at school for five or six years. As the number of failures in any Honours examination is infinitesimal, it may be imagined how far down the scale must come the deadline between pass and failure.

All these, for one type of undergraduate or another, are solid advantages, and the defects are a good deal harder to discover. But they exist, nevertheless.

There is, first of all, the shortness of the terms. If we allow four weeks as the average time taken up by examinations, lectures have to be crowded into something like twenty weeks of the year – and not only lectures, but contact with tutors, special coaching, library work, meetings of societies, organized games and all the other manifold activities of the undergraduate. The result is that for eight weeks on end John Smith of Trinity, anxious to profit to the full by his opportunities, is overworked, overstrained and over-stimulated – after which he goes home for the vacation, with few books in his trunk but his own (it is hard for under-graduates to get out books on loan from Oxbridge libraries), becomes Our Jack of Lower Back Street and spends any-thing from five to eighteen weeks in an atmosphere of Dad's politics, Mum's grievances, the homework of Lizzie and Bertie – and the wireless.

Bill Jones of Redbrick is, by comparison, much more fortunate. He has not to submit to these constant uprootings and transplantings. His ten-week terms, if more humdrum, have also been less hectic than the eight-week terms of the other. When they are over, he can still, if he likes, go to the University all day long and work in the library, or, if his home is not in the university town, he can take out books for the vacation. (Oxbridge undergraduates in whose home town there is a university have been known to attempt to make the best of both worlds by applying for permission to read in the library of that university because of being unable to borrow books from their own.) He may even be fortunate enough to establish vacation contacts with professors or lecturers, some of whom like to spread their work over a longer period by giving their more advanced students less individual time during term and continuing their direction of them during the vacation.

A second, and perhaps the principal, advantage of the modern over the ancient university is the greater care with which the former looks after its alumni. To that rare bird, the brilliant student, gifted with initiative, confidence and resource, this may be no help, but merely an irritation or even a positive disservice, but to perhaps ninety-five per cent it means a great deal. Let us see how the difference works out in practice.

At the older university there is nominally dual control, which means in practice a very uncertain control, generally of the wrong kind. The unit is not the university, but the college. The undergraduate is allotted, with fifty or more others, to an overworked and often jaded tutor, who, however carefully his appointment is made, cannot possibly be a specialist in all the subjects which the majority of his undergraduates are reading. The tutor, whose primary duty is to look after his morals and general welfare – the Oxford women's colleges have what they call 'moral tutors' – will also advise him as to the School in which he should read, and thereafter will supervise his work if he is competent to do so, and, if not, will sublet him to a 'director' or 'supervisor' who is. This will generally be a junior don, from the same or another college, who makes the greater part of his income by picking up such unconsidered trifles as the direction of stray undergraduates, and additional private coaching for such of them as need it. Sometimes the tuition is given individually; sometimes to groups of three or four at a time. Where the tutor or director has the requisite knowledge and skill, the system may produce quite good results; where he has not, and the undergraduate realizes that this is so, it is often possible to effect a change. But the very best of tutors can be only on the perimeter of his pupil's studies; he cannot know them (except through the pupil himself, or from anything that he may have picked up from his predecessors) from the inside.[1]

Outside the circle of these studies, then, is the College official, the tutor or supervisor, almost as detached an

1. Sometimes, though not for a reason that the University need be proud of, he can get a little farther. An Oxbridge undergraduate of my acquaintance went some years ago to a director who was able to discuss in detail with his groups of pupils an important course of lectures in his own subject which they were attending. He had been to the same lectures himself fifteen years earlier, had taken copious notes of them – and the lectures had not changed by so much as a paragraph in the interval!

adviser as the undergraduate's own father might be if he were a scholar in that field, while inside it stand the University officials, the professors and lecturers, the men who plan the course of instruction, who draw up the time-table of lectures, who deliver the lectures, who pursue (or ought to pursue) research in the subjects of them, who have (or ought to have) alert minds untarnished by routine contacts with innumerable pupils, and who are almost wholly responsible for the examinations on the results of which may depend a man's entire career. And with the men of this latter group, for anything the system provides to the contrary, the undergraduate, during his entire course, need have no direct personal contact at all.

Actually he does meet many of them. Some professors have tea-parties for undergraduates whose names they find on a lecture-list or with whose faces they have become familiar in the lecture-room. Some lecturers – though very few – invite questions, encourage discussions or play the additional role of tutors or supervisors. Where there is a voluntary organization connected with the subject, such as a Mathematical, Geographical or Theological Society, the lecturers, and even the professors, may occasionally take part in its activities. But, to sum up the situation in general terms, the undergraduate has the minimum of contact with those whom he most needs to know, and the direction of his work is not, as it surely ought to be, in their hands, but in the hands of men who cannot, in the nature of the case, be expected to feel the same responsibility for it.

Contrast the modern university, with its individual, and to a large extent autonomous, Schools, and its direct contact between the Head of each School and every undergraduate studying in it. The freshman wishing to read, let us say, for Honours in Modern History is referred by the Dean of the Faculty of Arts to the person best able to pronounce on his ability to do so – the Professor of Modern History. If the Professor accepts him, he becomes personally responsible for his guidance and progress. Either he or one of his staff will act as his director, tell him what lectures are best suited for him, recommend books, suggest plans for vacation study, discuss with him results of class examinations, advise him as to a career, send him out with a testimonial based on close, personal knowledge extending over his entire course, and, as likely as not, continue to exercise a decisive influence over him after he has gone down. This does not mean that the professor either has or desires to have as much control over the undergraduate as the schoolmaster has had over the boy. If he is wise, he will treat each as he needs, giving the able and resourceful man his head and providing more substantial help for those deficient in initiative. This is expert education which yields the maximum of fruit; the other is a haphazard system, at its worst little better than self-education by the undergraduate under exceptionally favourable conditions. The only reason why the superiority of the modern system in practice is not manifest is that the older system has the inestimable advantage of being able to work upon the best material. The ancient universities, like the ancient schools, skim the cream of the country's intellect, and then, in the next generation, point to the success of their alumni as proving the efficacy of their methods of education. If it were practicable to take two groups of students, of identical capabilities, and to subject each to one of the systems, the results might possibly work a revolution and there might be fewer multicoloured blazers beautifying the banks of the Isis and the Cam.

It may be contended by some that the control and direction actually exercised in the modern university are often only nominal: that the professor often does no more than send undergraduates to certain lectures, and mark their examination papers once or twice a year. This, no doubt, is so in extreme cases, but the corresponding extremes at Oxbridge are much more notorious. A Cambridge undergraduate of my acquaintance, for example, went through the whole of his university career without having once spoken to a professor. Another had a tutor who discharged his obligations by requiring him, once a week for two years, to translate to him at sight a passage from a volume chosen at random from his bookcase. And what about that famous institution, the Oxford essay, which has to be written, and then read aloud to the tutor, week after week, year after year, even by science students, so that the tutor may extemporize criticisms and suggestions for 'improvements in method or phraseology'?[1] An ordinary mortal would need to read an essay himself, and have ample time to think it over, before venturing such criticisms, but not the tutor from Oxford. Inspiration comes to him without effort – or does it?

A. L. Smith used to tell the story of how he once visited Dr Spooner of New College, and found him in his bedroom shaving with the door open, while an undergraduate mumbled inaudibly in the next room. When the voice ceased, Dr Spooner said, 'That's very bad. You may go away now.' 'Oh, so that's how you correct essays in New College, is it?' said A. L. Smith. 'Yes,' said Dr Spooner, 'that's how we correct essays in New College.'[2]

A fairer criticism of the modern university is that the undergraduate has no 'moral' tutor and gets little or no guidance other than academic. It might be said in reply to this that a student living at home has no need of a tutor standing *in loco parentis*. It is also an important consideration that whatever extra-academic help he does get comes from the Head of his School – for, if such guidance is to have the maximum of efficiency and value, it is essential that it should be given, not by a man to whom the undergraduate has been assigned in a purely arbitrary way, but by one with whom he shares common interests and who has that intimate knowledge of his capabilities and character which frequent contact brings. But the true answer is that any student living in a Hall of Residence in a modern university

1. Cyril Bailey in the *Oxford Handbook,* ed. 1932, p. 128. Several passages in Mr Bailey's essay may be profitably contrasted with the following view of an Oxford undergraduate: 'After two years the weekly essay becomes exceedingly irksome. One could benefit far more from discussion than from writing long expositions in "essay language". But tutors are most unwilling to excuse an essay. Unless you produce something concrete you are not being worked to full capacity!'

2. Christopher Hollis, in *The Tablet,* 6 September 1941.

enjoys all the advantages of the Oxford and Cambridge tutorial system in addition to those of an efficient system of centralized academic direction, and that it seems, as we shall see, as if one of the primary future aims of the modern university will be to have far more of its students, both men and women, in residence.

A third advantage of the modern university which, by its nature, cannot be discussed in detail, is its comparative cheapness. Its fees are small; subscriptions to athletics and to non-academic activities are compounded at a cost of £3 to £4 yearly; the library being more accessible, and therefore more useful, fewer books have to be bought; the non-residential student lives almost wholly at home, with the maximum of economy; and there are no large gratuities to pay and no subscriptions to a multiplicity of societies. Thus, although the boy who goes from Drabtown to Trinity is well provided with scholarships, he often finds life much more of a financial strain (for which reason concentration on his work, and happiness in it, become more difficult) than his former schoolfellow who lives modestly, but well within his means, at Redbrick. Far from lunching off venison in the Master's Lodgings, he is too often engaged in calculating over how many meals he can spread a piece of dry cheese or a pot of marmalade. No doubt the handling and spending of a greater amount of money is good for his character, and no doubt the standard of living at Oxford and Cambridge is much more healthily low than it was thirty or forty years ago. But many an ex-council-school boy could tell tragic tales of ignorance, debt and misery; and life at the older universities will not be really satisfactory until the standards, and hence the expenses, are much lower still.

II

And what of the university teacher? How many of those who have gone from Oxbridge to Redbrick, or from Redbrick to Oxbridge – and plenty of moves are made in either direction – regret having done so? Does the average 'provincial' professor wish himself in one of the so-called metropolises of learning? Once there, are the advantages that he reaps from the change at all substantial? Is migration from the one type of university to the other a process to be encouraged?

The question is a very different one for the boy or girl fresh from school and for the mature teacher. The latter will be influenced less by venerable towers, hallowed precincts and storied windows richly dight than by practical considerations of tenure, living conditions and finance. In these respects there is much less to choose between the two of them than one might imagine. But, on the whole, Oxbridge wins.

As far as stipend goes, the modern university compares quite well with the old. 'Before the war,' remarks the University Grants Committee in a report dated 1948, 'individual salaries varied greatly, as between one university and another. On the whole the salaries were higher in those universities which had the greatest income from endowments.'[1] In 1948 the standard rate of the professor's salary was £1,500 for London, £1,450 for other universities and £1,350 for university colleges. First-grade lecturers, previously the worst-paid group, got from £900 to £1,100; and even on the old salaries there were occasions when a comparatively prosperous Oxbridge don in his middle thirties thought such a post worth taking. Junior lecturers, as such, have always received much the same salary at each type of university, but at Oxbridge they have more perquisites, though probably also less time.

As against any advantage held here by Oxbridge must be offset considerably increased expenses. The Redbrick professor can establish himself in a flat near his work, in a good-sized house outside the city or in a cottage in the country. He can subscribe to student societies or be completely oblivious of their existence; he can be accessible or inaccessible to colleagues, students and visitors from outside; he can entertain

1. *University Development from 1935 to 1947*, London, 1948, p. 46.

lavishly or not at all. Most professors do, as a matter of fact, incur some expense here, but it is entirely voluntary; their whole life is their own to do as they like with. At Oxbridge, on the other hand, the professor is forced to keep up two establishments. He must accept rooms in college, involving certain expenses which are obligatory, however little he needs the rooms or uses them. His house cannot well be far outside the town, since the shortness of the terms means an intolerable crowding of engagements. The demands made upon him for subscriptions are numerous, and, more usually than not, difficult to refuse. Acquaintances from other universities and elsewhere drop in upon him and expect to be entertained at the High Table. Private entertaining, since everybody lives one on top of the other, cannot be avoided, and goes on constantly, quite apart from the bevies of undergraduates who, if one is a college official, have to be admitted even to the sacred privacy of breakfast. To many people these things are no burden, except financially; but, together with the artificially high prices which seem to rule at both Oxford and Cambridge, they explain why, again and again, the first thing a professor has to do after his translation to either from Redbrick is to consider carefully where he can economize.

But as well as increased expenditure there are increased opportunities, which may, and probably over a long period do, much more than counterbalance it. The inarticulate youth who moons over one's breakfast marmalade proves to be the son of a wealthy merchant who invites one to his villa on the Riviera. The American university president who tediously expatiates on democracy to the Senior Common Room has really come to find an occupant for a lucrative visiting professorship. That costly book which one had always wanted to bring out is, surprising to say, accepted without question by a publisher about whom a colleague has rung up a few days previously to ask if he may bring him round after dinner. At Redbrick such things never happen. One gives one's lectures, attends one's meetings and goes home. And what is more, none of them would ever happen if one stayed in the place all night. For to Oxbridge all the best people continually gravitate, whereas to Redbrick no one, if he can help it, ever comes at all.

From this develops another group of advantages, even more completely in the category of the imponderable. Except for the man who prefers to live strictly within the circle of his family, or to shun visitors and establish himself in the country, the amenities purchased by these additional expenses are well worth having. College society, with its wide and diverse social and cultural interests, is a pleasant and effective antidote to the narrowness inseparable from specialization: if the Redbrick man feels the need for such a society, he has largely to create it for himself; at Oxbridge, he has it ready-made. Both here and elsewhere he will meet interesting people, probably more than he could find anywhere else in the country, except only in London. Finally, there is the elusive argument of prestige. If a learned society is looking for persons on whom to bestow one of its coveted fellowships, it may perfectly well ignore Redbrick altogether, but it will certainly begin by asking: 'Well, now, first of all, who is there at Oxford and Cambridge?' A Cabinet Minister may need an educationist for a Royal Commission; a foreign statesman may want to recommend some English scholar for a decoration; an Eastern potentate may be seeking a temporary home for his son. Each of these, except for some rare and particular reason, will look first to Oxbridge and as likely as not there will be no need to look farther.

Then there are the students – and here Oxbridge has an advantage which to many conscientious and able teachers is irresistible. Only the minority of its undergraduates come from the Little Back Streets and the Drabtowns. Most have had the advantage of tradition and breeding, a cultured home, a public-school education, foreign travel in vacations, and so on. Those who have not are at least the pick of the municipal schools and among them are many intellectual pearls of great price. What man of ability will lightly renounce the chance of having a constant supply of such material to work upon? Should it not be the ambition of every man worth his salt to go where he can get it?

One might suppose so. But this advantage is frequently offset by a factor which sometimes a man who has made such a change discovers only when it is too late. The public-school boy, despite his natural advantages (or perhaps because of them) tends to be over-confident, to dissipate his energies over multitudinous interests, to cut lectures, to shirk difficult reading, to turn the vacations into holidays, and generally to take the line of least resistance in everything that concerns work. The brilliant boy from the municipal school, making heroes of the public-school men whom he is meeting for the first time, finds it only too easy to go the same way, and, especially if his tutor or director gives him too much rein, degenerates rapidly from a first-class man into a second.

The Redbrick freshman, on the other hand, makes a good pace from the very start. The transition from school to university produces no great upheaval in his habits; it is in every way a more natural one than the transition from Drabtown to Oxbridge. He finds greater freedom: fewer class hours; more scope for initiative; a better library than he has had the run of in his life, an equal and perhaps a more intelligent interest taken in his work and at the same time less check on it. Being keen and industrious (for were he not he would never have got to a university at all), he applies himself determinedly to his reading and finds in new methods, new subjects and new teachers the most powerful of incentives. Since there are few purely social engagements to compete for his interest, and the societies to which he belongs arrange their meetings at times when he would in any case not be at work, he is able to achieve the maximum of concentration. Then, again, he regards his professors and lecturers with greater awe than does his former schoolfellow at Oxbridge, whose companions at first rather shock him with their offhand talk about dons, until, very soon, he himself reaches their sophisticated level. At Redbrick, the general habit is to think of a professor as an extremely glorified assistant master – in fact, in some subtle way, as the superior of one's own headmaster – and of the lecturer as similar to professors in every respect save age and fame. Hence one is amenable to all their hints and suggestions, which may partially account for a phenomenon not uncommon at Redbrick – the sudden blossoming, about halfway through the course, of an apparently third-class into something approaching a first-class mind.

Now there may be two opinions as to which is the more agreeable type of pupil, and it should be added, to meet an obvious criticism, that women, at Oxbridge certainly, and perhaps also at Redbrick, are apt to reach a higher standard of industry than men. But anyone who has learned from personal experience how heartbreaking it can become to watch good material continually going to seed would probably prefer the industrious second-class man to the brilliant and lazy one.

Neither Oxford nor Cambridge, of course, is wholly indifferent to this waste of talent and some colleges renew or suspend scholarships each year according to the results of examinations. But sometimes the craft of the undergraduate is equal to this well-intentioned precaution. There was once a major scholar of a Cambridge college, who, having imbibed the poisonous fallacy that the education you get at the University has nothing to do with books, proceeded to squander his energies from the day he entered his College, and distinguished himself in his first-year examination by taking a bad third. The College promptly deprived him of his scholarship, whereupon he mended his ways, and in the following June, being an exceptionally able man, took a high first-class in the first part of his Tripos. Delighted at the success of their discipline, the authorities not only gave him back his scholarship but increased its value, the result of which, a year later, was that the man scraped contentedly through his Part II at the very bottom. No doubt, weighing his financial receipts for the three years against the disagreeableness of concentration, he decided that he had got as much out of both worlds as was humanly possible.

But Oxford and Cambridge are themselves more responsible for the existence of this type of pleasant scoundrel than they might be prepared to admit. It is because life there is too easy, because minimum standards are too low, that every college contains scores of men completely ignorant of what is meant by concentrated and methodical study or even by any kind of sustained mental exertion. Perhaps it is, partly at least, for the same reason that so little original work of merit is produced by the hundreds of teachers and resident graduates at each. What external incentive to research has the 'Junior Fellow', with the highest academic honours, morally sure of a competency whether he goes or stays, or the 'Senior Fellow', who has stayed to good purpose, is well on the way to amassing a number of remunerated offices, and, if a bachelor, finds his college quarters the most comfortable place imaginable to grow old in? For the moment, however, we are concerned only with the effect of this waste of undergraduate material upon the teacher, and it certainly seems to furnish the strongest of arguments against his leaving a modern university to go to Oxford or Cambridge.

There is one other argument of this kind – a more positive one: the possibility of doing pioneer work at Redbrick. After all, the place is not yet a hundred years old. Very few of its Schools have traditions, great names, sufficient equipment, more than adequate buildings, generously stocked libraries. Very few of them have students who come from all parts of the country because they can get there what they can get nowhere else. Not all of them have even enough students to allow the planning of a syllabus containing all desirable options or to justify the appointment of a staff varied enough to guarantee an all-round education. It is the privilege of the man who goes to Redbrick young – perhaps, though not as a rule, 'to save his soul'[1] – and who stays there, to play his part in the building up of all this – a

1. Flexner, p. 252.

process which, in the nature of things, cannot be completed quickly. The man who passes on thence to Oxbridge follows, as a rule, in the wake of a long line of predecessors, who have probably done a great part of this work for him already. If they have not, and he attempts to do it now, he may find himself cutting across academic red tape, vested interest and innate conservatism, and wish himself back in the keener air from which he came. In that case he will probably do well to brave the convention that Oxbridge is the undiscovered country from whose bourn no traveller returns and take a single ticket back to Redbrick.

Whenever I return to Oxbridge, I am reminded of a story told me in the United States by a self-made man who had just returned from his first visit to Italy. As he had travelled from one great city to another, and gazed on marvels of Classical, Medieval and Renaissance art which previously he had known only as pictures, he felt as if he had been transported to a dream-world: it just could not be real. But suddenly, while being conducted through the last of these cities, he emerged with a start from his dream-life and realized that he was still in the same world as the one he had left. It was then that he asked his guide one of those blunt but penetrating questions with which Americans in Europe are apt to startle, and sometimes to shock, their hearers.

'Say,' he remarked, 'this is all wonderful – all so mighty old. ... *But* ... *what have you done in the last hundred years?*

'I come,' he continued, 'from a city of 300,000 people, over two thousand miles from New York, the finest city of the American south-west. You'll find there a great railroad station, large blocks of modern apartments and offices, huge stores and hotels, a cathedral, a university, schools of all kinds and one of the finest residential sections in America. Yet less than a hundred years ago not a house was standing there: every square mile of our city was prairie. How does your progress since the eighteen-thirties compare with that?'

Now nobody would suggest that Oxford and Cambridge have done nothing for the last century. Fewer than a hundred years have passed since Newman quoted, with apparent approval, the remark of the Edinburgh Reviewers that 'a set of Lectures on Political Economy would be discouraged in Oxford, probably despised, probably not permitted'.[1] As for Cambridge, only forty years ago she had no English Tripos, and no professorships of French, Italian, Spanish or English literature. In fact, there was opposition to the creation of the last-named Chair, in 1910, on the grounds that it would be 'of a light and comic character – not only useless, but positively harmful'.[2] While, even in 1917, a member of the Senate, 'as a genuine and patriotic Englishman', could declare that 'the teaching of foreign languages was futile and to be deprecated in the highest degree'.[3] But despite flocks of benefactors, the progress of Oxford and Cambridge is slight by comparison with that of the universities which are already beginning to challenge their supremacy. For these, a century ago, did not exist. They were created from nothing and they have grown and prospered, largely on local generosity, and made scholars, including world-famous scholars, out of such material as remained to them when the choicest pieces had been eliminated. In the world that is coming they will of necessity be given greater opportunities and show that they can achieve greater results. But even were that not the case, it would still be a glorious and a happy lot to be both a university teacher and a pioneer.

III

At one time, the problem of choosing a university for a boy to go to (for nice girls never went to universities) was simple. There was Oxford and there was Cambridge. Some asserted that a university existed in London, but no-one had ever seen a building with such a title, though it was rumoured that a body of that name had been founded to conduct examinations. There was also believed to be a university

1. Newman, p. 161. 2. F. L. Lucas, in *Cambridge University Studies*, London, 1933, p. 259. 3. Ibid.

at Durham – wherever that was. In any case, the problem was easy to solve. There was Oxford and there was Cambridge: unless you had been to one of them yourself, and therefore wanted to send your son there, it mattered very little which of them you chose.

So all the boys who could afford it (and that meant all boys from 'good' schools) went to Oxford or Cambridge, while all the schools that were not 'good' sent those of their abler boys whose parents were prepared to forgo their potential earnings for three years to whatever local universities or colleges they might chance to hear of. Oxford, as H. A. L. Fisher wrote – with apparent complacency – in 1919, shared with Cambridge 'the special function of completing the education of young men, coming from cultivated homes, trained for the most part in our Public Schools, and destined for political life or the learned professions'.[1] In other words, while Oxbridge continued to win distinctions with its brilliant rich, Redbrick made a name out of nothing through the exertions of its brilliant poor; and, although Oxbridge still refers officially to persons who have received Doctor's degrees from Redbrick as 'Mr', and relieves Redbrick graduates of the trouble of wearing their gowns when they dine in college halls or lecture in the University, Oxbridge could not choose but become unofficially aware of Redbrick's existence.

Indeed, as the greatest pioneers of the new universities began to create Schools of distinction, it was impossible to ignore these universities any longer. At Manchester there was a galaxy of brilliance: Roscoe in Chemistry, Tout in History, Alexander in Philosophy, Toller in English Language, Ward and Herford in English Literature; and many more. At Liverpool, McCunn made a name in Philosophy, Gonner in Economics, Pares in Russian and Reilly in Architecture. Birmingham took Oliver Lodge from Liverpool, where he had already achieved pre-eminence, to be its first Principal – and later Birmingham had men of the

1. H. A. L. Fisher, *The Place of the University in National Life*, Oxford, 1919, p. 4.

calibre of Ashley, Bantock, Selincourt and Beazley. And these are only names set down at random: few people realize what outstanding scholars have worked in the modern universities and have been glad and happy to spend their whole lives in them.

Then there gradually dawned upon Oxbridge a most brilliant notion. It was being attacked, principally by adherents of that troublesome institution known as the Labour Party, as a class-nursery, the preserve of the privileged, the paradise of the idle rich, and so forth. So henceforth it would welcome the poor – that is, the brilliant poor – and the most valuable of its college scholarships, which had always, in theory, been open to other than 'good' schools, should now be so in reality. So Greek, which only the 'good' schools taught, and not always even they, was made an optional subject for the university entrance examination instead of a compulsory one. The number of scholarships and exhibitions offered for 'modern' subjects – especially for modern languages – was multiplied. Fees, at one time high out of all proportion to the value received for them, also began to come down: in many colleges, for example, the tutor's fee was halved. Simultaneously, economies in living were announced: in a few colleges an undergraduate no longer had to choose between ordering cooked dishes from the college kitchen at *à la carte* prices and breakfasting or lunching on his own bread and marmalade, but could go to the college 'Hall' three times, instead of once, daily, and enjoy a simple and moderately priced *table d'hôte*, in some cases at an inclusive terminal charge.[1] So greatly did the cost of living rise during and after the War of 1914–18 that, but for such economies, an Oxford or a Cambridge career would for many have been impossible. As it was, whereas living in general rose by over 100 per cent, Cambridge life rose by less than 30. In 1910, that useful guide, the *Students' Handbook*, represented the minimum annual

1. During the War, for obvious reasons, many colleges adopted an *en pension* scheme of this type. Previously, it had been favoured by women's colleges rather than by men's.

amount of pocket-money on which a careful man could 'do'
Cambridge at £150, £300 being needed to leave what it
considered a comfortable margin; in 1935, the increases in
these amounts were only £38 and £68 respectively.

The result of all this reform was that, here and there in
the scholarship lists, among the venerated names of Eton,
Harrow, Winchester and the rest of the 'good' schools,
there began to appear those of Puddlewick Grammar
School, Drabtown Municipal Secondary School for Boys,
and others which, to the old-fashioned don, must have
sounded quite too impossibly 'bad'. The scholars, however,
when they arrived, proved, after all, to be not quite so
alarmingly vulgar. Feeling themselves fish out of water,
they behaved quietly, took no liberties, made friends
chiefly with one another, and even subscribed with reasonable liberality to the things for which they were told their
support was expected.

The net influence of these immigrations upon Oxbridge
was excellent. The new men were always of marked ability,
for only if they had gained the highest scholarships could
they afford to come. So they challenged the brilliant
Etonians and Wykehamists in the Schools, and, by not
infrequently beating them, greatly stimulated keenness.
They raised the already high intellectual standard of First
Class Honours, in short, without in any way disturbing the
comfortably low standard of the Third (or Fourth). Which
suited Oxbridge very well; for if it is the few brilliant men
who bring her fame, it is the vast crowd of the lazy, indifferent or stupid who fill her coffers and provide hundreds of
tutors and coaches who might have become scholars, but
find it easier and more profitable to 'take pupils', with a
more than adequate living.

The new development was also an excellent thing for the
municipal secondary schools – and incidentally for any
headmasters of such schools who might be trying to climb
farther up their own particular ladder. When once Drabtown had been able to taste the pride of heading the Honours List on its Speech Day programme with the name of

John Smith of Trinity ('Major Scholar. First Class Honours, Mathematical Tripos. Smith's Prizeman') and the illiterate chairman of the self-important Governors had announced that the said Smith had beaten 'scholars from Heton an' 'Arrow', it was not likely that, when his three years of honour and glory had come to an end, Drabtown was going to resign itself to heading its Honours Lists with B.A.s of Redbrick.

Certainly not. Day in, day out, after morning 'prayers', boys standing in their uneasy and uneven ranks were exhorted, 'for the honour of the school', to strive, year by year, without fail, to carry the fair name of Drabtown to Oxbridge. Parents too, by suggestion rather than by exhortation, were encouraged, in confidential conversations, terminal reports, and letters, to envisage their boys wearing rabbit-skin hoods or conducting their families around the old-world colleges in that city. Instead of getting a Municipal Exhibition and entering Redbrick at seventeen and a half or eighteen, the abler boys were now persuaded (or sometimes dragooned, with feeble protests from parents) into staying on at school till they were nineteen, not only in order to take the Higher Certificate, quite unnecessarily, for three years in succession, but to have at least two attempts at the Oxbridge Open Scholarships. Many such boys merely became hopelessly stale and did worse at their second attempt than at their first: but they were conveniently forgotten – or relegated to Redbrick. The few succeeded, and in due course sailed away triumphantly on the sea of success – to return, of course, at frequent intervals, to Alma Mater *pour encourager les autres*.

Meanwhile, though very slowly, and only here and there, those modern universities which had been able to develop their outstanding Schools were challenging the older foundations for academic pre-eminence. The 'democratic' tendencies of Oxbridge, however, stimulated by the war of 1914–18 and the establishment of new and valuable State scholarships, developed rapidly. So year after year, to an increasing extent, Redbrick had the chagrin of seeing all the best boys and girls from its schools making for Oxbridge and the dubious consolation of welcoming those who had tried to do the same, and, for lack of brain, or possibly of application or efficient teaching, had failed.

The same process goes on to this day. 'Oxbridge if I can and Redbrick if I can't.' Headmasters almost to a man, and headmistresses almost to a woman, encourage their pupils to think of the local university as second-best. It never occurs to them to inquire seriously if mathematics or physics or history is better taught at Oxbridge than at Redbrick. To go to Oxbridge means, on the one hand, to bring honour to the old school, and, on the other, to get for oneself an indefinable 'something which the others haven't got'. So Redbrick loses two groups of undergraduates, each superior to the group it gets, and with the help of which it could very soon challenge Oxbridge everywhere. The first group is of children who leave the district young, for expensive board-ing schools elsewhere, and, having gone through them, would never dream of going on (or should one say 'back'?) to the local university; the second group is of boys and girls educated, usually at no cost to their parents, in local schools, who leave their native town just as they have a chance of repaying something of the debt they owe it.

That is the state of things which the new world must remedy.

IV

What is the ideal towards which we need to work – for no revolution which involves the building up of a new tradition can be accomplished quickly?

An England, surely, in which there are no longer two large residential universities for those who are either well-to-do or brilliant, and ten smaller universities, mainly non-residential, for those who are neither. Let there be twelve, of approximately equal size, all in the main residential, and each having certain Schools in which it excels the rest. Let the standard of admission at all universities, as well as the minimum standard for graduation, be raised, as nearly as is possible, to the same level, and let the Pass examinations be, not a bolt-hole for duffers anxious to idle away three years on games and social intercourse, but a test of genuine all-round (as opposed to specialized) ability. Let every boy or girl entering a university go where his or her particular subject is best taught. And finally, let a levelling of standards pave the way for the interchange of pupils where this is in the interests of the pupils themselves.

The first reform, which must precede all the rest, is the allocation to the modern universities of a Treasury Grant many times larger than at present. In each of the years 1931–5, for example, the recurrent grant of £107,500 given to Cambridge University was, with the exception of the London grant of £557,000, which had to be divided between twenty-six Colleges and Schools, larger than that given to any other of the universities and university colleges in England. Oxford was second, with £97,500. Liverpool came out third, with £86,000; on its heels came Manchester, with £81,000 (excluding the £14,500 of the Manchester College of Technology). Birmingham received £76,000; Leeds, £71,000; Durham (including both the Durham and the Newcastle Colleges), £65,850; Bristol, £56,750; Sheffield, £50,500; and the four others, between £14,500 and £35,000 each.

There is ample reason, of course, for giving a large grant to the vast University of London and its dependent institutions, with their student population of nearly 13,000 or about thirty per cent more than that of Oxford and Cambridge combined. Durham University is also in a special position, and so, perhaps, is Reading, with only some six hundred students, but over two-thirds of them resident in Colleges or Hostels. The position and future of the University Colleges would also need separate consideration. But meanwhile there is an unanswerable case for giving the seven remaining Universities – Birmingham, Bristol, Leeds, Liverpool, Manchester, Nottingham and Sheffield – first, a six-figure block sum for building purposes, and

secondly, a recurrent annual grant of a size out of all proportion to the grants given to Oxford and Cambridge. For
these seven Universities, together with more than one University College deserving of university status, have in the
past been largely dependent on private generosity, which
has now been strangled by taxation, and on municipal
help, which it is unlikely can be greatly increased. Oxford
and Cambridge, on the other hand, are flourishing institutions and likely to remain so. Their Chairs are much more
highly endowed than those of their poorer neighbours.
Their numbers are larger, so that they have a greater income from fees. The gifts they receive are more numerous –
for it is a curious fact that potential benefactors, even if
they have themselves once been poor, generally favour
universities which they know to be already rich. Their
endowments are large – and this is particularly true of the
endowments of certain colleges, which can afford to pay
young men comfortable salaries as Junior Research Fellows
and free them from College duties, without requiring too
strict an account of how they spend their time. There is no
case for the continuance of the present system, by which the
richest and largest institutions get most and the smallest
and poorest least. If the country wants two Universities to
absorb its best brains and the rest to languish for want of
intellectual nourishment, it can continue to give to those
who already possess. But if it wants a round dozen of universities, each developing to the full its latent capabilities,
it must give substantial help to those less able to help themselves, and so enable them to compete with their rivals.

There are three principal and fundamental ways in which
this large block grant and increased annual subsidy would
be utilized. The most urgent is the development of residential facilities. Most of the modern universities have their
hostels or halls of residence, but, though these are generally
full and their advantages are freely recognized, only a very
small proportion of undergraduates live in them. In 1934–5,
for example, less than 16 per cent of the total number of

students in University institutions, other than Oxford and Cambridge, were doing so. At Reading, in 1934-5, 68.3 per cent of the students lived in hostels, but this was by far the highest percentage in the country, the next highest, Bristol, showing 37.2 per cent, and the lowest, Sheffield, mustering only 9.5. Oxford and Cambridge are omitted from these statistics because, although 53 per cent of Cambridge students and 37 per cent of Oxford students (excluding the negligible proportion living at home) were in lodgings, these lodgings were subject to the discipline of the Colleges to which the students belonged.[1] In the report in which they published these statistics, the University Grants Committee referred to the large number of local authorities in Scotland which have supplemented their Bursary awards so that students may reside in the University hostels. Since 1936, the same excellent steps have been taken by certain authorities in England and it may be hoped that this tendency will increase.

But a much more radical reform is needed than that and it will cost money. Perhaps now that for years the country has been spending upwards of £5,000,000,000 annually on war as against less than £2,000,000 annually on its universities – let us try to envisage what that means: a ratio of nearly 3,000 to 1 – an outlay of this kind will not shock the public as much as, we may be sure, it would have done before 1939. 'You are not going to get some of these things put right,' declared Sir Charles Grant Robertson in that year, 'until the sense of national values has altered.'

A battleship costs £9,500,000. It may be essential at the present time but in ten years it is out of date. What could you not do with £9,500,000 for the Universities? Yet can you imagine any government in Great Britain daring to borrow, say, £20,000,000 to spend on education?[2]

In 1930 the Grants Committee disclaimed any intention of suggesting that the modern universities 'are expecting to transform themselves into institutions mainly residential

1. U.G.C., 1936, pp. 13, 17, 65.   2. N.U.S., 1939, p. 10.

in character'.[1] It dwelt, first, on the 'difficulty of securing the land and financing the buildings for any such large-scale transformation', and, secondly, on the desire which many students will always have, 'from motives of economy', to live at home. The possibility that the State could overcome both these obstacles did not apparently occur to the writers, or, if it did, they preferred not to put ideas into people's heads by mentioning it. Six years later, we find them recognizing the growing popularity and the solid value of halls of residence, but merely appealing to private benefactors to provide the capital for more of such halls, and, failing that, suggesting that the universities could find it by borrowing.[2] The time for appealing to benefactors has now gone by, and it is to be hoped that no responsible person or public body would any longer be content with the alternative. It should be an axiom that every university must have sufficient hostels to accommodate a very large proportion of its undergraduates, and every student should be compelled to reside, either within one of these hostels, or in lodgings affiliated, as it were, with the hostels, and under strict university control, unless he were specially exempted for personal reasons which would probably not affect 10 per cent of the whole. The mere fact that a student's home is near the university should not exempt him, for a large part of the gain of a university education consists in transplanting the student from his home and yet subjecting him to a discipline of a type which he would not have if he went to a distant town as a clerk in an office. The idea would no doubt be considered revolutionary: I remember the bitter complaints once made by some students who had been awarded scholarships for a short residential training course in the town where they all lived because they were not allowed to go home whenever they felt inclined. But in time

1. U.G.C., 1930, p. 43. Can a university, in passing, transform itself into an institution? Cf. p. 65, below.

2. U.G.C., 1936, p. 18. The picture which the Committee drew of the ideal hall of residence in 1921 and 1925 and summarized in 1936 (pp. 18–19) is wholly admirable and should be considered as a standard to be followed wherever new halls are founded.

it would certainly prevail. The total numbers of students at
the university would probably be reduced – but that might
not be a bad thing, for many think the present numbers too
high. The advantages are obvious. One has only to contrast
the present Redbrick University, situated in (or very near
to) the slums, with a Redbrick University City of the future,
lying well outside the municipal boundaries, with its Great
Hall, its playing fields, and, above all, its Greengates, its
White Gables and its Goldcrest, each creating traditions of
its own and gradually endowed by the benefactions of its
own former residents – the colleges, hoary with tradition,
of centuries to come.

But even to-day, the gain which such a reform would
bring, as regards the student's academic work no less than
his physical well-being and his all-round education, would
be immeasurable. More and larger hostels would soon be to
a great extent self-supporting, and it should be possible
for a student to live in hostel – or in college, as we should
probably say – more cheaply than he can to-day in lodgings.[1] Most important of all, there would no longer be any
great inducement, out of mere geographical considerations,
for a Birmingham boy to go to Birmingham University or
for a Manchester boy to remain in Manchester. Each would
go where he could get the best education of the type he
needed. There would be real freedom of choice.

Some of the money, again, would be used to provide
Redbrick with open entrance scholarships, which would
enable it to contend against the present-day overwhelming
advantage of Oxbridge. A Dean at a modern university can
tell a parent who, for financial reasons, is hesitating where
to send his boy that its expenses are much smaller and confined to essentials. But the parent will reply that practically
all its entrance scholarships are provided by local authorities

1. The average all-in cost of living at a hostel at present is about £3
weekly. Small as this figure may seem, it is a good deal higher than the
average all-in cost of lodgings in a large city, and even the difference of
a few shillings weekly may suffice to decide the student against living in
hostels.

or have been endowed by local benefactors, and are open for competition only to the children of ratepayers in certain areas, whereas at Oxford and Cambridge there are numerous entrance scholarships, provided from college endowments, which are open to the whole country. He might add, if he knew enough about the subject, that the colleges have further unallocated money which they use to provide still more scholarships for their own undergraduates, and also that local authorities supplement the scholarships they award by maintenance grants graduated so as to meet the higher cost of living at the more expensive university. If every modern university could offer a hundred open scholarships of £100 each (costing a mere pittance of £10,000 annually) to be awarded chiefly in the subjects in which its work was acknowledged to be of a high standard, a long step would have been taken towards the equalization of opportunity.

A third and most important reform is the development of special Schools within each university. When the new universities were in their infancy this was not possible. But they have now progressed far enough for it to be pretty clear which Schools within each university can be described as already pre-eminent, which of them would become so if they had the necessary personnel, buildings and equipment, and which are unlikely in the near future to rise above an average standard. A proportion of the increased annual grant, when it comes, should be allocated to the development of Schools in the first two classes.

Already, in the newer universities, schools exist here and there to which students come, not only from all over the country, but from many parts of the world. These, as a rule, have been developed by means of the administrative genius and scholarship of the men at their head, reinforced by private munificence. Let the State show equal munificence and it will be surprised at the results. In each of our modern universities there are professors – some still comparatively young, some now growing old and perhaps disillusioned – who have everything necessary for the building up of a supremely good School, except money. To obtain so small a sum as £50 for a piece of apparatus or a set of some learned review for the library they have to beg, to organize and even to carry on private intrigue: negotiations for the acquisition of such an amount have been known to occupy months: there are professors who will supply money out of their own pockets rather than waste valuable time in begging for it. No doubt when a man builds up a School in face of such difficulties he is himself the better for it, but those who might have passed through a mature School during the twenty years in which it has been a-building are very much the worse.

These are the necessary fundamental reforms, and little more is needed for their accomplishment than money. Probably, once they are in being, other reforms will follow, but there is no reason why we should wait for that. It may be, for example, that, when the schools – yes, even the 'good' schools – see how things are moving, Oxford and Cambridge will be taken down from the twin pedestals which they occupy in every really nice headmaster's study and will at least be dusted and regarded with critical eyes before they are replaced there. The question is: Who is going to make the start? It would help if in every area where there is a modern university a few strong-minded principals of schools would band themselves together and say: 'We have a duty to the university of this area and to modern universities in general. It will therefore be our normal policy to recommend boys and girls proposing to read for Honours to go to whichever university – ancient or modern – is doing the best work in their particular subjects, and to put before those who wish to read for a pass degree the advantages of going to the local university.[1] We realize that this policy may deprive certain pupils of the social advantages at present obtainable from residence at Oxford and Cambridge, but, quite apart from any doubts which

1. The 'pass' standards of all the modern universities are very similar; those of Oxford and Cambridge are, in the writer's view, lower than the rest.

may be cast upon the value of such advantages, we think this a small price to pay for the development of the university system all over the country.'

Finally, there is the question of interchange between universities, which, besides making for increased efficiency, goes some way towards the very real desideratum of giving undergraduates more experience. No-one familiar with American universities can fail to appreciate the advantage of a system by which a student can do part of his work in one college and part in another. The United States being so large, and its smallest colleges so often remote from any broad current of culture, this system of progression is almost essential to educational efficiency. But a system of interchange, both of teachers and students, would also be valuable here, and, owing to the shortness of distances, is perfectly practicable.

As to teachers, it would be well (if only as an antidote to inbreeding) for a rule to be made requiring every junior lecturer to spend at least one session in another university than his own – a longer period if he were a graduate of that university – before being promoted to the next higher grade. Any professor or senior lecturer who was an acknowledged expert on some part of his subject (and ought there to be a single one who is not?) should be encouraged to give courses of lectures at other universities in his speciality in exchange for similar courses given in his own university, when he finds such courses would be useful, by his specialist colleagues. There is no conceivable objection to this plan except the present lack of any machinery for its organization, and this could be provided by the committee of Vice-Chancellors and Principals which already meets, together with other committees, which should meet at least once a year, composed of the heads of departments in all the universities in each subject. There is no objection on the score of expense, while Birmingham remains at only two hours' distance from London and Liverpool, Liverpool is less than an hour from Manchester, and Manchester is but an hour from Leeds. Time is no bar – for, even if anyone could maintain that university teachers were pressed for time, little preparation is required for lecturing to undergraduates on one's special subject and it would be a great saving to have to lecture so much less on the special subjects of others.

Interchange of students mainly affects the graduate school, of which much more will be said later. Very occasionally, when an undergraduate shows a bent for some aspect of his subject which can better be studied elsewhere, he might advantageously be transferred, and a system of compulsory hostels would make such migration comparatively simple. But the great need is that graduate research should be rendered more efficient by the free interchange of graduates according to what they require and what each university can give them. Thus, if A, B, C, D are four university Schools in the same subject, which specialize in aspects of that subject designated E, F, G, H respectively, a graduate in A who wishes to study, not E, but F, would transfer for part or the whole of the course to B, a proceeding which would be much more natural if the professor at B had visited A to lecture on F during the A-man's course as an undergraduate. At present the only regular inter-university contacts in academic matters are provided by the appointment of external examiners. But at examination times everyone is hurried and the atmosphere is abnormal; it is during the teaching weeks that contact would be most fruitful.

It may be objected that such interchanges presuppose a fairly drastic levelling of standards: this may be so, and it is to be doubted if the firmest believer in university autonomy would consider some such degree of levelling by agreement likely to do any harm. At any rate, there is something wrong with some of our universities when a dissertation is recommended by a professor for a Litt.D. degree and his external examiner says that at his own university it would not be given so much as a Ph.D. and is worth no more than an M.A. Or consider the significance of the letters 'M.A.' At Bristol and Liverpool they usually mean that a thesis has been presented and always that at least two years have been spent, under direction, in advanced study. At Birmingham and Manchester they mean, under certain conditions, that no more than one year has been spent in advanced study. At Glasgow or Edinburgh they have nothing to do with advanced study at all and mean simply that an examination has been taken corresponding roughly to the English B.A. At Oxford and Cambridge they denote neither advanced study nor examination, but indicate that a B.A. has paid certain moneys to his college, together with a further sum to the university. There is an obvious case for some degree of standardization here and it might at least be attempted.[1]

And where, the reader of this chapter may ask, do we get the Battle of the Ancients and the Moderns? True, it has not yet begun and it is unlikely to begin to-morrow; but the moment for it is drawing perceptibly nearer. For centuries there were no Moderns at all. Since they came into being they have for generations been tied hand and foot for lack of resources and the Ancients have had everything their own way. During the last few decades they have partly freed themselves from their bonds and now lack only the munitions of war with which to do battle. But those munitions cannot much longer be denied them; and then let the Ancients look to their defences, for the battle will be upon them before they know it.

1. Since writing the above I have gone into the question further in an article in T.E.S., 23 October, 1948.

CHAPTER TWO

The Nature and Aims of a Modern University

I

WHAT is a university? That is a question which the Oxbridge freshman must often ask himself, on his introduction
to a place so different in every respect from the school which
he has left three months earlier. It will be some time before
he can give the question a satisfactory answer, and he will
probably not be helped by an extraordinary definition,
surely inspired by some demon of irony, to be found in the
Students' Handbook to Cambridge:

'The University of Cambridge is a corporation which,
in addition to the usual powers of corporations, such as the
ownership of property, possesses the rights of exercising
disciplinary authority over its members, returning two
representatives to Parliament and conferring degrees.'[1]

Even at the tender age of nineteen he may have an ink-
ling that knowledge is more important than proctors or
M.P.s. Later, when he has gone down, and is able to take a
more objective view of his university and to appreciate its
merits and defects in a way no undergraduate can, he might
evolve a definition which, though undoubtedly imperfect,
is perhaps as satisfactory as it is possible to find. The definition would be framed in words something like these:

*A University is a corporation or society which devotes itself to a
search after knowledge for the sake of its intrinsic value.*

Each phrase of this definition needs consideration. Let us
deal with each in ascending order of importance.

(1) *A corporation or society.* Not, it will be observed, an
'organization' or (as they often say in the United States)
an 'institution' or 'school';[2] still less a 'place'. A University

1. Ed. 1935–6, p. 1.
2. In many parts of the United States, especially in the Middle West
and West, undergraduates habitually refer to their university or college
as 'school'.

may be domiciled in one town or city, or even housed in a single group of buildings within a limited area, and it is often most convenient that this should be so. But it may equally well consist of several groups of teachers and students each housed in a separate town. Or, as sometimes happens on the Continent, two or three of its Faculties may be domiciled in one place and the remainder in another. Or again, the main body may have distant colleges affiliated to it, which are in a real sense a part of it. Or the whole of its members may be dispersed among twenty or thirty colleges, each with a separate individuality. We all know the story of the foreigner who, after being taken round all the colleges at Oxford (or was it at Cambridge?), inquired of his guide, 'But where is the University?' And it was no foreigner, but an intelligent undergraduate very near the end of his university course, who once remarked to me in genuine bewilderment: 'What I have never understood is, who *owns* the University?'

To both these questions the history of the word supplies the best answer. The medieval Latin word *universitas* meant a corporation, society or community of any kind, a body of persons collectively organized and considered in their corporate aspect. It could be used in a broad sense, to embrace all Christian people; it could be used in a narrow sense, to denote a relatively small group of captives languishing in a foreign prison.

When used in the particular sense of *studium generale* (a phrase which embodies the nearest conception in existence in the Middle Ages to our modern conception of a university), it would invariably be delimited by an appropriate phrase of qualification, such as *magistrorum et discipulorum*. More and more frequently scholars began to group themselves together to form a kind of guild for the purposes of mutual defence and protection, and it soon became sufficient to refer to such a guild simply as a *universitas*. For this reason our word 'university' properly denotes 'a body of teachers and scholars' – nothing less and nothing more. Yet the common conception held of it is that of a building, or of a set of buildings, *attended by* teachers and scholars, and nobody realizes that, in saying 'This bus passes the University', he means that it passes the buildings used or inhabited by the University, or that, if the buildings were all burned to the ground, the University would still remain.

There is a further important point to be made here. Many people talk of universities as if their name indicated that every kind of subject under the sun ought to be studied in them and they were places where knowledge in its most 'universal' aspect should be sought, a college of the liberal arts and a technical and commercial school all rolled into one enormous whole, with a syllabus in *x* large volumes. This is as erroneous a supposition as that the *studium generale* concerned itself only with knowledge of the most 'general' kind and specialized in nothing. The 'general' or 'universal' concept underlying each of these terms has reference not to the subjects studied but to the people who study them. These associations could be joined by anyone capable of profiting by them – i.e., without distinction of class, or age, or rank, or previous occupation – as they may still, with even fewer restrictions than of old. It is quite incorrect to think that every kind of subject should be studied at a university, and it is surely astonishing that Newman should not only have been so vague about the history of the word, but should have been so easily content to adopt the popular sense in which it is used and say that 'a University should teach universal knowledge',[1] asking

'What ought the term University to mean, but a place where every science is taught which is liberal, and at the same time useful to mankind?'[2]

(2) *For the sake of its intrinsic value.* If some would assent to the first part of the definition, a few would frankly disagree with the second, while many more would misunderstand it. Dr Lowell, one of the great Harvard Presidents, once drily defined a university as a place where nothing useful is taught. I would not go as far as that; to the extent that it was meant to be taken seriously, it was intended as a

1. Newman, p. 20.   2. Op. cit., p. 161.

sharp corrective to the mentality, only too common in America, which (to quote an equation which I have actually seen in print) puts the cultural value of modern language study on a level with that of typewriting. I can see nothing inconsistent with the nature of a university in the inclusion in the curriculum of frankly vocational teaching, provided this be recognized as an addition to the university's essential work and not claimed as a part of it. A technical college, a secretarial or domestic science school, a cramming institution are all quite distinct from a university. Both deliberate technical training and a certain amount of cramming may legitimately be indulged in during the course of university instruction, but education in a much broader and humaner sense must be the chief and ever-present aim.

(3) *The search after knowledge.* Here we come at once to the most vital, and yet to the most contentious part of our definition. Let me say at once that I must diverge fundamentally from the position of Newman, to whom the university is 'a place [*sic*] of *teaching* universal knowledge', and its object, 'the diffusion and extension of knowledge rather than the advancement'. 'If its object were scientific and philosophical discovery,' he adds, 'I do not see why a University should have students':[1] that we shall discuss later on.

That the search after knowledge is the essential function of the university is to me a basic article of faith; and if this book does no more than convert a handful of university teachers to that belief it will have fully repaid the time spent on it. It is in so far as our universities have declined from, forgotten or denied that ideal that they have failed in their duty. The definition is true historically: it was to *advance* knowledge, indeed to *possess all knowledge for themselves*, and not in the least to diffuse it abroad and convey it to others, that the earliest universities were established. It also holds together logically – for if existing knowledge is only to be diffused, let local authorities found *studia generalia* as they found elementary and secondary schools: they will only need to appoint superior types of school teacher, and

1. Op. cit., p. ix.

these are plentiful enough, as any scholastic agency will testify.

No: the primary aim of the university must be search for knowledge – re-search, as we call it to-day: not merely actual discovery, not merely even the attempt to discover, but the creation and cultivation of the spirit of discovery. Imagine a group of men, in any age, retiring from the life of the world, forming a society for the pursuit of truth, laying down and voluntarily embracing such discipline as is necessary to that purpose and making provision that whatever they find shall be handed on to others after their deaths. They pool their material resources; build a house; collect books; and plan their corporate studies. This, in its simplest form, is the true idea of a university.

But to do all this is not sufficient for them. Not content with discovering and leaving dissemination to others, they want to disseminate too. And, not content with doing this by means of books, they want to do it through living channels. So they seek contact with others, especially with the young, who are like-minded with themselves, and train them, first and foremost, to be discoverers of fresh knowledge – i.e., researchers – and secondarily, to be diffusers of the knowledge which they give them as part of their self-imposed task. And, as the effectiveness of a teaching inspired by such high ideals becomes manifest, more and more come to them to be taught – including many who have not the ambition, nor perhaps the capacity, to embrace research as a vocation, but who value, and desire, what we term 'the hall-mark of a university career'.

Here, as a natural development from the essential idea of the university, we discover its teaching function. In the original truth-seekers and the young people with whom they make contact we have the *socii* (the 'Fellows', now pretentiously termed 'Professors' and 'Lecturers' – words which obscure their main duty) and the *discipuli* (the 'Scholars', as they were called when part of a foundation, corresponding to the 'Students' or 'undergraduates' of to-day).

One more detail has still to be added. The young scholars must not only be instructed, trained, educated, before they are ready to engage in research, or, in their turn, to instruct others; they must be tested, licensed and given some status which will be a guarantee of their competence and fitness. Hence the lowest degree, that of Bachelor, and the successive degrees of Master and Doctor, the power to confer which can be bestowed on a society only by high authority – in this country by Royal Charter – and is recognized, almost the world over, as the seal of the university, differentiating it from any other educational institution, from elementary school to 'University College'.

But to the idea of a university only the 'Fellows', the researchers, are essential. There could perfectly well be a university which, like All Souls' College, Oxford, had no undergraduates at all; and, instead of teaching, replenished its ranks by the choice of scholars who had been taught elsewhere, devoting itself entirely and exclusively to the pursuit of knowledge. But there could never be a university which had no researchers at all and which engaged in nothing but teaching. A secondary school can never be a university, though in its highest forms, given scholarly teachers, there can be much of the university spirit. A university without research would be nothing but a super-secondary school.

Here, then, are the university's two aims: (1) *research* – patient and unremitting – including the cultivation of the spirit of research in even the youngest; (2) *teaching* – systematic and methodical, but also rich, stimulating and thought-provoking, so much so that again and again one finds the two aims merging and becoming temporarily indistinguishable the one from the other. Ruling and dominating each of these activities is the formation, both in *socii* and in *discipuli*, of character. For the discipline of conscientious teaching and application to learning cannot but make men better. And the discipline of research is as much more beneficent than this as research itself is a nobler activity than teaching and learning. Here one discovers that method, mental retentiveness, quickness of apprehension and skill in argument are of less moment than selflessness, humility, sincerity and balance of judgement. Here, without knowing it, one grows in honesty, generosity and love of truth – or fails as a scholar.

There still remains one concept to be elucidated and clarified – that of 'knowledge'. Admittedly the word is unsatisfactory: whenever it is used there insinuates itself the age-old antithesis between 'knowledge' and 'wisdom'. But the acquisition of knowledge does not mean the mere amassing of facts, either in the memory or in books and monographs, nor even the mere discovery of facts previously unknown or the rediscovery and restatement of facts forgotten. The prevalence of this factual conception of knowledge is, as we shall see later, largely responsible for the disrepute into which, in some circles, research has fallen, though, as far as my own experience goes, those who speak slightingly of it have not themselves always great originality or breadth of mind. As soon as one considers in some detail all that the pursuit of knowledge comprehends, its nobility and supreme worth at once become manifest. It includes, on the lowest plane, collation, comparison, revaluation and the shedding of new light on facts previously known, always provided that these activities are carried out in an eager and questing spirit. It includes the study, in the same spirit, of backgrounds to facts and events with the object of attaining a juster perception of them. It includes adventures, both critical and creative, into the unknown, whether with objectives envisaged beforehand or for purposes of pure exploration. It includes the interpretation of knowledge, whether factual or conceptual, hitherto available only to one class, community or language-group, for the benefit of others. It includes the perfecting of method, so that unknown lands may be provisionally charted by those who are unable to embark on voyages of discovery. It includes the re-examination, in the light of modern knowledge, of views and conceptions held by past ages; and not infrequently this activity, besides correcting the past, will re-illumine the present and even light up the future.

All that has been said can claim only to be a partial definition of a university, but it will at least give some idea as to what kind of person the *socius* and the *discipulus* should be. The *socii*, who have embraced university work as a vocation, will continue their pursuit of knowledge for as long as their powers allow. Compulsory superannuation may free them from their teaching duties and from the contractual obligation to engage in research, but they can no more regard their vocation as having ceased than can an aged monk, or a retired priest or doctor. Throughout their lives, too, they will attempt to stimulate the spirit of discovery in others – and this not so much of set purpose as because they cannot do otherwise. Their passion for knowledge should be infectious: none who know them should fail to be aware of it. The *discipuli*, apart from those who have found their vocation within the university, will, after a few years have passed, go out into the world, either to teach others, some of whom will, in due course, follow in their footsteps, or to pursue some other profession, which may take them far from the university atmosphere or may keep them near it. The extent of the influence of their years of study will therefore vary. But of all of them we can say this: when they go out from the university they should feel fuller, and yet emptier, than when they entered it; they should have an increased power, yet at the same time a keener sense of their own weakness; above all, they should be afire with a passion to discover and explore.

I I

This is the 'idea of a university' held by many teachers who regard university work, not as a means of gaining a comfortable stipend for only a few hours' work every week, but as a vocation to which their ideals and talents pledge them. But, both in the ancient and the modern universities, it is an idea in grave danger of disappearance. Some of the *socii*, who in the enthusiasm of youth were faithful to it, have allowed it to fade from their minds, and hence to evaporate from their teaching. As to the *discipuli*, the growing stress of life, the increasing difficulty of obtaining employment, the constant irruptions of worldly interests into the realms of the spirit, all tend to crush, in those who pass only three or four years in the university, the idea that their essential task there is to pursue learning for its intrinsic value. Only a few years ago the late Ramsay Muir, that well-known Manchester historian who to the great loss of academic life abandoned it for politics, said that he used to think his undergraduates 'had come to the university not as to a factory of ideas but as to a mere knowledge-shop; not to be forced to think about life, but merely to acquire the necessary fragments of dull and uninteresting knowledge which were required for examination purposes, and therefore might open the way to some unimaginative mode of livelihood.'[1] The reality in many cases is worse than that. Too often, not only at Oxbridge but also at Redbrick, the student is caught up in a whirlwind of lectures, games, examinations, dances, debates, friendships, vacations, worries – and who knows what else? – and, between preoccupation with the present and uncertainty as to the future, not only the most vital aspect, but any serious aspect, of a university career is forgotten.

Most freshmen come up to the university with two main ideas. One, a very clear idea, is that they have to amass a great deal of specialized knowledge in order to pass examinations, success in which will be important to them hereafter. This idea alone has been dinned into them both at school and at home, and, quite apart from that, it is a perfectly natural one, since lessons and examinations have been their principal concern at school, and the university appears to them as a kind of continuation school, and nothing more. The other idea, a much vaguer one, but very attractive to the adolescent and often the more potent of the two, is that the real purpose of the university is to broaden the undergraduate's experience, to enable him to pick up scraps of all kinds of knowledge and to give him something often vaguely described as 'general culture'. He hears little about this at school, except perhaps from some young master whose 'Varsity' days are not long past; whether he hears about it at home depends very much on the home itself; where he chiefly imbibes it is from former schoolfellows who have preceded him to the university. When he arrives there, he finds that Vice-Chancellors, Deans, tutors and all who deliver the well-known hortatory addresses to freshmen give this idea their most emphatic benediction; sometimes, in fact, they seem almost to be apologizing for the existence of lectures and examinations at all. The average under-graduate's reaction is to join every society, to attend every religious or political meeting, to read voraciously scraps from every kind of book and to discuss anything and every-thing with all and sundry. This phase, usually accompanied by neglect of academic work and by the most perfunctory attendance possible upon lectures, generally lasts until the examination lists at the end of the first year administer an already half-anticipated shock. The result of this shock, according to the strength of it, and to the temperament of the student, is either a reaction towards excessive specializa-tion, or the feeling that academically all is now lost, leading to a slightly diluted and disillusioned pursuit of 'general culture' for the remainder of the undergraduate's career.

Much of the responsibility for all this lies at the door of those who fail to point out that a truly liberal education, and the acquisition, not only of knowledge, but of a thirst for knowledge, are best attained through a conscientious self-application to the subject or subjects in which one has elected to specialize in all their varying aspects, together with a rigidly self-controlled study, over the greater part of the university course, of a limited number of other subjects, chosen either from their connection with one's main inter-ests or as providing a pure rest and relaxation from them. Thus an undergraduate reading for Honours in French would naturally select for subsidiary study Modern History,

English Literature and another language; his societies might be the International Affairs Discussion Circle and the Dramatic Club; and his hobbies, photography and botany. A specialist in Social Science might well read widely in the foreign language or languages he already knows, learn the elements of one other, join the Social Service Club and one or more of the political and religious societies and make a hobby of painting or music. If to these activities be added a care for physical fitness and attendance at debates or public meetings of current interest, the result should be an education both broad and deep, the maintenance of the sacred flame of desire for knowledge brightly burning, undimmed either by dilettantism, by ennui or by physical or mental fatigue. It should be impossible for anyone organizing his university career in this way to go down with the feeling that, on the one hand, he knows as much as he wants to of his special subjects, and, on the other, with a palate vitiated, through over-much tasting, for knowledge in general. 'Good-bye to all that' is the unhealthiest of cries which can come from a student after graduation. American universities significantly and inspiringly style their graduation day 'Commencement'.

III

The foregoing section applies with approximately equal force both to Oxbridge and to Redbrick, though Oxbridge, with its numerous social engagements and its long and alluring list of famous speakers, is more apt to breed the dilettante, and Redbrick, where the alternatives to lectures are less inviting, the dull and narrow specialist. But there are other reasons why the essential and inspiring central idea of the university is apt to be forgotten at Redbrick – or even never heard of. To each of these we must pay some attention.

(1) First, although, as we have said, the private lives of undergraduates differ very widely, in the average Redbrick home there is a severer economic pressure and the

undergraduate is never away from his family for long enough to be free from it. Anyone at all intimate with students' homes will be familiar with the types of reminder that, often in quite a kindly way, are for ever being hammered into them:

'Well, Aggie knows *we* can't do anything more for her.'

'This is her only chance to get on in life and she'd better make the most of it.'

'We've all pinched and denied ourselves to send you to college, my boy, so you just see you do well in your exams.'

'Tom'll have to help us with the expenses when he's finished at the University so it's to be hoped he'll get a good job.'

What boy or girl of nineteen or twenty can be expected to think of acquiring knowledge for its intrinsic value when young life's song has to be sung to a dad-or-mum obbligato of that nature? And how incumbent it is on the professor, going home each Friday afternoon to his warm, comfortable and quiet study, where he can pursue knowledge undisturbed over a long week-end, to imbue his students with this counter-ideal and keep it continually before them!

(2) Freshmen, again, are apt to be misled by the superficial similarity between the modern university and the secondary school which leads to it. Walking or cycling to the university, just as they did to school, they are apt to think of lecture-rooms as class-rooms, of lectures as classes, of professors and lecturers as teachers and of the Vice-Chancellor as a kind of super-Headmaster. The differences seem trivial: the lectures are fewer than the classes were and on occasion can be cut without penalty. Professors seem to know more than the masters did and are unimpressed by that argument previously considered irrefutable: 'The book says so.' There are about three half-holidays a week as well as the whole of Saturday. And so on. But too often undergraduates go through the greater part of their course without suspecting that there is more in it than this. And the university itself – by means of compulsory lectures, register-marking, class examinations, etc. – unconsciously

underlines the 'continuation school' idea. No-one tells the unsuspecting students that they are now members of a society with a common aim, toward which seniors as well as juniors are working; that upon them falls the onus of organizing their own work, both in term and in vacation; that every question they ask can no longer be answered with a 'Yes' or a 'No'; that they should learn how to use a library and aim at building up a small one of their own; that they should lose no opportunity of discussing their work, both with their contemporaries and with their seniors, so as to make it more real and living. These things it is surely the duty of the professor and lecturer to tell the student: how else can he be expected to learn them?

(3) Were the modern universities all residential, they could move out, as has been said, to the greatest good of the greatest number, into the suburbs of the great cities, or even into the country. But as, for generations to come, most of them are destined to be set in the heart of city life, the pull in the vocational direction which their environment gives must continue to be considered a drawback. Even indirectly, the constant roar and surge of city life puts the undergraduate continually in mind of his future. And direct reminders are more numerous and more potent still. Lectures are given on vocational topics in the Students' Union; the claims made by the Education Department upon undergraduates who depend for their maintenance on a Board of Education grant are always before them; the Department of Commerce, one of the modern adjuncts of the university course proper, organizes visits to works and factories; connections of all kinds are made with local leaders of industry. The world, students exclaim, is too much with them: little do they see that is theirs in the ideal of disinterested study – they have given their hearts (not to say their souls) away to the vocationists, who henceforward can lead them hither and thither at their will.

IV

So we come – rather despairingly, it would seem – to the crucial question: Is it possible, in a city university, to preserve and inculcate, in anything approaching its pure state, the fundamental idea which we have been considering? Provided the officers and teachers of the university themselves are true to the idea, I believe that it is. Some ways in which it can be done may be briefly suggested:

(1) The officers and teachers must not only hold the idea intellectually but must illustrate it by their own example. As we shall see later, the ideals of scholarship can be much better inculcated by practice than by precept, and it is not only the brightest and most suggestible students who model their attitude to their work upon what they sense to be the attitude of their professor.

(2) We must lose no opportunity of stressing the double aim of the university – research and teaching – and of putting research first. It is possible to fight the 'continuation-school' idea from the outset and it should be so fought. No-one is more susceptible than an adolescent to a fresh moral ideal, provided it be attractively presented.

(3) We must make it clear how closely scholarship is related to character, leadership and virtue. That sounds priggish, but only because it is unfashionable to write of such things in a natural way. The point is: Do we ourselves firmly believe that there is such a relation? If we do, we have no need to compose addresses or lectures on the subject – the fact will become obvious in our whole attitude to the subjects we teach, in our individual tuition, in the correction of essays, in chance conversations. The adolescent at the university is less sensitive to atmosphere and impression only than the child in the home: he often respects one professor, is indifferent to another, and despises a third without having the least idea why. It is largely a matter of latent ideals – or the absence of them.

(4) Far from stifling vocational aspirations, we must

encourage students to speak of them, relating both scholarship and vocation to the ideal of service, for which all true universities, in the past and in the present, have ever stood. 'The university', remarked a great American college president once, 'is the resting-place of those activities, those scholarly aspirations, those intellectual endeavours which make for spiritual insight, spiritual depth and spiritual beauty, but which cannot be transmuted into any coin less base than highest human service.'[1] In the ideal of service all three functions – research, teaching and vocational training – have their natural meeting-place.

(5) We must try to clarify in the undergraduate's mind the concept of 'general culture' and urge upon him the adoption of a definite policy of self-education. Dilettantism must be vigorously deprecated and its deleterious effects made plain. The linking together of interests and the importance of intellectual relaxation must be insisted upon. This is a matter primarily for the psychologist; and it would be useful to arrange, in every October term, a short course of lectures for freshmen, to be attended perhaps by second-year students as well, to which the usual hortatory address already referred to could be the introduction. Two or three of these lectures, at least, should be given by a practical psychologist.[2]

1. Nicholas Murray Butler, *Scholarship and Service*, New York, 1921, p. 63.

2. Since this book was first published, several universities have introduced this practice, which in time will probably become the rule.

CHAPTER THREE

The Organization of a Modern University

I

IF the first thing that strikes one about a modern university is red brick or dirty grey stone, the second thing is the extraordinarily complicated nature of its working. The machinery of the ancient universities is often criticized, perhaps with justice, but at least it is simple. If we disregard Convocation (the society of graduates which exists in all universities) at the one end, and at the other the numerous Boards which are concerned chiefly with programmes and lectures, their government is carried on by two bodies – at Oxford, a Congregation, composed of Doctors and Masters in residence, with its executive committee, the Hebdomadal Council; at Cambridge, a Senate and an executive called the Council of the Senate. At most of the modern universities there are Court, Council, Senate, and Boards of Faculties – a much more cumbrous hierarchy. Further, the contrast is even more striking in practice than in theory. Let us suppose that an Oxford or a Cambridge professorship falls vacant: the appropriate body appoints a Committee to elect to it; the Committee meets, makes an election and on the following day publishes the result. At most American universities, by the way, the procedure is still simpler: the Dean or departmental Head most nearly concerned chooses the professor and arranges the matter with the President.

But what happens when such a vacancy occurs at Redbrick it will need a separate paragraph to tell. In the first place, the Faculty Board concerned requests the Council to allow the Chair to be filled. Sometimes this request has first to be approved by the Senate, in which case a detailed preliminary report from the Faculty will be required – and, when received, will be debated upon by the Senate and Council – showing cause why the Chair should be filled at

all. This part of the proceedings alone may occupy weeks, or, if a vacation intervenes, months. If the Council agrees in principle to make an appointment, either the Senate, or the Faculty, or both jointly, will appoint a large Selectior Committee, which, as well as experts and semi-experts contains members of the Council and members of other Faculties than that concerned, who cannot possibly judge of candidates' ability in their own subjects. This Committee, after advertising, inquiring, selecting, and interviewing – a procedure which never takes less than two or three months – will report either to the Senate or to the Faculty Board which, alone or with the Senate, appointed it. Assuming that it reports to the Board of the Faculty, the Board deliberates upon the report and either rejects it (in which case the Committee begins all over again) or sends it to the Senate; the Senate then deliberates upon it and either rejects it (in which case both the Faculty and the Committee try again) or sends it to the Council; the Council then deliberates upon it and either rejects it (in which case the Senate, the Faculty and the Committee all try again in turn – and such cases do occasionally occur) or accepts it, whereupon, at long last, the news of the election is made public. This is the simplest example of the procedure. It sometimes happens that, for some personal reason, the Committee has to be dissolved and a new one appointed; or that the selected candidate withdraws while the Senate or Council is at the stage of approving him, and, if there is no *proxime accessit*, the whole of the lumbering and creaking machinery has once more to be set in motion; or that the Committee reports that no suitable candidate can be found unless £100 be added to the stipend – a calamity which may delay proceedings for months; or that the selected candidate requires to be paid £50 for moving expenses, which means that the Council has to submit the Senate's recommendation to its Finance Committee before pronouncing upon it. But even when no such further complication arises the procedure is highly wasteful of time and energy. Of time, for the election often takes as long as a year – it must be remembered that the Long Vacation lasts for three months and that neither the Council, the Senate, nor the Faculty Boards meet oftener than once every three or four weeks. Of energy, for if each member of every body concerned in the election of a professor attended all its meetings, no fewer than 150 persons would have a voice in the proceedings and several of them would serve on as many as three of the four principal bodies concerned. There is one university which consistently demands of all candidates for its professorships no less than sixty copies of their application and testimonials.

The only conceivable reasons to which all this unnecessary and wasteful formality can be attributed are either that the various bodies do not trust one another or that, for some reason which does not exist at Oxford or Cambridge, more people have to be consulted. There is, unhappily, some truth in the first suggestion: the Council, a lay body from the academic point of view, fears that the Senate may elect some myopic professor of the type familiar in fiction; the Senate, containing members from five, six or more Faculties, cannot trust any one of them to choose its man without fear or favour; the Faculty nominates its committee, but, lacking the boldness of Oxford or Cambridge, insists upon scrutinizing its decision in the closest detail. But the more important reason is the second. The modern university being what it is, a much greater number and diversity of people are concerned in its welfare. A description of each of the chief bodies which enact university legislation will give a pretty clear idea of who these people are.

First there is the COURT OF GOVERNORS, which technically is the University's supreme governing body, though many people think it the body which could best be dispensed with. It is a truly enormous corporation, running into several hundreds, but even more remarkable than the number of the members is the variety of the sources from which they are drawn. Let us take Bristol, whose Court numbers about 360. The list, occupying fourteen pages of the *Calendar*, begins with the Chancellor and other high officers of the

University. Next in precedence (observe how soon finance takes a hand) come 'life members' who have subscribed £1,000 and upwards to the University or are appointed by various corporations, ranging from an Oxford college to chocolate and tobacco manufacturers. Then come nearly forty persons appointed by the city and its various interests, such as hospitals, schools, and 'working-class organizations'; eleven representatives of County Councils and County Boroughs; thirty-six nominees of other universities, learned societies, and professional institutions; forty-three members of Parliament; and a huge and motley group of Lords-Lieutenant, Mayors, Bishops, heads of Nonconformist bodies, Chairmen of County Councils and Education Committees, Directors of Education, Chairmen of local hospitals and associations; headmasters and headmistresses of the leading schools of six counties. After a pause for breath we come to the whole of the University Council, the Deans of Faculties, the Professors and Professores Emeriti, the Librarian, the Registrar, twenty-nine representatives of Convocation, two representatives of the Readers and Lecturers, nominees of affiliated colleges, and finally a small group appointed by the University Council, ranging from the Presidents of the student body (who in other universities are members of the Court *ex officio*) to the 'Parliamentary Representatives of the University Constituency'.

It is intriguing to imagine what havoc this enormous body could work if all its members ever met at the same time and if those of them who had views on University education were to express them in turn. Fortunately there is no fear of that. The Court meets (to quote Bristol once more) 'at such times, in such places and in such manner as shall be prescribed by Ordinance or Ordinances', which usually means that a quorum is scraped together once or twice yearly,[1] to approve, after the minimum of discussion, reports and balance sheets and changes in the Statutes and Ordinances, to make some nominal elections and to fill up

1. It is a revealing fact that the quorum of the Bristol Court, with its membership of 360, is *twelve*.

vacancies in its own ranks. The exact functions in the different universities vary but slightly.

The chief value of the existence of a Court of Governors lies in its underlining of the many interests which have a stake in the University and the giving to those interests an opportunity for self-expression (of which they rarely take advantage) and a sense of responsibility (which it is to be hoped they value). It also ministers to the vanity and self-importance of a few persons regarded as potential benefactors of the University, if only by will. It may be defended as a harmless institution, which will be completely disregarded in the pages which follow, and is in practice without important influence.

At the same time, when a movement to simplify the administration of the modern universities begins, as some day it must, one of its first acts will no doubt be to sweep away the Courts of Governors in all of them. Busy public men living at a great distance have no time to attend their meetings, while local institutions and interests ought to comprise a sufficient number of graduates of the local university to be able to play a part in its government either through the Council or through a Convocation whose functions, on the abolition of the Court of Governors, might suitably be extended. The only persons really to suffer would be those who had recently subscribed their 'thousand pounds and upwards' in exchange for the privilege of becoming 'Governors'. No doubt, however, an Honorary Degree each would placate them.

If the Court of Governors may be regarded as mainly decorative, we come down to exceedingly hard brass tacks when we examine the functions of the University's real governing body, the COUNCIL. It is on the often difficult and delicate relations between this lay body with small academic representation and that purely academic body, the Senate, that high politics in the University largely turn. In the ideal university a Senate or Council composed of graduates and teachers would be completely autonomous, and the academic executive would neither be liable to be baulked and frustrated at every step, as at Redbrick, nor subject to highly disturbing cross-currents of college politics, as at Oxbridge. But a modern university, which starts its life without endowments, and on its running expenses generally has a deficit, cannot afford such luxuries as administrational idealism. Since much of the University's income is derived from municipal and commercial sources, municipality and commerce must have a part in university government. Hence the Council, a body of from thirty to fifty persons, most of whom are appointed by the Court of Governors or by local authorities, and very few – perhaps one-fifth or one-sixth of the whole – by the academic bodies. Those responsible for the Charters or Statutes of these universities when they were first drawn up took very good care that the academic voice should never sway the decisions of the Council, through which body practically every piece of university business must of necessity pass.

Whether summarized in a few words or detailed in a great many, the powers of the Council are tremendous. One Charter entrusts to it 'the conduct of all the affairs of the University': most of the others specify a list of its functions so long that nothing seems to be left for any other body. It is this all-embracing character that explains many situations and problems which the man in the street would find it difficult to understand. True, the Statutes often empower the Council to act only 'after consultation with the Senate', or 'after report from the Senate', but there is nothing in them to prevent it from rejecting all the Senate's representations without discussion. The Council is, of course, perfectly well qualified to 'select a Seal Arms and a Mace for the University', to 'have the sole custody and use of the Seal' and to deal with the University's revenue and property (though a committee appointed by the Senate would be equally so), but the large lay majority of the Council, many of whose members have never been to a university, and few have ever taught in one, is not in the least qualified, as Bristol requires of it, to 'promote research' (the Senate, by the way, has only to 'take cognizance of and encourage' research): it has probably only the foggiest idea of what research is. Indeed, it is often unable to appreciate the significance of the academic problems submitted to it. Yet it is the Council that elects to purely academic positions – namely, professorships and lectureships, that (in the words of the Manchester Statutes) 'institutes ... teaching offices', that can 'abolish or hold in abeyance after a report from the Senate any ... academic office in the University', and that can (in a wonderful all-inclusive clause) 'make regulations for any purposes for which regulations are or may be authorized to be made.'

Some of the universities give their Councils specific power to refuse to pass resolutions of the Senate or to refer them back for reconsideration; and all the Councils have in fact this power. It would be very easy to imagine acts of such bodies which run completely counter to any humane and cultured 'idea of a university'. Let us, however, describe some situations which, in fact or in effect, have actually occurred.

Take, first, general university regulations. Many professors believe that terms should consist of eight or nine weeks instead of ten. Ten-week terms, they say, give insufficient time for undergraduate reading (and directed reading, as will be observed later, is very much more important than lectures) and also insufficient time for good scholars on the staff to do their research. So in one university attempts have been made to obtain this reform. But no! These business men, whose work for the day normally ends when they step into their cars about tea-time, are quite unable to understand the position of a professor who started his routine work at about the time that they did, and whose real task of wrestling with ideas begins at about the time when they set about relaxing for the day. All they can make of the Senate's resolution is that 'these boys', who have quite enough holiday as it is, want more, and that their teachers, none of whom has ever spent a whole day, from ten to five, in an office, are supporting them. In vain do the academic members endeavour to explain things to them:

the idea that work means sitting in an office is so deeply
rooted that nothing can disturb it.

Then there are personal matters. The Senate has recommended for a Chair a certain candidate from another university by a large majority over some local candidate,
strong on the personal side, and well known to lay members
of the Council. They would not be human if they always
concurred in the choice – and yet it has been made by a
fully representative committee, which has balanced academic considerations against personal. Sometimes a reverse
type of interference takes place: recently, at one of the
newest of our universities, a particularly painful case occurred where a local man, academically about the best
qualified candidate in the country, was turned down twice
running by the lay majority of the Council on account of
certain extra-academic considerations which aroused their
opposition. Sometimes a question of principle is involved:
the Senate is advised by its experts that a certain French-
man is the best of the candidates for a Chair of French, or
an Italian for the Chair of Italian. Then some back-bench
lay member of the Council, whose education finished at
the elementary school fifty years ago, and who knows hardly
a word of French or Italian, sees his opportunity. A discourse, mainly irrelevant, on 'Britain for the British' con-
verts a few dubious members to the opposition, while others,
though not going all the way with it, suggest, as a *via media*,
that, if the matter were referred back, the Senate might
review once again the claims of the other candidates, so as
to get a unanimous election. In a case like this, the Senate
generally wins, but the heat engendered not infrequently
produces an effect upon other discussions.

It is perfectly true that, in normal conditions and over
any considerable period, very few cases of this type occur.
The lay members with little knowledge of things academic
usually confine themselves to the business side of their functions; the lay members who were educated at a university
are apt to be more troublesome, but are generally amenable
to the arguments of the academic members and sometimes

by viewing academic problems at a new angle can give
genuine assistance. If the Vice-Chancellor and the academic members of the Council have the necessary tact and
skill, relations between Council and Senate can be smooth
and even cordial. If the President of Council and the Treasurer have academic experience the Senate is more fortunate
still. Like so many other things in this country, the system
is entirely reprehensible in theory but in practice works
quite reasonably well. Yet every now and then it fails even
in practice, and, more important than that, it has the great
disadvantage of divesting the Senate of responsibility which
it should properly bear.

The SENATE is an academic body pure and simple, consisting of the Vice-Chancellor, its *ex-officio* chairman, and
the whole body of Professors. Most universities have some
further representation: they may include, for example, the
Chairmen or Deans of the Faculty Boards where these are
not professors; Associate Professors or Readers; non-professorial members specially elected by the Faculty Boards; the
Registrar, or Secretary of the University; and the Librarian.
The question of non-professorial representation is an unsolved and in some places a burning one. It is generally felt
that, let us say, a senior lecturer with twenty years' experience should, even if he is not the head of a department, have
a direct share in university government, as should also
every departmental head, quite irrespectively of his status.
Some universities solve this difficulty by giving the Senate
(or the Court on Senate recommendation) the right to co-
opt non-professorial members of the staff for a year at a
time, up to a stated number or proportion of the total membership – a provision which enables the Senate not to elect
any senior lecturer whose personality and Faculty record
suggest that he might be found stimulating but also
'difficult'. The general feeling to-day seems to be that the
initiative could come either from Statutes, or from the Faculty Boards, or from both. Some ultra-democratic persons
believe that the Senate ought to have representatives from
the student body, a development which would apparently

be favoured by that trade-union-like organization, the National Union of Students. This suggestion, as will no doubt
become clear to readers of this book, entirely conflicts with
its conception of university education and it need not therefore be discussed in detail. A better suggestion, of the same
type, is that the Senate might assign to the Faculty Boards,
or to certain of its committees, or even co-opt for limited
periods to its own body, a very small number of graduates
not on its teaching staff, to represent, as it were, the student
standpoint in a refined and matured form. Such a development would at first of necessity be experimental and it
cannot be regarded as pressing.

The Senate either initiates, or receives from the Faculty
Boards, all academic business, though, as we have seen,
none of this can become effective without the approval of
the Council. The person who holds a key position in both
Senate and Council is, as will be imagined, the Vice-
Chancellor. On him rests a very great load of responsibility
– a load, indeed, greater than he should have to bear. He,
with perhaps the co-operation of the Senate representatives
on the Council, has to interpret the views and standpoints
of each of these bodies to the other. And in his own personality he must hold the balance between them. It is on his
potential usefulness to both bodies that he is appointed –
though, as his appointment is the work of the Council, he is
apt to be more acceptable to the Council than to the Senate.
Very few Vice-Chancellors have succeeded in being equally
persona grata to both. The first question one asks about a
newly-appointed Vice-Chancellor is generally: 'Will he be a
Council man or a Senate man?' That remark reveals the weakness of the dual-government system more vividly than many
pages of argument. It will be a fortunate day for the modern
universities when their financial position is sufficiently
assured to enable the Senate to be master in its own house.

Of FACULTIES the numbers differ. Bristol and Liverpool
have five: Arts, Science, Medicine, Engineering, and Law.
Sheffield adds Metallurgy. At Birmingham, Commerce
takes the place of Engineering. Leeds substitutes Technology

for Engineering and has a Faculty of Economics and Commerce, subjects which in some universities come into Arts; it has no Theological Faculty, but gives divinity degrees as well as a B.A. in Theology. Manchester has nine Faculties – Arts, Science, Law, Medicine, Music, Commerce and Administration, Theology, Technology and Education. Reading has only three – Letters, Science and Agriculture – but has independent Schools of Art and Music and a Department of Domestic Subjects. Each Faculty is subject, in all but quite minor matters, to the control of the Senate, but this control is more reasonable than that of the Senate by the Council, since the interests of the Senate and of the Faculties are both academic. A tussle between the Senate and some Faculty (or, more rarely, many or all of the Faculties) is not unusual. The joint opposition of the Senate and a Faculty to some act of the Council is quite common. But an alliance between Council and a Faculty against the Senate is all but unknown.

It would be quite incorrect, however, to describe the Faculties (or, more exactly, the Faculty Boards[1]) as committees of the Senate. They are that neither in their origin, nor in their constitution, nor in their functions. The 'Faculty System' perhaps needs a little detailed explanation. It is a system which has grown up with the university much as the college system has grown up with Oxford and Cambridge. That comparison is not exact but it gives a better idea of what a modern Faculty is than the 'Committee-of-Senate' definition. Oxford and Cambridge have recently created what they call Faculties, but they have no more established the Faculty system in the Redbrick sense than Redbrick, if it dignifies its hostels with the title of Colleges, will be creating the Collegiate system of Oxbridge.

To begin with, were the Faculty Board a mere Senate Committee, it would consist almost exclusively of professors. It

1. The Faculty is the sum of all the teachers and students connected with a certain group of subjects. The Faculty Board is the Committee or Council governing the Faculty and consisting of ex officio (and also sometimes of elected) members who are teachers in the Faculty.

does, indeed, comprise the whole of the professors in the Faculty, as well as the Vice-Chancellor and the Dean, but there is a very large non-professorial element as well. Here, again, practice differs slightly: all heads of Departments (or Schools) are generally included, and some universities specify that a percentage (one-third or one-fourth) of the total membership of the Board shall be non-professorial. As a rule, the Board itself elects these members, but sometimes they are nominated by the Senate, and at Bristol they are actually chosen ('after report from the Senate') by the Faculty. One may hazard the generalization that on the Faculty Boards of most modern universities are to be found most of the senior lecturers, and that all the Boards elect men and women who may be described as 'ministers without portfolio' – lecturers who have often spent many years in the service of the university, and who, though not always supremely brilliant in scholarship, can view the many problems which come before the Board with an experienced and unprejudiced eye. Apart from the enrichment of its discussions by such members, their presence often serves as a barrier against the enthusiasms of 'departmentalists', as all heads of Departments who have their own special studies very much at heart are apt to become.

It will be unnecessary to describe the organization of Faculty business, for the mass of detail involved by such a description would obscure the main lines which this chapter is attempting to represent clearly. It has already been shown what a multiplicity of meetings are needed for the election of a single professor. Both the Senates and the Faculty Boards have numerous permanent committees: some of them useful, sifting the business before it comes up to the body concerned or dealing with the applications, grievances, faults and problems of individual students as only a small committee can; others, superfluous and time-wasting, reviewing and formally approving routine matters or resolutions which have already been passed unanimously by other bodies. One or two characteristic developments of the Faculty system are worthy of mention. At Manchester there is a General Board of Faculties, consisting of all the members of the individual Boards, which can make representations to the Senate on matters affecting more than one Faculty. In all the universities, Faculty Boards avoid much waste of time by appointing committees, representative of groups of subjects, to discuss such routine matters as set books, time-tables and the appointment of examiners. Where these committees include all, even junior, teachers in their subjects, they prove a valuable, if somewhat elementary, training-ground in administration and they guarantee that every member of the staff has some share, proportionate to his or her seniority and experience, in the government of the whole body.

Most of the universities have also special Departments or Schools within their Faculties, which, because either of their size or of their success, or of both, possess a greater individuality and freedom than others: such are the Departments of Dentistry, Pharmacy and Bacteriology at Manchester and the Schools of Veterinary Studies, Architecture and Education at Liverpool. These, and others like them, may, under such a development as has already been envisaged, become more and more important, for they would furnish both justification and bases for decentralization, and around each of them would be built the edifices which would attract the very best students from all over the country.

II

Young as the modern universities are, it will be seen from what has been said that they have already developed certain distinctive characteristics of which they are justly proud. The chief of these, perhaps, is the democratic constitution which gives administrative duties and responsibilities, if not as many as could be wished, to almost the entire staff. One who, besides having long experience at Oxbridge and Redbrick, has both studied and taught in foreign universities, served as a delegate to conferences held at universities in Europe, visited almost all the universities of one of the

Dominions and made an intimate study of university life in the United States may perhaps be allowed to give a word of personal testimony. In such circumstances one talks freely with numerous professors and lecturers of every type. Some, perhaps the majority, show hardly the slightest interest in the general policy of their university; others ride their own hobby-horses at the expense of the community; others become tremendously excited and enthusiastic over some burning question and then lapse into lethargy till some other controversy arises. Nowhere can one find anything approaching the sense of responsibility and the personal interest in university policy which marks the modern universities of Great Britain.

Partly, no doubt, this is an expression of the truly democratic spirit of our country, which in the universities of the United States is apt to be honoured more in theory than in fact. Partly, one cannot deny, it is attributable to the potential sources of discord between academic and non-academic interests, which continually key one up to preparedness for trouble. But chiefly it seems to be due to the widely spread representation on our administrative bodies and to the thorough discussion to which even the smallest piece of business may be subjected.

This system, however, has its drawbacks. Thoroughness can be carried too far. It is bad enough that time and energy should be wasted over the election of a professor – and some of the best men lost into the bargain, for not every professor or lecturer who has already a good post will be prepared to undergo a long period of suspense in order to get another. But it is much worse that the appointment of even a junior full-time lecturer, whom none but his future professor is really competent to choose, should involve an almost equal multiplicity of meetings, at least in the early stages. Procedures differ, but there is often the preliminary 'leave for permission to elect', the discussion on the Faculty Board, the election of a committee (sometimes including experts from other universities), the unavoidable advertisings, inquiries and interviews, the composition, by this committee, of a report to be debated, first by the Faculty Board and then by the Senate, each time subject in theory to 'reference back'. All this involves an expenditure of several hours for anything up to eight or ten people and of several minutes (in exceptional cases, of hours) for anything up to a hundred and fifty. The selection of the right man could be done more efficiently by the professor and his senior lecturer, as experts, with the Dean or Chairman of the Faculty Board to help them by assessing the general capabilities of the candidates at the interview. But this is only one of many instances where time seems no object. The sceptic should attend the meeting of some Faculty Board, which begins with the reading in full of the previous meeting's unabridged minutes, often including pages of some revised syllabus, lists of examiners and so forth. Not only does each Board have a dozen standing committees, but any of its meetings may see the appointment of any number of *ad hoc* committees. 'Oh, refer it to a committee!' is the usual cry when a private motion is raised. And each time six or eight members of the Board submit cheerfully to being deprived of from one hour upwards – and sometimes also to coming specially for the purpose from their homes – to transact business which could generally be done by two or three. Much of this unnecessary committee work falls upon a few men who are either particularly suited to it or particularly good-natured, or occasionally both. In a later chapter we shall see the effect of this on very different activities.

The other great disadvantage of this thoroughness is delay. We are often told that democracies are slow by nature, but there can be few snails in the political garden to compete with a modern university. Committees on legislation have been known to drag on for years, while legislation itself may be sent by a Board to the Senate, amended by a Senate Committee, sent on by Senate to Council, rejected by a Council committee and sent back to Senate, eventually finding its way back to the Board, which is to be warmly applauded if it has not forgotten what its original resolution was. For all business has to be got through in three terms of ten weeks each, and as each of the main bodies – the Faculty Boards, the Senate and the Council – meets only three or four times a term it can be imagined how many months a series of such legislative journeys will occupy. Any kind of election which passes through all its stages in six months is considered rapid, and although, when some sudden resignation makes it necessary for the Senate to act with unconstitutional haste, a temporary appointment (but not a permanent one) can be made within a few weeks, the person appointed is, as often as not, approaching the end of his first term's work before he receives an official letter from the Secretary of the University informing him that he has been chosen.

III

Departmental organization has already been touched upon and all that remains is to fill in details. Briefly, the system of unified control over undergraduates may be described as excellent for the Honours-man, but unsatisfactory for the Pass-man, though perfectly capable of adaptation to his needs and better than any other system in existence.

The freshman who enters a well-run School in a modern university is more fortunate than he probably knows. His work is unobtrusively supervised from the outset; a guiding hand extended to him where he needs it; and additional tuition provided where he is weak. His programme is arranged by those best qualified to arrange it, for neither he himself, nor anyone outside the School, is as competent to do this as his professor. Most important, perhaps, of all, he is free to consult his professor or lecturers at will. In the United States and some of the Dominions, this last privilege is emphasized by the assignment to every university teacher of one or more weekly 'office hours' during which for the stated period he must sit in his room, as though it were a confessional, awaiting consultation. Within reason this system might be introduced over here, though one experienced Dean who tried it reported that it seemed to make undergraduates no more assiduous in their attendance upon him than when he had left them to chance finding him in. But that, as he added, might be because after many years his habits had become generally known.

These facilities constitute only the minimum which the freshman may expect to enjoy. If he is fortunate, he will find that the School he has joined is an entity with as much character as the school he has just left. Some Schools invite well-known men to lecture to them on current events and undertake their entertainment. Others build up solidarity by concentrating on the social side and organizing winter tea-parties and summer rambles. Others link up with former members by means of a periodical news bulletin or by inviting them regularly back to the University. In one way and another such a School can make the undergraduate feel that in joining it he is joining a small community within the larger university society, and, if it has any post-graduate activities, he will realize that he can remain a member of that community, if he so desires, for the whole of his life. This last feature is particularly valuable; for the young graduate, with his academic links suddenly snapped, may feel lonelier during his first year or two after going down than he would ever have thought possible. The head of a School, if gifted with sympathy and understanding, can often do more for his pupils immediately after they leave him than at any time when they are with him, except possibly during their first term.

These are, of course, voluntary extensions of the single-control system and no essential part of the system itself. But system and extensions all leave the Pass student out of account, which may be one of the reasons why so many of our undergraduates read for Honours. The would-be Honours-man, on his very first day at the University, is sent by the Dean to the professor under whom he wishes to read, and, in many cases, the relations thus created are never broken. The Pass student, or the would-be Honours-man who has failed to gain admission to the Honours School, is sent to three (sometimes four) professors, each of whom assigns lectures to him and leaves him ruefully wrestling with a time-table which seems to assume that he can be in three places at the same time. Further visits, if he is brave enough to make them, will straighten out these difficulties; but he finds himself, even so early, contrasting his lot with that of his companion taking Honours, who, when lectures assigned to him clash, goes to the professor of his Honours School and is advised what to do. The unfortunate Passman, in short, belongs to no one, and, unless he drifts into a closer connection with one or another of his Schools, remains an academic outcast throughout his career.

It would be a good thing if undergraduates reading Honours were always adjured to look after the 'Pass' people with whom they are in continual contact, and to instil into them as much of the community spirit as they can. The undergraduate departmental society, at least, where it exists, can be (and usually is) open to Pass and Honours students alike. But the real problem is that of supervision. And here we may refer to a determined attempt at its solution which has been started in one or two modern universities – nothing less than an adaptation to Redbrick of the tutorial system of Oxbridge, though in a modified form invented by the University of St. Andrews, and known as the 'Regent system'.

St Andrews, describing the aim of this system as 'to facilitate close contact between students and the teaching staff', defines the regents' duties as 'to give friendly advice and assistance to students placed under their personal supervision'. Only scholarship-holders are affected, though 'other male students' may be included on the request of any Dean. As adapted in England, the system consists in the allotment of all first-year students (sometimes the second year, too, is included) to a number of 'tutors', mostly young lecturers, who, for a small annual honorarium, see them, singly or in groups, several times a term, help them to co-ordinate the various parts of their work and to organize their time, and invite them to discuss their private interests, home circumstances and anything else they like. Care is taken in the selection of suitable tutors: undergraduates

reading Honours, for example, often find themselves allotted to a lecturer in their own School. But, since few of
the tutors have much experience to draw upon, one would
suppose that the success of the scheme with different groups
must vary greatly according to their personalities.

Without first-hand experience of the system, one cannot
comment upon it in any but a tentative fashion. Judging
particularly, however, from what I have heard of it in Scotland, I should take its chief defects, if applied to English
conditions without modification, to be two. First, for reasons already suggested, *every* undergraduate reading for
Honours should be tutored by a member of the staff of his
School: this should be a part of the regular work of the
School, whose teachers should neither need nor accept
remuneration for it. Secondly, the system should be extended to the senior years – which, if the first amendment
were adopted, could be done at little greater cost than now.
The times when an undergraduate chiefly needs direction
seem to be the first year, when everything is new to him and
the self-adjustment from complete and rigid to partial and
relaxed control is difficult to make, and the last year, when
the future is opening out with rather terrifying rapidity,
and as often as not he is hesitating about his career, and yet
the final examination is imposing a strain which usually
brings its reaction when the tension is over.

It is by no means certain, as a matter of fact, that the
Regent system, at any rate in the hands of young tutors, is
a solution of the pass-man's problems at all, for the co-
ordinating of the work, in three or four subjects each, of
perhaps a dozen undergraduates, is a task which can be
properly performed only by a teacher of long experience.
But the introduction of the system is an excellent innovation and it may prepare the way for an eventual solution
which should probably be purely academic. It might consist in the carrying of one of the Pass subjects to a higher
standard than the rest, the direction of the undergraduate
then falling to the School of the subject thus chosen. After
all, it is quite unnatural to expect anyone to study three or

four subjects for three years to an equal standard. Everyone who has any right to be at a university at all has some preference for one subject or type or work over another and this preference ought to be recognized. To recognize, even to encourage it, and to make such choice compulsory would go far towards killing two birds with one stone.

IV

The life of a well-established, middle-aged professor in the Arts faculty of a modern university can, if he likes to make it so, be one of the softest jobs to be found on the earth's surface. He may live ten, twenty, or sometimes even fifty miles from his work, and come in for only two or three days a week; he may have a cottage in the country and run down to it at irregular intervals for two or three days at a stretch; or he may even have his house and family at the distant seaside, go home on Friday afternoons for long week-ends, return on Tuesday evenings, and spend the rest of the week between bachelor flat, lodgings, or club and the University.

What does his *essential* work consist of? Well, assuming that he has students (and there are professors who frequently have none, and, far from endeavouring to obtain any, actually discourage the idea), he may have to give anything from two or three to nine or ten lectures weekly. If he is conscientious, he will alternate his courses scrupulously with those of his lecturers from year to year and by reading and research keep each set strictly up to date; if he is not, he will deliver the same lectures, prepared twenty years previously, every session, pulling the notes of each out of a drawer just in time to give them a dust-over before delivery.

Besides lecturing, he has a number of duties which will be precisely as substantial as he cares to make them. Apart from the moral obligation to engage in research himself, which, once he has been appointed for life, he can disregard, if he likes, for his entire career, he is expected to supervise the research of graduate students: but, unless he is the kind of man to inspire research, very few graduate students will

come near him, so that falls to the ground. He can hardly
escape having to set and mark a few examination papers,
but these, like Christmas, come only once a year – or, very
rarely, twice. From time to time, he will be asked for testimonials, but these are largely written according to formula
and only the best professors spend long over them. He may
sometimes have to put in ten minutes or so advising an
undergraduate who has failed in an examination, found his
work too difficult, decided to change a course of study, or
got himself into one of about a score of other situations which
are periodically arising. He will receive regular summonses
to meetings of the academic bodies; and probably he will
spend an occasional hour or two in attendance at these, although he has no obligation to do so beyond a moral one,
and, even if his absences are commented upon, they will
involve him in no penalty. This seems to be the whole of a
professor's essential minimum of work and it must not be
forgotten that it applies only to the thirty weeks in the year
which are not vacation. It would probably be no exaggeration to say that, if his conscience will permit him to do so
little, he need do no more than ten hours' work a week for
from twenty-six to twenty-eight weeks in the year – say the
equivalent of thirty eight-hour days out of three hundred
and sixty-five. If he has no students, almost the whole even
of this vanishes.

Before going farther, it is only fair to say that he is paid
very badly too. A lecturer of thirty – a man, it must be
remembered, of the highest academic distinction – receiving
the modest stipend of from £500 to £600 a year, will think
himself very lucky if he suddenly jumps into a Chair with
its salary of £1,450.[1] He does not reflect (or perhaps even
know) that by the time he is sixty he will be lucky if he has
increased that salary to more than £1,550. That is no wage
to give a type of man who has the ability, and has had to
pay for the expensive education, of a barrister, a Harley

1. The figures given in this paragraph, and on p. 109, are those which
were current in 1949. They are tending to rise with the increasing costs
of living.

Street specialist or a high-class business magnate, any one of whom earns from five to twenty times the amount, or of the headmaster of some leading public school who, between salary and perquisites, earns as much as two or three professors. The difference is that the professor has a much easier life than any of these. Apparently it does him very little good, for he generally seems to die a few years after his retirement, and by no means infrequently succumbs while still in his decorative and loosely fitting harness. In another sense it certainly does him a great deal of harm: unless he is an exceptional man, he will be driven into some other kind of activity which seldom makes him a more useful member of his profession. The remedy is obvious: make your professor work as hard as your headmaster, barrister or business man, but pay him better too. A professorship might begin at £1,200 for a man of thirty, but the age and experience of the candidate should be taken into consideration and a man of forty should not be offered less than £1,600. There should be a biennial increment of £100, so that at sixty a man would be earning £2,600, at which point increments might cease, except that either then or at any point in a man's career his salary should be raised for exceptionally distinguished achievements. With this more generous remuneration, however, should be coupled much more ample requirements and more stringent tests, to which subject we shall return later.

If it be asked where this additional money is to come from (and the amount necessary would be increased by a no less essential amelioration of the salaries of lecturers) the reply would be as follows. First: if the modern universities are to pull their weight, they will, as we have said, have to be much better treated by the State. Secondly: if every professor had to do a full day's work, the universities would need fewer lecturers. Thirdly: all Schools should have lecturers, not professors, at their head, unless, over a period of years, they have had a fixed and agreed minimum of (a) undergraduates, and (b) graduate research students, the position of each School to be reviewed whenever there is to be a

change of head. Fourthly: by means of inter-university arrangements most of the Schools which have few or no
students could be eliminated. Instead of six or eight universities each with minute and from time to time non-existent Schools of (let us say) Experimental Psychology, Russian,
and Palaeography, Experimental Psychology might be
taught only where a laboratory exists or the subject fits best
into the general programme; Russian only where an existing
Chair or Lectureship is endowed, and Palaeography where
there are strong schools of Medieval Literature or History.
No effort should be spared to make these Schools, where
they exist, as efficient as they can possibly be and to encourage anyone who wishes to read in one of them to matri-
culate in the appropriate university. Apart from the labour
and skill needed for making the initial adjustment, the only
disadvantage of the plan would be to give an undergraduate
a rather smaller choice than at present of the subjects which
he takes without specializing in them. But there are already
so many such subjects that this would matter little. The
financial gain would be considerable; the gain in general
efficiency would be enormous.

Returning to our main theme – the life of the individual
professor – the reply often made to the complaint that
university teachers are underpaid is: 'Yes, financially; but
they are amply paid in free time.' That, as we have seen,
is very true, the assumption being, presumably, that time
is money. And many – perhaps most – professors add very
substantially to their incomes by engaging in all kinds of
other gainful occupations for which their training or individual talents fit them. Some of them, during July and
August, mark stacks of school examination papers or teach
at vacation courses. Others lecture for their university's
Extension Board or for the Workers' Educational Association; or, if their subject is a popular one, or they have some
attractive hobby – such as Natural History or foreign travel
– take up popular lecturing. Some go in for journalism,
specialize in translation, write novels, travel books and

plays; compile text-books; give broadcasts; and so on. None of these occupations is in the least reprehensible, and all of them may be described as in the broadest sense educational; yet many professors, whether out of necessity or from choice, undoubtedly carry them to excess. It is not good that a man with only two or three students should compress his university work into two days a week and spend the rest of the time earning money by writing text-books, or that another man, paid £1,450 a year for fifteen or twenty hours' work a week over less than thirty weeks, should shake himself free from university duties for three months at the end of June and should then settle down to devote fifty hours a week for three weeks to the intensive marking of School Certificate papers in order to earn an additional £100. The university teacher certainly needs leisure, but he needs it for reading, research and recreation of the mind, not for routine work which seldom benefits any part of him but his pocket.

Another – an unremunerative – type of work with which the professor occupies his time is university administration and politics. As has been said, it is an excellent thing that a university should be controlled and organized to the extent that it is by the Senate and the Faculties, and this should mean that, during term, a part of the working week of each of their members is devoted either to the normal meetings or to such special duties as attendance at committees for filling Chairs, library committees, departmental meetings, and so on. But there are two abuses of the system. First, committees of Senates and Faculty Boards are as a rule too numerous, too large and too frequent in their meetings: about this enough has been said already. Secondly, the well-known tendency to overwork the willing horse is nowhere more observable than here. The few people who are clearly fitted for committee work (and sometimes no less clearly unfitted for the more essential activities of university life) are elected to committee after committee, until for half their time they are serving tables, their term-life is spent between lecture-room and committee-room, and they come home at night unfit for anything but relaxation.

A few of them eventually become deans or vice-chancellors or pass out of university life altogether; but the majority remain in their Chairs and become as familiar a type as the public-school House-master or Games-master in his 'second-boyhood'.

Such professors, of course, lead an active and a happy life – to some extent, too, a profitable one. Not being, as a rule, scholars by temperament, they welcome every stormy debate as a break in what might otherwise be a monotonous existence. 'Who in the profession,' inquires a recent writer, 'has not seen such a person transformed by the prospect of a tiff in the senate, chafing to reveal a vigour, an ingenuity, a dash which would astonish the ten or twelve generations of students who have passed without suspicion of such oases of vehemence through the desert of his official ministrations?'[1] The aspersion is perhaps undeserved as regards the teaching of such persons, but it is as a rule only too accurate as regards their pursuit or direction of research. The Committee-man hardly ever sees research in its true perspective, for, in an atmosphere heavy with argument and thick with ordinances, resolutions and points of order, creative thought does not readily flourish.

The 'committee-man' type of professor often tends to look down upon those of his colleagues whom he terms 'departmentalists', as though they were self-centred people insufficiently concerned about the progress of the university as a whole. There are, of course, such, but the majority are no more one-sided in their interests than is the committee-man. The development of an individual School is a most fascinating task. So far as the university ordinances and regulations allow, on the one hand, and within whatever financial limitations there may be on the other, the head of a School is his own master and has innumerable opportunities for promoting its welfare. He will study his staff, so as to get the very best and most understanding work out of them. He will cultivate each of his students; be a guide,

1. P. Mansell-Jones, 'Where modern universities are wrong', in *The Criterion*, London, 1936, xv, 604.

philosopher and friend to them as no-one else in the university can be; and keep in touch with them after their graduation. Departmental activities of a social kind can, and should, be organized largely by undergraduates, but even so an eye, and occasionally a finger, has to be kept on these enthusiasts. And sometimes there are other institutions which have to be run throughout by the staff if they are to prosper. Then there are the local schools which have to be interested in this particular School and that aim cannot be achieved without frequent visits. All these things are well worth doing.

This section began with a description, which the informed reader knows well to be no exaggeration, of the work of a professor who does as little as he need. What has followed makes it unnecessary to compile a detailed account of the work of the professor who does as much as he can. For several hours each day he is occupied in those admirably complementary activities which form his essential duties – teaching and research – the former predominating during term, the latter in the vacation. Literary work of a broader kind than his profession demands will keep him from the specialist's groove; contact with the schools will help him to understand his freshmen; occasional lecturing in a broadly educational or a frankly popular way will take him out of his study into the world. Finally, by means of well-chosen committee work, he can leave an impress, heavy or slight, upon the constitution of the university, and by developing his School to the utmost he can not only find another way of doing this, but can exercise his interests both as a specialist and as a man. As all-round and satisfying a life as it is easy to find, and as full and busy into the bargain, yet tranquil and free from worry as are few others.

V

Of equal interest to professors, who formed the subject of the last section, and to lecturers, who are to be dealt with in the next, is the subject of superannuation.

The policy now current both in the ancient and in the modern universities of retiring all professors and lecturers, without distinction, at the age of sixty-five, is on the whole a good one. Certainly nobody who has worked in a university where each individual case is treated separately and has had experience of the jealousy, ill-feeling and inefficiency which can result from that method would be opposed to the fixing of a definite age-limit. The limit of sixty-five is probably not too high. Civil Servants, after retiring on pension at sixty, not infrequently take up considerably more strenuous occupations than those they have been holding and the university teacher has perhaps even an easier life than the average Civil Servant. No generalization can be drawn from isolated cases, and it is as unfair to refer to Oxbridge dons of years gone by who went on lecturing till they became legends, and died, still lecturing, at ninety, as to second-grade lecturers at Redbrick whom inadequate salaries and consequent financial cares seem to have robbed of all their vitality by fifty-five. As a general rule, a man who at sixty-five has done well over forty years' research and teaching ought to be ready to give up his teaching and spend what years of power he has left on research alone. Perhaps sixty-seven would be a more exact limit, but seventy, in most cases, is too high.

Some universities, though making sixty-five the normal age for superannuation, allow re-appointment for one session longer, or even for two sessions, provided the Senate (which generally means, in practice, the Board of the Faculty involved) so desires. This modification of the strict rule is particularly useful when for some reason it has proved impossible to make a new appointment immediately; and, provided it does not become the thin end of a wedge, and thus admit the disadvantages of the old haphazard system, it seems unexceptionable. What is not so is a too common custom of retiring a professor who has been earning (let us say) £1,500, and then, soon afterwards, when some minor vacancy occurs in the School, taking advantage of his not having left the locality by inviting him temporarily to do this

work at a salary of about £400. The emeritus professor seldom refuses the invitation: for one thing, he may be intellectually quite active and never have wanted to retire at all;
for another, he is interested in his old School; for a third,
he is often glad of the money. But the bargain is an iniquitous one; for, granted that part of his former salary was
paid him for administrative work, which he will no longer
have to do, his long experience and presumed scholarship
should make his value at least double that of a junior lecturer. It is surely illogical of a university which proclaims
that a man is too old to continue his work at sixty-five to
engage anyone above that age at all. But it is undignified,
as well as illogical, for the body which, on a professor's
retirement, made handsome verbal acknowledgement of his
services rendered over a long period of years, to re-engage
him at the salary of a man just entering the profession.
There were once two professors at the same University
whose names had for years been closely associated with each
other. One of them, at sixty-five, was re-appointed at
£1,100 for a further year, while the other, some years later,
was compulsorily retired at the same age, though his School
was only a small one, and in the very next session, the new
election having been delayed by the cumbrous working of
the machinery already described, was re-appointed for a
year, not merely to do the work of a junior lecturer, but as
'lecturer in charge of the School', at the stipend of £450.
The Universities might at least agree upon a minimum
figure reasonable for a professor re-engaged without
administrative obligations; or, if they expect him to do the
whole of his former work, offer him the whole of his former
salary. It is hardly in the best academic tradition to save a
few hundred pounds by taking advantage of a former
colleague's good nature, or penury, or both.

More even than on his generous allowance of time, the
scholar on the permanent staff of a university can congratu-
late himself on enjoying security of tenure; the professor is
given a formal appointment terminating only at the age of
sixty-five, and the senior lecturer, though his appointment

has periodically to be confirmed, is in practice in the same happy position. Next in value to security, and bound up with it, come the benefits of the Federated Superannuation scheme which both professor and lecturer have to join on their appointment. Now that this is over thirty years old, few whole-time university teachers are not members of it, and the improvement which has taken place in conditions of retirement since it was founded removes one great blot from the profession. It is a contributory scheme, under which the member pays in five per cent, and the University ten per cent, of his salary – a generous apportionment of the cost. So many assurance companies co-operate in the system that the member can choose the kind of policy best adapted to his individual needs, circumstances, and responsibilities. Further, the scheme embraces not only all the universities and colleges in receipt of Treasury Grants but Government scientific staffs and a great many colleges and research institutes not assisted from the Treasury. Broadly speaking, this means that a university teacher can pass to almost any other type of institution in the country to which he is likely to want to go without either the trouble or the financial loss which ceasing to belong to the Federated System might cause him. To compare this with his position at the beginning of the century, when each university had its own scheme, often confined to the senior members of its staff and not transferable to the scheme of any other body, is to note nothing less than a transformation in comfort and security.

VI

The professor, enjoying a tenure so secure that, until the date of his retirement arrives, it is almost impossible for him to be ejected except for some grave delinquency, has, as we have already remarked, practically no external stimulus to do more than the minimum either of research or of teaching. The lecturer, on the other hand, has a great deal. Some lecturers come into the profession in their thirties or forties, either from schoolmastering, or occasionally from scientific research or from industry. But the majority begin in their twenties, either immediately after taking their first or second degree, or sometimes at the end of an intermediate period which they describe in their applications as 'devoting some time to research', but for which the more usual term is 'unemployment'. At whatever age they enter, however, the large majority of them find themselves near the bottom of a ladder of which the highest rung, a professorship, seems incredibly remote, and which they have nevertheless, for their own comfort, to climb in the shortest time possible.

This ladder, known as the 'grading scheme', varies so much in different universities, and, even in the individual university, is so frequently altered that, even if a detailed description of it were possible, it would be sure before long to be out of date. There are generally three grades, the second – like the second-class in Honours degrees – being often divided into two parts. The lowest grade, that of the 'Assistant', 'Assistant Lecturer' or 'Junior Lecturer', is admittedly probationary in character; the first year of the appointment is openly so. The salary here usually begins at £400, and, in the course of three or four years, rises to £475.[1] If the lecturer is either a poor teacher (without being bad enough to have merited previous dismissal) or shows no sign of doing any research, his appointment then ceases. If, on the other hand, he is considered promising, he mounts a grade, with increase of salary to £500 or £550, rising by small increments yearly; but, unless promise has matured into performance, principally assessed on the basis of published original work considered by external experts (who are often consulted at this point) to be of merit, he will remain in that grade – or even in its lower division – for life or until he has found that its maximum salary – generally between £700 and £800 – is less than he can get in some other profession. Once, however, he has won the hall-mark of scholarship – and by this time he will normally be between thirty-five and forty – he is advanced further either

1. See p. 100, n. 1, above.

into Grade I (if Grade II is not subdivided), or into the higher division of Grade II, where security is practically as complete as in Grade I and chances of election to a Chair in another university are good. Should no such chance come off, promotion to Grade I, or to a Readership, ranking above a Grade I Lectureship, with a salary of between £900 and £1,100, follows often as a matter of course. Nothing that has been said here takes any account of the excellent and prevalent system of granting family allowances, about which no generalization is at present possible.

The salary scale under the Grading Scheme is not an ungenerous one, especially in its lower stages. There was a time when a Grade III lecturer was paid about as much as a senior porter, and certainly, allowing for the cost of living, no more than a superior parlourmaid or a nursery governess. The result was that he was compelled to find additional remunerative employment and so did little or no research, which meant tardy promotion or even the loss of his job. To-day, a young man or woman has usually enough to live simply but comfortably upon without allowing any other paid activities to interfere with essential university duties.[1] The only important exception is the case of the lecturer in some modern language or in any other subject that necessarily sends him abroad for purposes of study. For such periods, as also in rare cases where a man's research demands the purchase of expensive books or apparatus, the university should be (and sometimes is) in a position to supplement his salary by a grant.

It is in Grade I that the shoe pinches, and there is a good case for a further revision of the salary-scale here. The reply is sometimes made that senior Grade I men are generally disappointed and continuously unsuccessful candidates

1. A.U.T. (p. 13) considers that 'the problem of Grade III is not the salary, but the years of service and the prospects of promotion', neither of which seem to me unsatisfactory. The observation, however (p. 12), that 'many Grade III teachers do work of a Grade II character' raises a more serious matter: 'the impression that universities are obtaining higher academic service for unsuitably low remuneration' is discussed elsewhere in another context.

for Chairs at other universities, which may be perfectly true. But it does not follow that their repeated failures are due to incompetence: Chairs being few in number, the principal cause will always be keenness of competition. Other causes are an inability to 'interview' well; a reputation, possibly undeserved, for being 'difficult'; a dislike or incapacity (discovered too late in life) for administration or the controlling of subordinates; the inability of the electors to appreciate the value of the candidate's research; the selection of a type of research which does not lend itself to piecemeal publication; and so on. For these and many other reasons a Grade I lecturer who fails to obtain a Chair may be an able, scholarly, and in every way estimable member of a staff, while his long experience makes him both a greatly prized adjunct to a professor newly appointed to a large department and an invaluable member of boards and committees for the enactment of university business. He must not, therefore, like so many senior assistants in secondary schools, be turned into a soured and disillusioned man, ploughing moodily through his fifties and awaiting release in the form of superannuation on a pension so small that it will need to be supplemented by the marking of examination papers in cartloads. There should be a grade, in short, higher than Grade I, carrying the title of Reader or Associate Professor, for which no lecturer should be eligible who has not gone through the whole of Grade I and election to which should require a two-thirds or three-quarters vote of the Selection Committee and the Senate.

These adjustments being made, the position of the lecturer may be considered satisfactory: what is a good deal less so is the way in which he enters the university's service.

In the first place, there is the manner of his appointment. Neither the unquestioning acceptance by the Senate of an informal selection made by the professor nor a full-dress committee with representation from outside the relevant Faculty will do. To face a board of eight or ten inquisitors at the age of about twenty-three is an ordeal from which the candidate to emerge the most successfully will be not the best, but the most self-assured. On the other hand, it would seem unwise to throw on a single man, however eminent or competent (and professors are not necessarily good judges of character) the sole responsibility for the election of a colleague whom it may prove difficult to dislodge for some forty years. A better method is to make all regular junior appointments, and to confirm all junior appointments made in emergency within the year for which they are held, by means of a committee of three, two of whom should be experts and the third the executive officer of the Faculty. Alternatively, the professor might be allowed to make appointments to Grade III lectureships, which, as has been said, are probationary, the appointments to be confirmed by committee at the end of the first year. All elections to higher grades would be made by committees, which the candidates, who would be at least in their late twenties, should be fully capable of facing.

A more serious question is that of the candidates' qualifications. It seems to be assumed in all universities that anyone with a First-Class Honours degree and an inquiring mind is capable of lecturing and teaching – to say nothing of researching – without any sort of technical preparation. 'Why,' undergraduates who intend to become schoolteachers frequently ask, 'do we have to spend a year after taking our degrees in obtaining a diploma testifying that we have studied and practised the technique of teaching, whereas if we were going to take up the equally difficult work of university lecturing and had good enough degrees to be acceptable from the academic point of view we could get posts without having had any training whatsoever?' They might go on to ask why ordinands, at their training colleges, are made to take courses in the preaching of fifteen-minute sermons and even in such a simple matter as the reading of Scripture, while university lecturers, who have to lecture for hours on end, generally on more complicated subjects than those of the ordinary parish sermon, are accepted without any kind of preparation. There seems to be no answer to these questions except that universities are

amateurish bodies which have never faced up to certain
elementary facts and perhaps never will.

The results of their laxity are appalling. Some lecturers
have not even enough idea of speaking to make themselves
heard. A few years ago, in a report to be referred to in the
next section, students of the Birmingham Arts Faculty com-
plained of the 'inaudibility of lecturers' in large classes:
'It becomes difficult,' they said, 'for those students seated
at any distance from the lecturer to hear his voice.' And
this is not exceptional. Many an eminent professor, delivering an inaugural lecture, on possibly the only occasion in his
life when he will have any audience beyond his unfortunate
students, is content to mumble through an ill-written script,
stumbling over phrases he cannot decipher and failing to
kindle a spark of interest in an audience which has attended
out of politeness. Nor does he seem to mind very much that
this should be so. In most cases he knows his stuff and believes himself to be passing it on satisfactorily to others, but
whether or not he is putting it across with the maximum of
efficiency is simply of no interest to him. Indeed, the whole
idea of 'putting it across' is foreign to his ideas and perhaps
distasteful – 'a vulgar Americanism', one dear old colleague
of mine used to term it. His attitude is that the undergraduate must take him as he finds him and be thankful.

What remedy can we find for such a state of things? The
Birmingham students (whether inspired by exaggerated
respect or by a sense of humour cannot be stated) suggested
that classes might be made smaller. An alternative would
be for lectures to be made better – by means of training.
The University Grants Committee seems to think the young
lecturer can undertake his own training, much as the Victorian father believed that his sons could undertake their
own sex education. 'Young University teachers', remarks
the 1936 Report, 'might be more systematically encouraged
to take serious thought as to the best manner of presenting
a subject. In this connection careful preparation is essential.'[1] But few who are not born lecturers will find this

1. U.G.C., 1936, p. 21.

counsel sufficient. The universities who employ them should see to it that they do more than 'take serious thought'. Till this happens, a professor might at least be expected to hear some of the lectures of his newly-appointed lecturers during their first terms and discuss both the preparation and the presentation of their work with them privately. This is admittedly an ordeal, which one would gladly spare them were there any alternative method of training, but until the universities take their responsibilities more seriously there seems to be none – and, after all, every school-teacher has to accustom himself to supervision.

The revelations produced by such visits as these are incredible. I have heard a young lecturer intone his lecture with his elbows on the desk, his head on his hands and his eyes fixed all the time on a manuscript from which he read word for word. I have seen a man talk for five minutes on end with his back half-turned from the class and for part of that time looking out of the window. I even knew one youth so fixed in his habits that he could only lecture extemporarily by pacing six steps in one direction in front of his audience and then turning round and taking six steps in the other: if he interrupted his progress his inspiration at once vanished and he was forced back to his lecture notes which he would then read almost word for word. And yet he was a thoroughly good scholar and knew his work through and through.

Then there is the all-important matter of organizing a lecture-course which also needs experience or training. For a beginner to plan his course and time his lectures without being instructed how to do so is probably exceptional: the method generally favoured is to get through as much as you can in each hour and hope that, by the end of the session, you may have covered the syllabus, omitting chunks of it as soon as you discover that you certainly will not. In this respect there seems to have been a falling-off since the last generation. Then, the syllabus was invariably covered, though most of the lectures were factual and often trivial in content, delivered in dull and monotonous tones, and as lifeless as though the lecturer were deliberately trying to suppress his own personality. To-day there may be more personality but there is certainly less method.

The only effective remedy is, of course, to subject all would-be university lecturers to a specific course of training. It would be best to make this, with slight modifications, the normal full year's course for the training of teachers. Quite apart from the efficiency of such a course, the break of a year between graduation and one's first post gives valuable time for mental recuperation and an adjustment of thought after a period of intense specialization, while the study of such new subjects as psychology, method and the history of education broadens the outlook in a way from which no specialist can fail to benefit. But the minimum requirements of efficiency would probably be met if a short and purely technical course, compressible into the three months of the Long Vacation, were organized centrally (say in London) and required to be taken by all candidates for lectureships. Training in reading aloud, the delivery of a lecture, the teaching of a class and the planning both of a syllabus and of a single lesson or lecture, would be better than no training at all. This type of instruction could be conveniently worked in with either existing or *ad hoc* vacation courses, the members of which would provide the necessary audiences. The essential thing would be the practical examination at its close: no candidate ought to be accepted for any but a temporary post in a university until he had passed it.

VII

In any discussion of the lecture system in vogue at the modern universities, prominence should be given to the results of agitations and inquiries carried on by student groups during the past decade at Glasgow, Birmingham and Liverpool. It may be worth while briefly to describe each of these in turn.

At Glasgow the agitation began in December 1932, when the Students' Representative Council, declaring that 'all was not well with the Arts degree' set up a committee to investigate what a student orator termed 'an academic chaos, a cultural quagmire'. Progress was slow: only in May 1933 was a questionnaire sent out to all Arts students, of which, if we may judge from outspoken comments in the *Gilmorehill Globe*, an ephemeral student-periodical, but little notice was taken. It was not until March 1934 that seven recommendations were made to the Senate, four of which dealt broadly with the lecture system:

(i) That attendance records should be either abolished or regularized;

(ii) That students should be given printed synopses of lectures;

(iii) That worked scripts should be returned at special tutorials held after class (i.e., terminal) examinations.

(iv) That no class should contain more than 150 [*sic!*] students.

Nothing practical, it appears, resulted from these recommendations. In October 1934, when Sir Daniel Stevenson was installed as Chancellor, the irrepressible *Globe* suggested that they should be submitted to him personally by the student body. Shortly afterwards, as is the way of such publications, the *Globe* itself came to financial grief and the matter lapsed.

The Birmingham inquiry, carried out in 1936, was a more business-like affair, inspired partly by comments on the subject made by the University Grants Committee in that year[1] and partly by a student-debate held in the Union at the end of the Lent Term at which a motion approving the lecture system was lost by 87 votes to 21. A mass meeting of the Guild of Undergraduates followed, at which four propositions were carried, viz.:

(1) Lecture notes should be distributed: this would make unnecessary 'a large number of lectures which consist of mere dictation'.

(2) Lectures should survey 'basic principles' rather than be 'as at present a dictation of a conglomeration of facts.'

1. U.G.C., 1936, pp. 21–3.

(3) 'In the time thus liberated', tutorial classes, each of not more than six students, should be formed.

(4) A joint committee of University authorities and Guild representatives should study the practicability of the foregoing recommendations.

At the same meeting propositions recommending the reduction of lecture-hours and the abolition of compulsory attendance at lectures were rejected.

In the following week the Guild set on foot a methodical inquiry (which, if an onlooker may be allowed to say so, did it great credit) 'on the grievances against the present system' and issued a printed report of twelve pages to be referred to shortly. Nothing very definite resulted, but the undergraduates' evident dissatisfaction with the fare provided for them produced a considerable effect.

At Liverpool a similar inquiry was held, and a report prepared, by a Committee of the Guild of Undergraduates, during the session 1937-8. Less is disclosed about the origins of this inquiry, but the Committee was clearly under the influence of the Grants Committee Report for 1936; each of the Departmental Societies reported, both on the general points raised and also on matters connected with their special interests in which they saw need for reform. Though, as at Birmingham, some of the conclusions reached showed imperfect understanding of the issues involved, the report was indubitably, as it claimed to be, 'a sincere effort on the part of the student body to present what it considered to be a genuine opinion of the Lecture System as at present instituted'.

It may be added that the National Union of Students also debated this subject at its Southampton congress in April 1937 and 'emphatically endorsed the opinions expressed by the Grants Committee, that more time should be allowed for discussion groups, tutorials and seminars, and that lectures should be reduced to an absolute minimum.'[1] Similar opinions were expressed, without a dissentient voice, at the Cambridge conference of 1941.[2]

1. N.U.S., 1937, pp. 52-3.   2. N.U.S., 1941, pp. 22, 24.

The question which apparently provoked the greatest diversity of opinion at Liverpool was one which at Birmingham hardly carried any weight at all: viz., whether attendance at a minimum number of lectures should be exacted as a prerequisite for admission to a degree examination. In the Oxbridge of long ago one went to lectures or not as one pleased, but, as at that time most lecture-courses had to be paid for separately, one often persisted in attendance at courses which proved to be inefficient or useless so as not to feel one was throwing away money, though, to do them justice, the lecturers never passed round the attendance list from which they made out their invoices until the second lecture of the course: the first taste was free. At the Oxbridge of to-day, where the student pays a single fee and for this may attend not only the lectures in his School or 'Faculty' but those in certain others, the temptation for the undergraduate who likes his money's worth is still strong, though for a different reason. But attendance at these lectures is in practice quite voluntary: no-one stands at doors and 'takes names'. At the modern university, where the register is marked at each lecture, the theory is that 75 or 80 per cent of the maximum number of attendances is required from all candidates for examinations, the idea being to prevent the university degree from becoming an 'external' one and to maintain the closest possible contact between teachers and taught. All Schools are required to send in periodical reports on attendances, but it would be interesting to learn if absences have ever cost any student exclusion from examinations and consequent loss of a year's studies. The issue raised in the questionnaire was if this system was a good one.

Though answers ranged from an emphatic affirmative to an emphatic negative, the majority thought, as more decidedly at Birmingham, that the system should continue. On the whole I agree. Those who disliked it wanted greater freedom in the university than at school, an opinion which seems to be supported by the Report of the University Grants Committee for 1936: the idea of compulsion, it says, is 'appropriate to a mental age considerably younger than

that of University students'.[1] But even under our present
system the undergraduate has more freedom than at school,
for at school, when allowance has been made for illness and
other unavoidable causes of absence, 100 per cent is the
compulsory requirement. Some of the societies suggested
that the minimum should be 50 per cent; but this is meaningless, for of what use is it to anyone to attend every other
lecture in a course? My own objection to the removal of
compulsion is this. With a voluntary system, if your lectures
are of any use, you will still, on most days in the year, get
practically everybody. But on a wet morning, or on the day
after some late evening function, or during an epidemic of
colds, or on some fine day in summer, you will get practically no-one. The moral result of removing compulsion,
that is to say, will simply be to popularize the line of least
resistance; the academic result, to lower the standards
of efficiency. I would gladly exempt any undergraduates
from the whole of my lectures who thought they could do
equally well without them. But if they are to attend any
of them, it is reasonable to expect them to attend virtually
all.

That there is little demand for a change in the system
seems clear from the high actual attendances, which are far
above any postulated minimum. The following figures were
supplied by a School of moderate size and no great distinction for the Michaelmas Term of 1941:

	Per cent present	Per cent excused through illness, etc.	Per cent absent without stating any cause
1. First Year (all lectures combined)	84	6	10
2. Higher Years other than Honours	90	5	5
3. Honours Courses	98	2	0

This record supports the contention that it is either tradition, or the value of the lectures, or both, that maintains

1. U.G.S., 1936, p. 22.

the attendance at them, and not the existence of any kind of external regulation.

In all discussions on the lecture system – at any rate ever since the versatile and plausible 'Q' published his *Lecture on Lectures*[1] and prefaced it with a famous quotation from Dr Johnson – it has been customary to speak of lectures as if they were the natural and traditional rivals of books. 'Lectures were once useful', Boswell reports Johnson as saying; 'but now, when all can read, and Books are so numerous, Lectures are unnecessary.'[2] The antithesis is surely an entirely false one. Lectures and books are no more rivals than teaching and research, than Medieval and Modern History, than English Language and English Literature. They are (or should be) complementary, each helping the other.

The difference between the two is rather like tuition received by correspondence and tuition given viva voce. The impression left by the personality of the tutor whom one meets in the flesh is the deeper and more vital; yet when his inspiration has faded it is almost impossible to recapture, and one turns gratefully to the marginal notes written on one's manuscript by the man at the Correspondence School. They at least are as black and legible as ever. So with books and lectures. 'Q', as devil's advocate, states the case for books generally:

'The reader of a book can take it at his own *tempo*, not hurried by the lecturer's pace. He can bend his mind to it at his own convenience, not catching up his gown to attend on a time-table, not pushing for a seat if he be late and the seats are crowded. If he find a difficulty here and there, he can pause at any point, turn back, re-read. No continuous strain of attention is required; for, while the spoken lecture may induce somnolence, and the printed page a somnolence even deeper, yet with the advantages of privacy, you can lay the book at any point face downward on your knee, turn back on awaking, and recapture your interest. You cannot

1. London, 1927.
2. Boswell, *Life of Dr Johnson,* cit. Quiller-Couch, op. cit., p. 5.

do this with a lecturer – who, moreover, has possibly by this time gone home.'[1]

Yes, but are these really advantages at all? It is true enough that one can read a book without concentrating on it, whereas an able lecture almost forces concentration upon one; true enough that many undergraduates leave the university without knowing what concentration on a book really means. But can taking up a book and going to sleep over it be dignified by the name of working? It is to be feared that the devil's advocate was pleading with his academic tongue in his only too human cheek: for the real advantages of books over lectures we must look elsewhere.

Books are solid and permanent: they cannot evaporate or disappear. They have been carefully written and their theme is developed in the clearest form of which the author is capable. They can (as 'Q' remarks) be studied at the learner's own pace and to some extent he can adapt them to his methods. They involve no long walk or train journey; no periods of time wasted, as between two lectures; no subsequent investment of time in the re-writing of notes; no enforced postponement of the next instalment of study for a week or a fortnight. All these are substantial advantages.

But think also of the deficiencies of books. First of all, their number. How shall the student who relies on books alone know which to buy or borrow? Even if the library catalogue at his university has a subject-index (which is unlikely) he will find, under 'English history in the sixteenth century' twenty-seven works by nineteen authors. Let us suppose that he has taken advantage of a hypothetical new regulation making lectures voluntary and decided to study the sixteenth century unaided. Which of the twenty-seven works shall he choose? A pocket manual or a standard authority in three volumes? That single-volume history published quite recently looks the sort of thing – but, alas, it is 'out' and may not be back for as long as a fortnight. So he takes the pocket manual, but on sitting down to it discovers that its style is over-compressed and that the

1. Op. cit., p. 12.

library copy has lost its first eight pages. So he goes back
with it to the library and starts to wade through a larger
volume. But this, though interesting enough, appears to
give disproportionate space to very minor matters and soon
he can no longer see the wood for the trees. Half a term
passes in experiments of this kind and his progress is negligible. If a slacker at heart, he gives up the struggle. If a
sensible man, he puts his pride in his pocket, borrows a
companion's notes of the lectures he has missed, and returns
to the fold, only to find that in the very first lecture the
professor had mapped out the whole of his year's reading
for him.

Then there is the trustworthiness of the authors. How can
an inexperienced undergraduate possibly know that A's
views on Victor Hugo are exaggerated by his political bias;
that B has a prejudice against the Romantics; that, though
C enjoys world-wide fame as a critic, his book on Hugo
happens to be one of his *juvenilia*; that D is interested chiefly
in Hugo's dramas and the chapters in his work on the poetry
are not worth reading; that E, though we have to put him
in the library, is a hopeless dilettante and only an odd page
or two of him is worthy of serious study? But the lecturer
knows all this perfectly; and half an hour of his frank and
informal talk on the books available will save weeks of
aimless or misleading study. Nor could his comments ever
be printed in a book: they are too direct and personal for
that, and, as new works appear, they change continually.
Besides – there is a law of libel!

Next come questions of emphasis and selection. For the
purpose of some particular lecture course, only part of a
book is needed. The course, let us say, is on a certain English poet: who is to tell the undergraduate that there is more
criticism on that author worth remembering in a few pages
of Courthope or Saintsbury than in half the monographs
upon him to which the uninstructed student would naturally
turn? Or there is an Outlines of European History course of
twenty-five lectures and on two of these lectures the only
standard work in English is a heavily footnoted tome of

800 pages. Who except a lecturer is going to pilot the student through that work so that he can study the most essential part in the short time at his disposal? Or again, just one phase of a literary movement, just one philological rule is particularly difficult for the partially trained mind to assimilate. The author of the standard treatise on the subject is not writing for partially trained minds and if he were to dwell at length on those particular points he would throw his whole book out of proportion. The lecturer, on the other hand, is speaking expressly to the immature, and he knows, by experience, where he may safely skip and refer to books, where he may go quickly, where he must dictate and explain, where he must repeat and recapitulate, and even, in lectures of a less formal type, where he should catechize.

In all these, and in many other ways, lectures are complementary to books, not substitutes for them. 'I cannot see', remarked Johnson, 'that Lectures can do so much good as reading the Books from which the Lectures are taken.'[1] It seems so simple; and, if lectures were merely 'taken' from books, it would be. But a lecture is the fruit of perhaps twenty years' reading which the hearer cannot possibly compress into a term or two. It contains the wisdom of a score of books; and, even if the books were at his elbow, the student would not have time to read them. It is the product of a mature mind with long experience of what students need and can assimilate; it is often presented by a forceful personality; it stimulates, challenges and provokes in a way that nothing can unless it comes through the human voice. Let it be granted that, as the students we have been speaking of would say, there are bad lectures, given by professors who ought to have been appointed to research Chairs or to no Chairs at all. But their badness is generally notorious; they can often be avoided (bad lectures, for example, have a way of 'clashing' with good!) and sometimes, as through the private intervention of a sympathetic tutor or director of studies, they can even be

1. Quiller-Couch, op. cit. p. 5.

reformed. And let us not forget that there are also bad books, written by authors who ought never to have handled a pen; to say nothing of books good, even excellent, in themselves, but too advanced, or too obscure in style, for the adolescent. And the chief difficulty about all these is that there is simply no way of recognizing them. Some of the most unsuitable books for the student are published by the best houses, printed on the finest paper and written by men whose names are known even to the undergraduate. If he is no longer to attend lectures, then all books too advanced for learners must be bound in blue, badly written books in red and books of the first importance to students in green. And even that revolutionary reform will have made the lecture only one degree less indispensable.

To return to the reports, two of the three expressed dissatisfaction with the types of lecture given and there can be little doubt that there is grave cause for complaint under this head. Nor is the dissatisfaction anything new. 'Only one lecturer that I went to as an undergraduate', reports Mr F. L. Lucas of Cambridge, 'was better worth hearing than reading.'[1] Similar testimony can be elicited from any group of university-trained men, of any age: no wonder, then, in this generation of outspoken undergraduates, that it should be heard from the classroom as well.

It is surely axiomatic that no lecture course should ever be given, the material of which could be obtained by the hearers direct from books, unless, as sometimes happens, the material available in this way is of such a kind as to be unintelligible without simplification and commentary. But evidently this principle is not generally observed. To the universal Birmingham complaints of 'mere dictation' of a

1. *Cambridge University Studies*, London, 1933, pp. 292–3. It is true that he adds: 'That exception was a brilliant one.' As a report recently issued by the National Union of Students of its Arts Faculty Conference quotes the complaint of a Cambridge delegate, from the English School, that lecturers dealt too much with 'text-book facts', and an Oxford undergraduate wrote in 1942 that 'the subject-matter of nearly all our lectures can be found in books', things have not apparently changed greatly since the undergraduate days of Mr Lucas.

'conglomeration of facts' may be added the evidently keenly felt grievance of the Birmingham science student:

Much valuable time is wasted in writing down large masses of detailed information dictated in the course of a lecture. In many cases lectures become large dictation classes, in which there is an advantage for the quick and legible writer but which lead to considerable confusion for those who are slower, or else are trying to follow the meaning of the lecture as it proceeds.

With this compare the more urbane criticisms of Liverpool:

The necessity for a certain number of lectures to keep pace with modern developments is obvious. What we do urge is that factual lectures are a waste of time and energy; yet so many of the lectures we receive tend to be mere recitals of facts ('animated dialogues with one part left out') which are written down automatically, almost subconsciously, to be re-read only before examinations.

I would not condemn 'factual lectures' as unreservedly as these young reformers do, for a scholar's personality can make them as indispensable as any. Part of the criticism may be due to a failure to realize that the lecturer brings a trained mind to the tasks of selection, simplification, explanation, arrangement, and emphasis, and that what to the inexperienced listener may seem like random dives into 'the book' are in fact highly skilful adaptations of it – and of others which he may not know. Yet, when all this has been said, it will probably be generally admitted that there is a residuum of truth in the undergraduates' complaints and that the standard of lecturing, in content, as well as in delivery, needs to be greatly raised.

One very definite demand is made by all three groups of students – that they should be provided with printed or typed notes of their lectures. At Birmingham, such notes were actually supplied in the Faculties of Medicine and Law, a fact which no doubt stimulated the other Faculties to ask for them. This innovation, assuming that the notes provided were full enough and compulsory attendance were abolished, would certainly oblige professors and lecturers, if they wanted audiences, to give their discourses the maximum of attractiveness. At Liverpool, a plebiscite held on this and other matters in March 1937 resulted in a demand for printed lecture notes by 70.6 per cent, and only 20.7 per cent voted against them. In the departmental inquiries summarized in the report practically every society asked for them. The arguments were well put at the time by an anonymous writer in *Sphinx,* the student magazine, as follows:

'Full advantage cannot be taken of lectures owing to the necessity for note taking. One has to decide between taking down a rough outline of the lecture, which means missing out many of the finer points, or taking down verbatim any special statements of the lecturer, and perhaps losing the thread of the discussion. The result is that, unless one loses a good deal of valuable time in copying up the notes, one only has a rough outline of the lecture; at the same time, it is impossible to concentrate upon the lecturer, and each point cannot therefore be driven home by the lecturer to its fullest advantage.

'It would be to the advantage of both the student and the lecturer to provide a printed outline of the lecture, as is in fact done by certain lecturers in other departments, which would be sufficiently full to suggest the main points of discussion, and so avoid the necessity for taking notes. The outline would constitute a reminder of the lecture and, at the same time, serve as a basis for discussion for Tutorials.'

Any undergraduate who may read this book will not, I hope, accuse its author of lacking sympathy with the student's point of view, and I appreciate that point of view here perfectly. Nevertheless, I am convinced that it is a mistaken one. Lists of the titles of lectures, showing how much ground is to be covered each week and indicating the preparatory reading that should be done for each lecture, might be distributed at the beginning of a good many courses. They would be useful to the student for the organization of his reading, especially when he was obliged to be absent or was anxious for any reason to get ahead of the course. But to distribute lecture notes is a procedure cramping to both lecturer and student. To the lecturer – because, if he is efficient, his courses have to be continually revised, new material has to be added and emphasis must be shifted as his experience of his classes grows, or as new books on the subject appear. To the student – because, as has been suggested, he may be tempted to think that, if he has the notes, he has everything, but, most of all, because in the very taking of notes which the undergraduate just quoted finds so difficult consists a valuable part of university education.

There are many and diverse ways of 'sitting under' a lecturer. At one extreme there is the man who sits rigidly in an attitude of apparently deep dejection, only emerging from it occasionally to jot down a single word or phrase which strikes him. At the other extreme there is the kind of listener one sometimes finds in University Extension courses – sitting bolt upright from the moment you mount the dais, with bunch of pencils ready sharpened and shorthand notebook in position, preparing to take down every word that is to proceed from your mouth, to transcribe it all into longhand on the next evening, and eventually, no doubt, to reproduce a large part of it in the sessional examination.

The average able student learns by experience how to summarize the main points of a lecture *without* 'missing out many of the finer points', and, by the time he goes down, is expert in an important art which without his university training he would never have learned: précis-writing, not from a printed passage (as at school, where this is one of the most valuable things one learns), but from the spoken word. The university-trained man can take down, mentally or in writing, as few others can, the gist of a speech, and yet preserve any important thoughts in it which do not affect its main outline. That art should be cultivated and preserved, not allowed to die.

The skilful and considerate lecturer will help him by remembering that he has both to write and to listen and

not therefore adopting the rate and technique of a popular
speaker. By occasional repetition, by variation of rate and
emphasis or by saying from time to time 'I suggest your
taking down this passage *verbatim*', and then frankly dictat-
ing, he can make his task much easier. The young lecturer
will do well to inspect notebooks occasionally, not so much
for his students' benefit as for his own: there is no other way
in which he will learn so much of their failings, their needs
and their capabilities.

Another reform asked for, in some shape or other, by all
three groups of students was the seminar. Glasgow asked
for it in connection with the terminal examinations – and
is it not amazing that these valuable means of instruction
should be so widely used as mere tests, the undergraduates
never seeing their papers again? At Birmingham the Arts
and Science Faculties were particularly clamant for small
tutorial classes: in Arts there was 'general complaint' about
this; in Science 'all departments ... are strong in support of
individual tuition of students, and supervision of work,
which is neglected until the student reaches an advanced
course'. At Liverpool, some 55 per cent of those who took
part in the plebiscite referred to asked for more tutorial
classes. The National Union of Students voted similarly,
as we have seen, in 1937,[1] and in 1941 the 'Arts Commission'
of its Cambridge congress passed a resolution asking that
'tutorials and seminars should be extended and that discussions should be held following on lectures', by 141 votes
too, without abstentions.[2] The position, apparently, is that
everywhere seminars already exist but many more are
asked for: no doubt this is partly a reasonable request and
partly the result of modern youth's urge to express itself
even if it has nothing to say. But here, as elsewhere, the
great force behind the students – a piquant situation when
one comes to think of it – was the University Grants Committee, which in its 1936 Report expressed itself thus:

'Lectures might be fewer and need not be compulsory
if a greater use could be made of the seminar or tutorial

1. Cf. p. 117, above.   2. N.U.S., 1941, p. 24.

system. The distinctive advantage of this system is that the teacher meets the individual student or a group of students small enough to make possible a real discussion in which all present can take part, so that between the minds of student and teacher there is real give and take. ... Students can there ask their own questions, submit their own difficulties, and in some subjects even argue and defend their own ideas. ... Students are thus enabled in discussion with the teacher and with one another to develop, to clarify, and to correct their own ideas, and this is far more stimulating and educative than any mere assimilation of the ideas of the teacher however excellent those may be.'[1]

This is a great advance upon the reply made by an Oxbridge professor to a daring freshman who accosted him just as he had gathered up his manuscript and mortar-board and was about to sweep down from the dais and out of the lecture-room.

'Please, sir,' he said (from which mode of address it will be gathered that he had not come from one of the 'best' schools), 'is there any time when we can come to you and ask questions about your lectures?'

'There is *not*,' replied the professor, witheringly, and then added, feeling that he might temper the wind to a lamb but recently shorn of the childish privileges of school:

'*We don't do that sort of thing – HERE.*'

Indeed, the Grants Committee is more drastic in its recommendations than the would-be modernly minded 'Q', to whom it seemed that 'in ... lectures all interruptions should be ruled out' but that, in return for this concession, 'the lecturer should confine his words within fifty minutes or even less; and that afterwards, in a retiring-room, he should listen to any listener's difficulty, or – if he be tired and the difficulty serious – appoint a time to discuss it privately in his college rooms'.[2]

This delicious suggestion, which reads like a slightly profane rubric from the Prayer Book, is altogether too Victorian to be taken seriously (how A. C. Benson would have graced

1. U.G.C., 1936, p. 22.   2. *Lecture on Lectures,* p. 47.

that retiring-room!)[1] and must be enjoyed as one of the best pieces of questionably conscious irony that its gifted author ever perpetrated. The assumption underlying it, however, is rather an unfortunate one – namely, that the lecture is a discourse which should normally be not question-raising, but doubt-dispelling (if not, indeed, thought-quenching) and that only on rare occasions will questions arise other than of the type: 'Did you say Johnson or Thomson?' or any other demand be made upon a giant brain exhausted after the exertion of a fifty-minutes' reading from typescript. The stimulating lectures of 'Q' himself would certainly never come within this category, and, if he were taken at his word – presumably the last thing he expected – there would be a thronged retiring-room followed by a whole series of college meetings, which would, in fact, constitute nothing less than the 'tutorial system' in its most complete form.

Let us go back, then, to the recommendations of the plebiscite and of the University Grants Committee.

There are always inexplicable critics, and one of them once laid it down that 'any marked and special attention to the individual work of students by a specialist teacher comes perilously near to coaching, which is not the function of a college'.[2] But, with the exception of such a critic and of the most hidebound conservative, everyone will agree that anything which makes possible 'more individual tuition and more personal contact between staff and student'[3] is intrinsically desirable. But the question is one of the best use of time. First-year, or 'Intermediate', students take

1. The Birmingham science students raise the sympathetic if somewhat ungrammatical objection to a similar proposal that if 'the question is asked during the Lecturer's free time, ... the answer is curtailed, due, frequently, to the Lecturer's domestic arrangements'. 'In some cases', they add, darkly, 'questions are not welcomed.' An Oxbridge under-graduate, writing privately to me on this subject, goes further. 'There is little of the "Any questions?" attitude', he says, 'about most of our lecturers.'

2. L. E. C. Hughes, 'Perspective on lectures', in *The Universities Review*, London, November 1940, vol. xiii, p. 3.

3. U.G.C. 1936, p. 11.

four (more rarely three) subjects, and, if twelve hours weekly is to be a maximum allowance of lectures – as it surely should – this leaves each subject with a maximum of three to four hours, out of which it is difficult to see how more than one hour can be a tutorial except where numbers are so small that the distinction between lecture and tutorial vanishes. In a language-subject, indeed, one of the hours must always be devoted to prose composition, one to literature and at least one to conversation, and what happens, in that case, to essay-writing, history and philology? Can anyone, for that matter, maintain that one weekly lecture is enough to guide a student through the whole range of a foreign literature, or even over a period of two centuries? There is more time in Honours courses; but here, besides essays in the foreign language, translation from and into it, conversation and a much longer period of literature, there are (in both the languages, if two are taken) History, Institutions, General and Special Philology and the reading of old and pre-modern texts, to say nothing of periodical additional lectures on such subjects, the importance of which is continually being urged to-day, as Politics, Painting, Architecture, Music and Folk-lore, without some knowledge of which no language-course can be considered adequate. So that the question of Tutorials comes to this: Shall the undergraduate have less time for himself and more time in the class-room?

Nor is this the only problem. 'Q' seems to think that any body of undergraduates, after listening to a lecture on Wordsworth's Theory of Poetry or the Initial Organization of the American Colonies can at once absorb its content and that 'difficulties' will then emerge as clearly and crisply as the stamp from the slot-machine on the insertion of the requisite coin. Unfortunately minds – even, sometimes, mature minds – do not work like that. Before a tutorial class in any literature, for example, can be worth anything, the students must, not merely have listened to a lecture, but have read widely, and thought as deeply as they are capable of thinking on what they have read, both *about* the literature (i.e., in critical works) and *of* the literature itself. Otherwise the questions they are asking and the difficulties they are submitting will be of a kind to which they can perfectly well find out the answers for themselves by reading – and it is much better that they should. This means either that all the necessary reading for each lecture must have been done by all the undergraduates before it is given (an excellent plan, but, till libraries have numerous copies of every important book or undergraduates can afford to buy everything they need for their reading, a counsel of perfection) or that the tutorial classes on a lecture course must be held a term, or even a year, after the course itself. The latter is quite a feasible arrangement, for the tutorial class will assist the student's revision, but it means that each one's number of class periods will be exactly doubled, a state of things which the very critics of the lecture system are most anxious to avoid.

Were all Schools small, with no more than half-a-dozen students in each year, it would be practicable to a great extent to substitute tutorial classes for lectures, for the lecturer could then ensure that the necessary reading was done beforehand, or arrange the order of his classes to fit the progress of the reading, and, as no splitting of classes would be required, there would be no additional expense. But imagine a First Year Honours Shakespeare course, which at present is given twice weekly to one hundred and fifty students (that ideal maximum so much desired at Glasgow) being treated tutorially! This would mean fifteen classes of ten each or ten of fifteen each – more than the work of an additional lecturer, and for one course alone. Then, too, as everyone thinks he knows something about Shakespeare, and every member of the class would have read a few of his plays at school, the discussions, unless rigidly controlled, would be long, fierce, rambling and often irrelevant: any hard-working student would gain far more by spending the same hour quietly with his Bradley. If it were compulsory to treat such a course tutorially, the doubling of the time spent on it and the expense of an

additional lecturer could not be avoided, but two alternative
methods could be employed, either of them better than
that described. One would be to wait until the whole course
had been completed and then to hold the tutorial classes,
not for discussion of individual lectures but for more advanced discussion ranging over the whole field. The other,
a system in vogue at a well-known American university,
would be to attach to each large School a number of young
graduates (preferably graduates of that same university
reading for a higher degree – they would not then require
full-time salaries) to each of whom would be allotted a
group of students and who would be responsible, among
other things, for seeing that before each lecture their students read as much as possible from the prescribed authors.
Then, either immediately or very soon after the lecture,
the groups would meet their leaders, discuss it with them
in the light of their own reading and have the benefit of
another and a more mature view on it than each other's or
their own. Such a practice as this is perhaps the sole way of
meeting the views of the out-and-out 'tutorialists'. It will
make great inroads into the university's finance and into
the undergraduate's time; and some may doubt if the gain
will be proportionate to the outlay. But it does at least take
the difficulties into consideration, as the tutorialists' facile
generalizations do not.

Indeed, though one is always anxious to be sympathetic
to suggestions made by the Grants Committee since it so
frequently itself shows sympathy, wisdom and discernment,
it must here be taken gently to task for enunciating the
most unexceptionable principles without recommending
financial provision for putting them into practice. Any
tutorial system, as the Committee agrees, involves more
generous staffing; and 'the policy implied of moving in this
direction as strenuously as means will permit is one which
has our cordial sympathy'.[1] But let the Committee face the
facts. Here is a small university, in the Arts Faculty of which
there is a total of 324 weekly lectures. Let us suppose that

1. U.G.C., 1936, p. 23.

one-third of these (a high assumption) either exist only on paper, as a few probably will, or are seminars, language-classes or other lectures already tutorial in character. Let us then, for the sake of economy, abolish one-third of the 216 others and provide each of the 144 which remain with just one tutorial class weekly, though some of these classes would have over 50 students and for efficiency would need subdividing into five or six. However, for these classes let us provide 12 young graduates at the minimum salary of £350 a year each and taking 12 hours' tuition weekly. The cost of this inadequate tutorial system, in one Faculty alone of this small university, would be £4,200 a year, not more than half of which sum, at the very most, might be saved by the cancellation of 72 lectures weekly. If the tutorials of one Faculty cost £2,100, the cost to the entire university would not be less than £7,000; and the whole of the universities would need considerably over £80,000. And we have not done yet. 'A tutorial system,' says the Grants Committee, 'in which the junior members played the only or even the main part would be very far from what we have in mind.'[1] So even professors (at £1,450 each) are to be brought in, then! Well, let us assume that the average tutor's salary which the Committee has in mind is only £700 (i.e., to every three classes one professor and two junior lecturers, or three rather poorly paid senior lecturers). That means over £160,000 a year for a tutorial system of almost minimum adequacy. Does the Committee see any prospect of recommending such an additional sum? And, if it can be obtained, is it certain that a tutorial system of this kind is the best thing to buy with it?

It is really worth while asking, indeed, if the whole question of lecture *versus* tutorial has not been made too much of and if the emphasis has not been shifted from the more important question whether the undergraduate is made to feel that the responsibility for covering his syllabus and reading round it is really his. It is most instructive, if also rather surprising, to observe that the Grants Committee assumes all lectures to be the 'mere assimilation of the ideas of the teacher':[1] actually, of course, all good lectures present many other ideas and view-points than the teacher's. If the learned signatories to the report honestly think that, what wonder that the undergraduate should? He certainly does. And one reason why the spoon-feeding lecture, 'taken' from books or made up exclusively of the lecturer's own ideas, is bad, is that the student comes to think that if he learns his lecture notes his whole duty is done. Tell him specifically, on the other hand, that he must organize his own work, and that his professor's task is to help him, whether by lectures or by tutorial classes, to do so, and you put both professor and student on their mettle – the latter, to be his own master and ask for such help as he needs and seems not to be getting; the former, to provide the type and amount of help asked for if he thinks the request a suitable one. Once those ideas were inculcated and both parties were working jointly towards the same object, we should hear very few more complaints about compulsory lectures or demands for the substitution of one form of teaching for another. For the problem would in effect have been worked out as between each teacher and each class, and the question which we began by asking would have solved itself.

VIII

Of the examination system at the modern university two features merit special mention.

One is the obligation to appoint an external examiner, generally from another university, who sets many of the papers, marks some or (occasionally) all of them, takes part in the viva voce test (which most universities make a part of every examination leading to a degree) and sits in committee with the other examiners in the School or the Faculty for the determination of results.[2] There are external examiners

1. U.G.C., 1936, p. 22.
2. Flexner (p. 253) asserts that only one college in the whole of the United States appoints external examiners for the bachelor's degree. In the award of higher degrees, however, external opinion may play an important part, as I know from personal experience.

at Oxford and Cambridge, but they are sometimes external only in name – i.e., they may be resident members of the University with considerable knowledge of the courses taken, so that the clean bracing air of outside opinion is not felt. It is unnecessary to point out how valuable this is to all concerned – to the University and to the individual School, which it helps to keep up a high standard; to the examinee, who can be sure that any possible personal prejudice for or against him is removed; and not least to the external examiner himself, who is able to make a private comparison between the methods and standards of a colleague's School and his own.

The other outstanding feature is the custom, in the modern university, at every examination, of taking into account the classwork of the candidate during the period covered by it. Sometimes this is observed very literally and strictly – i.e., at the Examiners' meeting details are laid on the table of each candidate's work during his career in the School. More ordinarily, it is thought sufficient to refer to the course records in 'borderline' cases or to give the external examiner some general idea of each examinee's capability and past. Contrast this practice, especially when carried out with the maximum of conscientiousness, with conditions at Oxford and Cambridge, where a man may be examined for his degree by two or three dons none of whom knows anything of his record or has ever spoken to him, and where, on the other hand, the professor of his Honours School, the very person who ought to have most to do with the examination which may so largely determine his career, may not be an examiner at all.

These things will seem of very real importance to all except those who hold (or act as though they held) that a man's degree matters little and that what matters is the education which he gives himself. To talk in this way, as many do, is to create an artificial opposition between things which should go together. Self-education is important, but the only examination ever held upon it is a long-drawn-out one which lasts throughout the candidate's life and the results of which are never proclaimed except by the Recording Angel. What a man is assessed upon in this practical and imperfect world has to be his achievement in that other examination of which the results are published by university senates and which stamps him with the triple seal of his University, of the School in which he has read, and of the type and class of degree which indicate how he has profited by his opportunities. It may be, and generally is, vital to an examinee's career whether he has passed or failed, taken an Honours or a Pass degree and been placed in a First Class, a Second or a Third.

That being so, it is surely a duty only less incumbent upon his teachers than that of stimulating in him the zeal for knowledge and discovery to leave no stone unturned that he may be given the class of degree which he deserves. No trouble is too great to take over the assessment of a candidate whose performance seems to be hovering around some borderline. If he is a clear First it matters little whether his mark be called 82 or 85 per cent, or his letter A+, A++ or (to quote the expressive Oxford notation) A+?+. But if the line between First and Second is drawn at 75 per cent, it matters a great deal if his total is to be 73 or 77. If the examination results are inconclusive, or there is evidence that the candidate was for some reason unable to do himself justice at the examination, one is thrown back on two possible sources of further evidence – the viva voce and the internal records. In an external, or in what may be called a 'pseudo-internal', examination, the former alone is available – and the candidate's nervousness may make the problem harder instead of solving it. In a genuinely internal examination, one has the course-records.

But here comes a fresh difficulty, which bodies that conduct purely external examinations may thank their stars they are not called upon to solve. What if the records and the examination results are frankly and flatly contradictory? The helpfulness of the records is clear if they show that an examinee whose papers and viva are B?+ has consistently done B+ work over a stretch of three years. But what if the records are A and the examinations C? Or, worse still, if the records are C and the examinations A? Should one light-heartedly strike a mean and award some kind of B? Or should the higher or the lower mark be disregarded?

The answer can perhaps be found by asking another question. What do we want the class which we award, the indelible seal which we set on our student, to represent? Surely the whole of his career, from beginning to end, and not one hectic week in his last June. Surely his ability, plus his industry, plus the success with which he stands up to the ordeal of Finals. And, since success in coping with an ordeal is a good test of character, it seems to follow that the last of these considerations should be given equal weight with the other two, save only if it can be established that the candidate has been physically indisposed during the examination. (This, in passing, is where terminal or yearly class examinations are useful, as the strain on the examinee is less severe than in the Finals.) So the three questions the examiners should ask when judging the course-records and the examination results would seem to be:

(1) What do the records show the candidate's industry to have been over the whole course?

(2) What do the records plus the examination results show the candidate's ability to be?

(3) What do the examination results alone show the candidate to have achieved when confronted with a test (or with two tests if the Finals are spread over two years) based upon the entire programme?

Not all examiners would agree with this method of adjudication, arguing that it places too high a premium on industry and that their concern is merely with results, and not with how they were obtained – assuming, of course, that they were obtained fairly. To this argument the reply would be that (1) the system, even on the face of it, gives only one-third of the marks to industry, and that (2) the course-records do not in reality register pure industry, but sustained industry plus ability, which is a very different thing. But really the precise way in which the records are used matters very little, provided they *are* used; and to realize the immense superiority of the genuinely over the nominally internal system one has only to contrast two meetings of, let us say, three examiners, in one of which two examiners are well acquainted with each candidate and have his whole record before them, while in the other all they have to judge is half-a-dozen three-hour papers and only one of the three knows the candidate even by sight.

Neither the Birmingham report, which was confined to the lecture system, nor the Glasgow recommendations, which had a wider scope, made any direct criticism of the conduct of examinations. The Liverpool report, however, made the interesting suggestion that there should be a re-examination for unsuccessful Finalists at the end of the Long Vacation after their failure. One of the Departmental Societies suggested that discretion to permit such re-examination should rest with the Dean of the Faculty; it is doubtful, however, if any Faculty Board would be willing to accept such responsibility – still less would any Dean. The idea of re-examination presumably comes from the practice obtaining in most, if not in all, modern universities of holding a Supplementary Examination for First Year ('Intermediate') candidates each September, and allowing those who have failed in June (sometimes only those who have failed in a single subject) to sit again. But that is a very different thing. The freshman has just completed a year marked by an entirely new type of routine, different methods of instruction, and counter-attractions to academic work of which previously he knew nothing. He may hardly have effected his necessary self-adjustment by his first June. There is, therefore, an excellent case for his being re-examined, either on his whole course or in the subjects in which he has failed. But if, after a three-year or a four-year course, a candidate is not ready for a test by which he stands or falls, whether with the chance of sitting again in a year's time, or for good, there must be something seriously wrong with either his work or his character. And the admission of course-records as evidence before judgement is given seems to destroy the last vestige of a case for re-examination in any year above the first.

One other question often raised among undergraduates is that of class examinations, which some – whether they are held terminally or yearly – dislike, as savouring too much of spoon-feeding methods and the atmosphere of school. In theory many university teachers dislike them too, and for the same reason, though in practice they find them extremely useful. Perhaps the best arrangement would be for the Head of a School to hold them only in courses where he judged them to be needed. But, as a rule, regulations prescribe their being held either once or twice yearly. Once should always be sufficient: at Easter for freshmen, who need two terms for self-adjustment before being examined at all; at Christmas for higher years, for Easter results will not be published till late April and that is too near June to allow the candidate to extract the maximum of profit from them. There is something to be said for the practice of holding the terminal examination at mid-term, so that the lecturer may fill up any obvious gaps or go over any imperfectly covered ground before the vacation. If that plan were generally followed, it is to be hoped that the Glasgow undergraduates' recommendation of tutorial treatment of the worked scripts might become general too.

The advantage of holding class examinations will be obvious, and most industrious students of methodical habits, who like to know just how they are progressing, welcome them; so, to that extent, does the methodical professor. The professor, on the other hand, who trusts to impressions in dealing with students and the student who likes to tackle his programme in his own way, find them irritating. On the whole, they may be said to justify themselves, though, perhaps, the more individually and departmentally they can be organized the better.

CHAPTER FOUR

The Twofold Aim : (1) Research

IT will be generally agreed that the university has two chief aims, research and teaching – or, as the Leeds Charter calls them, 'the advancement and dissemination of knowledge'. These blend so frequently, and at times so completely, that it is often more accurate to describe them as one single aim which can be regarded from two aspects; it is convenient, however, in a book like this, to discuss them separately. In doing so, in this and the next chapter, we shall extend the meaning of the word 'research' to include graduate teaching[1] and the organization of what in America is called the 'graduate school', but, on the other hand, we shall exclude one most important aspect of it – the incitement of the undergraduate to discovery and adventure, as it will be more natural to treat this under 'teaching', a phrase here delimited to mean 'undergraduate teaching'.

First of all, let a proposition be re-stated which will serve as a foundation for the whole of this chapter: that the promotion of research (using that phrase, for the moment, in its wider, not in its narrower, sense) is (or, more correctly, should be) the chief part of the aim of every university. Research and teaching form one twofold aim, but the parts played by each are not equal. The spirit of research must permeate all genuine university teaching, but, though in any university of to-day there will in practice always be teaching, it suffices for the ideal university that there should be research.

One admirable little book on the universities cuts clean across this proposition by declaring: 'A purely teaching university, still less a ''research institute'', is not really a

1. It will be observed that the pleonastic adjective 'post-graduate' is avoided throughout this book.

university.'[1] This dictum needs modification. A 'purely teaching university' is almost a contradiction in terms, but a 'research institute' can certainly be a university unless there is some sinister shade of meaning in the word 'institute' which the author has not made clear. If it means a free association of persons formed in order to undertake research, then this *is*, in the purest sense of the word, a university. Its only defect, from that point of view, lies in the uncertainty whether or no those who compose the association are fitted to undertake and direct research, and, if they are, whether or no those who succeed them will be. It is convenient, therefore, not to consider such a body as a university unless and until it is empowered by authority to grant degrees which will ensure fitness and continuity. But this is in no sense a matter of principle.

Let us now be perfectly frank and say that this primacy, or anything approaching it, appears to be conceded to research only by a very small minority of university teachers. Few, perhaps, would take Newman's extreme view and exclude research from the university altogether, but most, at least in their heart of hearts, give it only a secondary place. They would subscribe to the dictum that 'the modern university is in practice mainly a teaching (and of course an examining) institution'[2] and whole-heartedly declare that this is as it should be. Not many, it is to be feared, would go farther than the University Grants Committee did in 1936, when it reminded us that 'a University is *not less essentially* concerned to increase than to impart knowledge'[3]; still fewer would endorse the assertion of Sir James Irvine that 'a university is responsible for enlarging the boundaries of knowledge rather than for colonizing the territory it explores'.[4]

1. Sir Charles Grant Robertson, *The British Universities*, London, 1930, p. 59.
2. P. Mansell-Jones, 'Where modern universities are wrong', in *The Criterion*, London, 1936, xv, 598.
3. U.G.C., 1936, p. 24. Italics mine.
4. In *The Obligation of Universities to the Social Order*, New York, 1933, p. 53.

Here is an actual example of the view of research most widely prevalent. In the early part of 1940, two professors, A and B, were talking about the havoc which the War had wrought upon the staff of the Arts Faculty of their University.

'You know,' said A, 'poor old C has lost so many of his lecturers that he's had to give up his research altogether.'

'I should think better of him,' replied B, 'if he had given up his teaching altogether.'

There, in its most extreme form, is the antithesis. If for any justifiable reason, a professor is unable to continue both his teaching and his research, which should he sacrifice?

In practice, of course, lest the hungry sheep should look up and not be fed, he might temporarily suspend his research until adequate provision could be made for the teaching which his staff had relinquished and then resume it again. But, if no such provision were practicable and he were left with the choice between research and teaching, classes and lectures must be reduced in number, for research comes first. That is B's view – and the view expressed in this book.

But A thinks quite differently. So C 'does research', does he? And very nice, too! Gives the place a tone, don't you know! Raises it a cut above secondary schools and all that! Quite right and proper! And such a suitable hobby for a professor; much more appropriate than gardening or collecting stamps! How better could he use his super-abundant leisure? But of course one can't expect to have the leisure to indulge one's hobbies in war-time. Research, in short, is not an essential, but an extra. Not an integral part of one's work: a mere luxury.

This chapter begins by stating the view that it is at least as culpable to neglect one's research as to neglect one's teaching; as reprehensible to reach the end of the session without having put in a year's honest research as to have constantly failed to make an appearance in one's lecture-room.

The word 'research' has fallen into some disrepute in this country because it has been consistently misunderstood and misinterpreted. This is due largely to the direction in which graduate study has developed in the United States. Undoubtedly much of the advanced work done in that country is admirable, both in itself and because of the encouragement which it gives to the spirit of inquiry. But unfortunately it has not all been of the right kind and it has not been confined to those who are capable of undertaking it. Thousands of students who should never have proceeded beyond a first degree have been allowed, if not compelled, to sit, first for their 'Master's', and then for their 'Doctor's'; and not only so, but the attainment of a Ph.D. has been made a *sine qua non* for all grades of university and college post above the lowest – that of instructor. From the huge number of universities and colleges in the United States – one American in every 125 acquires a 'college education' – some idea can be formed of the number of such aspirants and hence of the number of Ph.D. degrees conferred annually. The result of this is that research is undertaken, from no spirit of adventure or inquiry, but as a piece of drab routine of which the only cheerful aspect is that one day it will all be over. And that attitude, in turn, prompts the graduate student, or rather his director,[1] to choose a subject which makes the least demands on qualities which he either does not possess or has no desire to use – such as imagination, critical insight, judgement – and calls into play chiefly the industry and perseverance without which he would never aspire to a higher degree at all. Hence the prostitution of research by the choice of unworthy subjects – the theses on dish-washing, cheer-leading and the buying of women's garments by mail which many people thought fables until Dr Flexner rendered a service to education, and

1. It is a perfectly normal thing for an American M.A. to 'go to' his professor, who will 'give him' a subject to write on for his Ph.D. 'An American professor of mathematics once said that the choice of subjects for dissertations was actually the most trying part of his work' (A. J. Grant in L.M.U., p. 35).

enlivened an admirable book, by giving chapter and verse for them.[1] Hence, too, the insistence on factual research of a trivial kind which characterizes not only theses in the United States but also articles in learned reviews and papers read before learned societies.

Now, although in most Arts subjects factual research will play only a minor role, there are at least two legitimate fields for it in the Arts Faculty Graduate School, as also for research of any kind the intrinsic value of which is apparently small. First, it is a simple and generally a necessary type of investigation for the young worker who seeks primarily a training in method. One cannot leap into the ring and become a champion without endless preliminary sparring. In fact, the wise teacher will encourage this type of research on a small scale even in the undergraduate. 'Suppose you go and find that out for yourself', 'Has it ever occurred to you to wonder why ... ?' 'Those two books seem to contradict each other: why not investigate the matter and discover if they really do, and, if so, which one is right?' are all salutary suggestions. A considerable part of a first thesis should normally be factual, even when the writer has already shown excellence in insight and judgement. Secondly, factual research is involved in almost every major piece of investigation if this is conscientiously carried out. No biographical or critical study, for example, can be complete without it, and again and again the results of investigatory articles of a factual type, which appear in learned reviews, are later embodied in books of much wider scope acknowledged to be authoritative. There is, therefore, at least in the Arts subjects of which I can speak from experience or definite knowledge, no justification for a generalization enunciated some years ago in terms which, excessively simplified though they are, it may be useful to quote because they express in striking phraseology ideas to which, privately, if not openly, many professors subscribe:

Investigators may be divided into two main classes, those who strive for enlightenment, and those who grub for facts. The first

1. Flexner, pp. 102-4, 153-5.

are the searchers, to whom we are indebted for basic discoveries, new methods, fresh valuations and alternative interpretations. These are the major contributors to progress. They are rare beings, of outstanding insight and very exceptional ability, who add significantly to our grasp of the scheme of nature. The second are the re-searchers, who churn over the old ground, employing the time-honoured methods of others upon hitherto untested materials and untried compounds. These are the minor operators, who amass results by routine procedures and need possess only a reasonable measure of skill and talent.[1]

To both the antithesis itself and its implications one must take the strongest objection. The 'searcher' has to be a 're-searcher' too: his 'basic discoveries' will not be made without much 'churning over the old ground', done either by himself or by someone else; and often the nature of his task makes it essential that he, the 'major operator', should be the 'minor operator' too. The 're-searcher', on the other hand, if he really has 'skill and talent', will not be content with a life spent in minor operations but will be as eager as his colleague to make 'basic discoveries', though no true scholar, young or old, will allow failure to make them to deter him from proceeding on his chosen way. At any moment, the 'searcher', baulked of his major hopes by lack of time or opportunity, or merely by chance, may find himself condemned to 're-search', or, while still keeping his ambition in view, may find that a mass of 're-search' has to be done before he can push his discovery any farther forward. At any moment, the 're-searcher' may discover that the result of some minor piece of factual investigation has illumined a whole tract of knowledge and enabled him to proceed with his studies upon a higher plane, and become a 'major contributor to progress'.

Where factual investigation – or, in the elegant language of the critic, 'grubbing for facts' – ceases to be beneficial, and can even become extremely harmful, is where it is regarded as an end in itself and leads to nothing but a kind

1. G. F. Herrenden Harker, 'A Plea for the Sabbatical Year', in *The Universities Review*, April 1935, vol. vii, p. 112.

of itch to do more and more investigation of the same type
– a tendency, unhappily, often encouraged by electors to
Chairs and committees on promotion who evaluate candidates' publications by the 'weight and measure method'
and are often more influenced by the length or brevity of
the list of published work which they submit than by the
testimony of experts as to its value. Let us imagine, for
example – I take this merely as typical and diagrammatic
– that we read in the *Review of English Studies* an article on
the activities of the poet Wordsworth during the first three
months of the year 1798. Our first reaction, perhaps, is to
exclaim: 'How in the world can his activities during those
particular months matter?' But some time afterwards we
read a new biography of Wordsworth by the author of that
article and find that the information it revealed has thrown
fresh light on the *Lyrical Ballads*: if his next article discusses
the activities of Scott in the year 1805, our comment upon
it will probably not be so hasty. On the other hand, some
younger and less gifted man, finding or believing it incumbent upon him to 'do research', may be attracted by
the type of investigation exemplified in the Wordsworth
and Scott articles and proceed, industriously but point-
lessly, to pour forth articles on the activities of Milton in
1654, of Cowper in 1782, of Shelley in 1813, of Byron in
1820 – and so on. In the literatures which have been most
assiduously studied – notably English, French and German
– almost every part of the life and work of every major
author has been thoroughly examined, and it is tempting
for the young researcher, seeking a theme in following which
he will never be accused of plagiarism, to take the most
insignificant author he can find and treat him as his betters
have been treated, though in all probability no-one will be
in the slightest degree the wiser for knowing anything whatever that he is likely to discover.

Matters go from bad to worse when from the factual in
literary investigations we pass to the statistical. Here too, at
least in some of the best-known fields, American researchers
have set us a bad example. They discuss foreign influences

in literature in dissertations of the type which a critic once pithily denoted by the formula 'Jones in France', and they conclude that, because seventy-two of Jones's plays were performed in France during 1860 and only thirty-six during 1870, his influence was twice as great in the earlier year as in the later. Or they discuss the poet Brown's use of colour, and, after counting all the colours used in his works, they describe green as his favourite because he uses the word 'green' 582 times, yellow coming a poor second with 347. It never occurs to them to include colour-evoking substantives, to attach any importance to the cumulative effects of colour-phrases in certain positions, to distinguish between vivid and conventional epithets, or between the literal and the metaphorical, and so on. Incidentally, such researchers not only miss in Jones or Brown all the things that most matter, but they soon blunt and deaden whatever critical faculties they themselves may originally have possessed. There is said to have been a very minor French dramatist in the seventeenth century who left 270 plays, mostly bad ones; and in a certain American university legend has it that a 'scholar' once ploughed through the whole 270 in less than six months in order to write a monograph on that dramatist's use of the first personal pronoun: in order to do this he read one play every morning and one every evening, Sunday being a holiday. This is no doubt apocryphal but it is really characteristic of the soulless industry of much that proceeds in great quantity from the United States and in less but still considerable volume from our own country.

What, then, will be the definition of a research which is at once the inspiration and the crown of a liberal education? Even if we leave until the next chapter one important aspect of it – the stimulation of the spirit of research in the undergraduate – it will be much wider than any commonly envisaged. First, it will comprise all original work of a scholarly kind, such as investigation, criticism, the intelligent publication of texts, appreciation based on scholarship, and certain types of imaginative and creative activity. It will, of course, include the presentation of facts or ideas either in a new light or (as a rule) in such a way as to bring them within the reach of those from whom they would otherwise be excluded. It can further be extended to the keeping abreast of contemporary investigation and thought in one's own field and to a critical receptiveness of new ideas in that field or in any other which one may have studied. Finally, it takes in, not only the pursuit of all these activities oneself, but the encouraging, stimulating and training of others to pursue them, and participation in the activities of bodies devoted to their furtherance.

Such an interpretation of a fine word which has become debased in current usage not only restores its dignity but creates an ideal which must attract men and women of every type who have the smallest degree of scholarly ability. To reveal hidden knowledge, to present fresh modes of thought and to train one's successors to do both these things are among the noblest activities in which anyone can hope to engage. And, of all people on earth, members of universities – and, most of all, university teachers – have the greatest opportunities, and obligations, to engage in them.

(1) For, in the first place, they have two things which are essential to research – time and tranquillity of spirit. By comparison with busy administrators, they live a life as sheltered as the schoolboy's. They are untroubled by the financial worries of the business man; by the uncertainty of the civil servant or the officer in the fighting services as to the part of the world where he may be sent to-morrow; by the thousand crises that may beset the headmaster of a boarding-school; by the constant broken nights of the physician; by the shattering calls made on the nervous energy of the priest. The professor, as we have seen, is certain, and all lecturers above the junior grades are reasonably certain, of a fairly satisfactory living wage, and of complete security of tenure, until the age of sixty-five. Teaching, preparation for teaching and the necessary share in administration will not occupy the average man, at the very most, for more than four or five hours a day, excluding

Saturdays and Sundays – and in most callings a working day is taken as comprising eight. And even this goes on for barely more than half the year. What other profession has an annual vacation of some twenty-two weeks? Certainly, one would think, if academic longevity does not reach a high figure, it ought to.

With such wealth of time at his disposal, a conscientious professor might well smile ironically at attempts made to represent him as overworked. The University Grants Committee, in its 1930 report, reminds the Lords Commissioners of His Majesty's Treasury that the university teacher may have but little time for research in the course of a morning's routine work: 'A piece of research', they remark solemnly, 'is not like a piece of knitting which can be taken up at odd moments, and a free hour or so between lectures is seldom of much use.'[1] Of course not, but such free hours can be used, not for flicking newspapers or gossiping in the Common Room, but for clearing up odd pieces of routine which otherwise would be done on the next free day – a day that research will then be able to claim. The Committee appears to deprecate the very just observation that 'the men and women of genius, who make the really important contributions to knowledge, are not deterred by the most discouraging conditions.'[2] But that is the truth. 'If we are to effect anything,' once wrote that veteran scholar Dr F. S. Boas, 'we must definitely allocate certain portions of our time to investigation, and refuse, save in exceptional circumstances, to surrender it to any other purpose.'[3] The writer cites the rule made by one scholar to devote the first hour of his working day, week in, week out, to research: no such scholar, we may be sure, would ever plead shortness of time if he were a university professor. One may venture to regret that the Grants Committee should have administered soothing syrup to a profession which enjoys far too much time, instead of what it chiefly needs – an iron tonic.

These observations will be ill received by many university

1. U.G.C., 1930, p. 35.   2. U.G.C., 1930, p. 34.
3. *Teachers and Modern Language Research* (Cambridge, 1919), p. 4.

teachers, who look as shocked when laymen gird at them for always being on holiday as the bank manager does when his neighbours envy him for 'closing at three'. The conscientious professor will say, and rightly so, that he works as hard as any other man, though if he is honest he will agree that the conditions under which he does so are nearly ideal. But the point is that, if that is true of him, it is because he is faithful to his obligation to engage in research: he could not possibly make a full-time job – for term and vacation – out of administration and teaching.

In the report just referred to, the Grants Committee quotes a letter written 'at his Vice-Chancellor's request by a scientist of world-wide reputation who is now at the head of a large scientific department in a modern University'[1] which might seem to contradict the picture of the professor's life just given. The gist of it is as follows:

(a) His lecturing hours are not heavy but routine duties encroach so much on his time that his research and reading can be done only in vacations.

(b) The direction of from twenty to thirty men doing research work, together with his own research and reading, constitutes a whole-time job. Departmental administration and attendance at university committees constitute another.

(c) In practice, administrative duties win in the competition against research because they are urgent, whereas research can be put off. 'The consequence is that the time for doing research always seems to be just round the corner and never arrives.'

The obvious moral of this letter is that the department of the scientist in question was understaffed – probably only temporarily, for he would never have achieved a 'world-wide reputation' had he not had time for research, and indeed he admits that in the past he has 'managed to do a good deal'. But in reality the striking thing about this letter, quoted by the Committee as evidence that the senior professor is badly, and perhaps irremediably, overworked, to the detriment of the research 'in virtue of which he was appointed to his position', is the evidence which it provides

1. U.G.C., 1930 pp. 36-7.

of the pleasantness of the places in which his lot has fallen
For, in the first place, the writer admits that he has hi
vacations free, which, when a reasonable period for com
plete and necessary holiday has been deducted, amoun
to about four and a half months yearly, or one-third of hi
whole time. Secondly, the writer is said to have 'felt himsel
to be in some measure to blame' for not having deputec
some of his responsibilities – which, of course, he was, for a
department with thirty research students is not without it
Associate Professors, Readers or Senior Lecturers. Thirdly
being a distinguished and senior member of the Senate, h
must carry more than ordinary weight with both the Senate
and the Council: is it not his duty to use that weight to
secure the modification of a system in which university
committees are twice as numerous, and three times as
large, as they need be? If they permit such a system to continue, overworked professors have only themselves to blame;
they are very differently placed from other scholars, who,
though not of 'world-wide reputation', are just as anxious
to do research, but have to use such odds and ends of time
as a time-table over which they have not the slightest con-
control allows them. Let them think of the schoolmaster,
engaged in the wearing task of teaching – and, what is more,
controlling – classes of lively boys from nine o'clock till
four, who has then to mark a pile of exercises, and perhaps,
in a boarding-school, supervise 'prep', before settling down
for what is left of the evening to the writing of a Master's
or a Doctor's thesis. What tales of heroic persistence under
conditions like those could not the tutors of such an institution as University Correspondence College unfold! Or let
them think of other scholars, this time, indeed, of 'world-
wide reputation', who made their name, not by following
the easy path of undergraduate, lecturer and professor with
twenty-two weeks of uninterrupted vacation, but by attending night schools after eight-hour days in offices, taking
external degrees – perhaps, for lack of means, without
tuition – at London University, and only gradually throwing
off the grinding shackles of their employment. By contrast

with these and many other types which have made good,
the life of the university teacher is a bed of roses. If he does
not see to it that his research comes first, who else will?

(2) Then, again, university teachers have opportunities
for research which are denied to many others. They have,
for example, at their very doorstep, the Library of their own
University, and perhaps, at their elbows, a Departmental
Library, containing books largely of their personal selection, as well. Distances in Great Britain are so small that
they are never impracticably far from the Reading Room
of the British Museum. Their names, or the names of their
universities, will serve as an introduction to foreign scholars
working in their particular field who might pay no heed to
a letter from an unknown private investigator. They have
the time, and they usually either have, or can obtain, the
means, to travel in pursuit of their researches. They have
pupils, or younger colleagues, whom they can train to collaborate with them: scientists, indeed, frequently build up
contributions to learning upon experiments carried out in
their university laboratories by their own juniors, while all
university teachers can test their theories or throw out
feelers of thought in seminars and advanced lectures.

Further, university teachers are in a far better position
than private researchers in the matter of facilities for publication. It may be granted that for one's articles, and still
more for one's books, it is not always easy to find an outlet:
learned reviews are apt to reply that the articles occupy
about five times as much space as they can spare, while
publishers are singularly dubious as to whether the books
will pay even their bare expenses and very properly remind
one that they have to make a livelihood like anyone else.
But the holding of a position at a university will at least
ensure that one's work is looked at, and several universities
have their own Presses, to say nothing of research funds,
which have helped many a struggling lecturer towards a
Chair. Then, too, a university teacher is in constant touch
with older colleagues who can give him the benefit of their
experience as to publication, in addition to much other

advice from which the independent researcher is as a rule cut off.

With so much time, then, and so many opportunities, it is our bounden duty to pursue and encourage research to the utmost of our capacity. Who else can be expected to do it if we do not?

(3) Prominent among the various reasons why every university teacher should be a researcher is the effect of research upon himself and his pupils. If our teaching is to be fresh and our Graduate School active we must be active ourselves. A lifeless professor means a lifeless school. To the Grants Committee we owe the preservation of a splendid and vivid figure of speech which deserves to be engraved upon the wall of every Staff Common Room:

'He who learns from one occupied in learning, drinks of a running stream. He who learns from one who has learned all he is to teach, drinks "the green mantle of the stagnant pool".'[1]

More about this, as it affects undergraduate teaching, will be said in the next chapter, but its importance for graduate work alone should be insisted upon here. Apart from the fact that there is no means of keeping the mind alive like scientific investigation or the systematic practice of original thought, it is clearly impossible – though the fact seems often to be forgotten – to direct the studies of others unless one is a student oneself. The man who lectured on Shakespeare without ever having read him, or even without reading him frequently, would soon be found out and derided as incompetent to the point of dishonesty. I still remember going, as a boy, to a popular 'travelogue' on India and realizing with nothing less than disgust, from something the lecturer happened to say halfway through, that he had never been to India in his life. Yet there are many professors whose standards are not much higher. They supervise the research of their graduates, never having done any themselves, or having done it so long ago that it

1. U.G.C., 1936, p. 43. From the Inaugural Lecture of Mr A. J. Scott, first Principal of Owens College, Manchester.

s no more than a memory to them. This is equivalent to saying that they are trying to cultivate in their students qualities which they have either never possessed or have deliberately allowed to rust through disuse – which, as Euclid would have said, is absurd.

Critics delight to call in question the value of research carried out by young graduates – and naturally it is often only at the second or third attempt that such research reveals any intrinsic worth. But even if it were never to have any at all it would be worth their while to undertake it for the sake of its effect upon their character, and worth their professors' while to direct it for the sake of its effect upon him.

(4) Another reason which impels a scholar to make a habit of doing research work is both an idealistic and a practical one. Through the study of his chosen subject he has gained a great deal over a long period of time – enjoyment and benefit for the mind, stimulating companionship, a broadening of interests, a strengthening of moral fibre, an enriching of the inner life. Ought he not to try to repay this by adding something permanent, however trivial, to the store of knowledge available in the field where he has for so long been able to dig freely for his own good? We are continually being urged, in the purely moral sphere, to leave the world a little better than we found it: is not the exhortation valid in the sphere of scholarship as well?

(5) And this prompts a further reflection, which should appeal particularly to those who stress the teaching function of the university, and declare that it is their duty, and their desire, to devote themselves primarily to teaching. If they really think this, and have the ability to do original work, how can they possibly neglect research and publication? For if they have written and published, their teaching and influence on teachers, will go on, with unabated force, for years, perhaps for generations, after their death. If, on the other hand, they have done neither, their influence, after their retirement or death, will persist only through their pupils and their pupils' pupils – that is, in a progressively

more diluted form. Nor will they achieve more, if as much
by publishing conventional text-books, for these seldom
outlive their generation. The only way in which they can
continue their work after retiring from the lecture-room is
through research, in the broad sense being given to that
word in this chapter. Few spectacles in the academic world
are as exasperating and saddening as that of the teacher
fully capable of doing original work of merit, contentedly
and even complacently, spending his best years between the
lecture-room and the committee-table and honestly believing he is doing all that is required of him. The man with
some physical disability who lives his life in solitude but
makes his name as a great scholar through his books will do
the greater good of the two. The happy man is he who can
combine what is best in both.

(6) A less personal, but very potent, incentive to original
work should be found in its importance to the university.
If, as has already been suggested, university education is to
be decentralized and democratized, not only in theory but
in reality, the modern universities will maintain a high
position only through the pre-eminence of certain of their
Schools in research. Even to-day those which are known
outside their own area are known for that and for that only.
Oxford is famous for its Rhodes Scholars; Cambridge for its
now no longer existent Senior Wranglership; both Oxford
and Cambridge are well known for the Boat Race, for their
Union Societies, for their Colleges. But there are no
Wranglers or Rhodes Scholars at Redbrick, and who ex-
pects young England ever to wear favours on the day of the
football match between Leeds and Sheffield or who ever
finds a series of articles in an illustrated weekly on famous
Halls of Residence in the Universities of Lancashire and
Yorkshire? No: if one visits universities abroad and talks in
the Common Rooms about Oxbridge, a conversation at
once ensues about its venerable colleges or quaint customs
or famous Chancellors, and as often as not degenerates into
a discussion as to whether they *really* do as good work there
as at the 'newer institutions'. If one starts a conversation

bout Redbrick, as likely as not no-one will ever have heard
f it, or will inquire sceptically: 'Oh, is that the name of a
British university?' But if its name should be known at all,
he reaction to one's remark will be: 'Oh, yes, that's where
Sir James Brown has the famous School of Social Science',
or 'Yes, I've heard of their great Physics Department', or
Why, their *Review of Foreign Affairs* comes to the Library
here: it's one of the very best things of its kind.'

So, if every other incentive fails, we can always labour at
our research work as a contribution, however small, towards helping to build up a future for the university of our
adoption.

To anyone acquainted with the universities, it is a truism
to say that neither at Oxbridge nor at Redbrick is the
amount of research done either by teachers or by graduate
students anything approaching what it should be. At the
former, a few exceptional persons – some of them professors,
some Fellows of colleges – do work of great distinction and,
wherever specialists meet, their names are inseparably
linked with the subjects which they profess; but the remainder, who constitute an overwhelming proportion of
the whole, produce practically nothing. At the latter, there
are fewer outstanding scholars (though Manchester, for its
size, could probably rival either Oxford or Cambridge)
but the average is higher – chiefly, however, because the
younger men are forced to produce in order to gain
promotion.

A little factual research will make the state of things
clearer. One university has on its official list of Professors
Emeriti four from the Faculty of Arts. Their average age in
1942 was seventy-one; their average length of service, as
full professors (i.e., with adequate salaries and complete
security of tenure), was sixteen years; the average number
of books they have published, according to their own returns
in the current *Who's Who*, is three. In seventy-one years,
sixteen of them spent in a professorship, and six in retirement, one might have hoped for more.

But, it will be said, there are also articles contributed to learned journals. Well, here is a tabulated record of such publications compiled by members of a certain Arts Faculty covering a session some years before the Second World War. It includes text-books, and also reprints and re-editions of books published years before, but omits articles appearing in newspapers and popular magazines, which hardly enter into the discussion. The figures are striking enough to merit abulation:

Number in Faculty	Number reporting no research at all	Number of books published	Average	Number of articles published	Average
PROFESSORS					
20	10 (50%)	3	$\frac{3}{20}$	20	1
LECTURERS					
80	56 (70%)	10	$\frac{1}{8}$	35	$\frac{7}{16}$

Twenty professors who in their twenty-two weeks of vacation produce a single article each and three books between them! Eighty lecturers, each the proud author of an eighth of a book and less than half an article! Certainly, if the universities can boast even a very few productive workers, they must carry an unconscionable number of pure passengers.

What can be the reason for this lack of productiveness? The academically minded Oxbridge undergraduate trustfully assumes that all to whose lectures he listens have distinguished themselves by their writings; and, when he becomes a Junior Fellow, gets to know them, and discovers they have not, he is still idealist enough to imagine that they must all have the uncompleted manuscripts of epoch-making works secreted somewhere in a romantic background. For the 'Oxbridge tradition', he is told, is to labour all one's life at some one great task: the resulting work may not see the light till after one's death, but 'there must be no premature publication – that is the Oxbridge tradition'. Then, while still in his twenties – and still an idealist – he accepts a lectureship at Redbrick, and soon begins to observe to himself, in perfect good faith, that, to judge from the number of his new colleagues who seem to have written nothing, the 'Oxbridge tradition' is observed there also. Gradually his confidence becomes shattered, but for a long time he continues to believe that some of the most reverend of his seniors spend their week-ends labouring at vast works which fortunately have escaped the awful fate of premature publication. Only as he becomes intimate with them does he discover that what they labour at is golf or gardening, quite content if they publish one article every two or three years.

Whether or no their unproductiveness is due to a love of the open air, it is most certainly not attributable to lack of time. In the Faculty of Arts referred to above as having 324 lectures weekly there are seventy-eight professors and lecturers, so that the average time which each spends in the lecture-room (exclusive of graduate work and a few hours in interviews and the like) totals almost exactly four periods of about fifty minutes each. A few senior men are admittedly overworked with committees, but at most they would hardly number more than a dozen. The great majority of the members of the staff have no such duties at all. The only explanations one can find are that the staff neither believe in research nor are forced to do any. Practically every lecturer of any standing and every professor who has ever been a lecturer has a certain amount of past original work to his credit. But once the lecturer becomes a professor, or has risen to as high a grade as he judges himself likely to reach or thinks it worth working for, all such activities come virtually to an end. That is not cynicism, but a conclusion which will probably be found inescapable if figures are taken over any number of years in any one university.

How can this state of things be remedied? Only by more drastic measures than, in the present state of opinion, any Senate is likely to agree to. In other words, opinion must be educated first. Once that is done and the time-squandering committee-system reformed, several necessary, if distasteful, reforms must be adopted.

(1) *More care must be taken about new appointments and promotions.* Here there will be an outcry: 'But we do take the greatest care to see that no-one is appointed or promoted to a high grade or a Chair who has not good original work to his credit.' True, we do. But we think only of the past. If he has already done creditable research, we assume that he will do more – though with the examples of ourselves and our colleagues around us, we ought at least to feel some doubt about it. What we need to consider more are the candidate's plans for research in the future. Only a man who has mapped out his own work for ten years ahead and inspired the Selection Committee with confidence that his performance will correspond to his promise should be considered for a Chair or a Senior Lectureship at all. And, having ascertained what his plans are, we ought to see that something approaching them is carried out. In other words, there should be

(2) *Short-term appointments.* More outcry: 'But a man who has the fear of dismissal hanging over him can't be expected to do research.' An obvious retort would be that he could hardly do much less than the average professor with a life appointment does at present. As a matter of fact, lecturers on a short-term tenure are often more productive than any others, though their abnormal activity is apt to cause a reaction once they have permanent appointments, and no-one wants men to do research merely from the fear of losing their jobs. But it would be quite reasonable to appoint all professors for ten years at a time, or, where the electors are doubtful about the appointment, for two periods of five years, followed by periods of ten years. In such cases it should be understood that the appointments are genuinely terminable failing satisfactory production. This should also be made clear to Senior Lecturers, save perhaps in rare case where they are appointed less on their research than in order to organize the bulk of the administration of the School and the teaching.

(3) *Annual Reports.* At Birmingham there is a 'University Research Committee', the first duty of which is to 'receive

and consider reports from each Department showing the research work in progress and in contemplation'. If every university had one of these, and every member of the teaching staff, from senior professor to junior lecturer, were required to report fully, at the end of each session, not so much upon work 'in contemplation' – there would be plenty of that! – but upon work completed and published, upon fresh work actually begun and upon the state of work still in progress, it is probable that the importance of research would bulk larger in the academic mind, and certain that the Research Committees would be able to give valuable if sometimes embarrassing evidence to the committees considering the claims of members of the staff to reappointment and promotion.

(4) *Reciprocity with other universities and Sabbatical Years.* An earlier chapter outlined a system of reciprocity whereby professors and lecturers who have specialized in certain aspects of their subject would give the benefit of their special knowledge to other universities than their own. This practice might well be extended to allow graduate students to migrate from their own university to another if the professor there is more competent to help them. Both these customs would relieve the university teacher of much extraneous and not always profitable work and allow him to concentrate more upon the part of the field which he has made his own. This in no way means that he should become narrower in his interests: just the contrary. But whereas it is an excellent thing for a medievalist (let us say) to read, lecture, conduct discussion classes and even write upon the history of the nineteenth century, it is irritating and unprofitable for him to have to spend a large part of his time for two sessions on some extremely insignificant treaty or set of letters on which one of his graduates wishes to write a thesis when his opposite number in a university fifty miles away has worked in great detail on the history of the years in question, and perhaps even has the very matter itself at his fingers' ends.

The question of reciprocity, however, opens up a much

wider question – that of the Sabbatical Year. To my own mind, until some of the academic and financial reforms already described have been effected, there is little to be gained by adopting such a project. It is popularly believed that every university teacher in the United States has one free year with salary in every seven and that he spends this year in improving his mind by foreign travel or study. It would be more accurate to say that in *some* such universities he is offered the choice between one year's leave on half pay and half a year's leave on full pay; and that, as often as not, he declines the offer for financial reasons or accepts the half-year and spends it a few hundred miles from his home as a pure holiday or even uses it to earn (or, as Americans say, 'make') more money. If a similar scheme were set up here, it is doubtful if the results would be in the least better and they might very easily be worse. The sabbatical year *as a right* seems to presuppose a much higher academic standard, both intellectual and moral, than we have attained at present.

As a *privilege*, however, leave of absence should be asked for, and given, much more than it is. As a rule, apart from cases of illness, it means that a professor has been invited to lecture, or attend a conference, in some foreign country or that the Government or some public body wants him for some important piece of specialized work. In all such circumstances, the necessary leave is, with few exceptions, unquestioningly and willingly given, as of course it should be. For the professor, who seldom makes much financial profit out of the change, gains greatly in experience; the university acquires further prestige; and the junior staff and students lose nothing if suitable teaching arrangements are made – they may even be the better for being shaken out of their normal routine.

There are two directions in which this practice might well be extended. The first is that of exchange professorships, both within the British Isles and between this country, the Dominions and the United States. These should be encouraged, and, as far as possible, arranged, by a central organization representing the whole of the British universities. But, as their utility consists in the broadening rather than the deepening of the teacher's mind and concerns general education rather than research, this is hardly the place to deal with it in any detail. The second direction, which is more relevant and probably needs fuller exposition, is the granting of leave purely for purposes of original work and investigation.

It would be a healthy sign in any university Faculty if there were no time in the year at which some of its staff were not on short or long leave for this reason. If we really spent our Easter vacations, for example, on original work, instead of persuading ourselves that we need an extended rest after the trying winter, how useful it would be for us occasionally to have either March or May, as well as April, to devote to it, and how easily, in most Schools, could the lecturing work be adjusted to free us! Nor, while the time-tables of university teachers remain as they are, would it be much harder, without assistance from elsewhere and without any expense being caused to the university, to free a small number of senior lecturers in the Michaelmas Term, and of juniors (who are needed less for June examinations) in the Summer Term, for the same purpose. The Summer Term, with only five or six of its ten weeks used for lecturing, would seem pre-eminently the time when juniors should be freed for research. To have either of these terms at one's disposal means a period of six months on end – from June to December or from April to October – for concentrated study. The busy Head of a large School is harder to spare – though often it is he who needs the time most. He has to be at his desk in October, to deal with enrolments, and to start the session on its way, and again from March to June, to set and mark examination papers, preside at the viva voce and examiners' meetings, attend scholarship committees, write testimonials, advise students who are going down, and so on. Unless he has an exceptionally able substitute the only short period for which he could be absent is from about mid-November to early March, or alternatively for the whole of the Lent Term, according to the practice of his university with regard to class examinations. This would give him only four months on end, to his junior's six, and it is doubtful how far a conscientious Head could immerse himself in his work if he were in any doubt as to his Department's well-being. On the whole, it seems better to meet the needs of a Head by giving him a genuine Sabbatical year, when necessary, and importing a substitute from outside to fill his place – or rather, that of his senior assistant, who would normally take it.

There is one condition, however, which should invariably characterize so admirably liberal a policy – that of control. There must be no risk that time granted for research should be spent on seaside holidays, or on the marking of school examination papers. Juniors should submit their proposed programme to their professor, through whom the request for leave would naturally be made, and, though the very nature of research precludes the invariable production of positive and tangible results, they should be required to satisfy him on their return that the time had been well spent. The professors' own requests for leave would be considered by the Research Committee of the Senate, which, either before they left or after they returned, would obtain any external evidence it thought necessary. This in all probability would be seldom, for a genuine and mature investigator will long since have proved his fitness and as a rule he can forecast what he is likely to accomplish in a given time much more accurately than a junior.

Old-fashioned critics may think such control as this unnecessary: may the time soon come when it will be! Yet if a Research Committee grants a professor as little as £20 in aid of publication, it requires a copy of the publication to be lodged with it upon its appearance, or, if the grant is made for the purchase of apparatus or rotographs, it insists that these shall become university property. Why, then, if it makes a grant of time (which sometimes may also involve the remuneration of a substitute) should it not have equally definite assurance that the time has been well used?

Thus far we have been speaking mainly of the teacher's research rather than of the student's; a discussion of the work of the Graduate School has been left till last because in the Arts Faculties of our universities this institution is still in a rudimentary stage of existence.

Those who have directed and lectured to graduates in the United States may easily be tempted to hope that it will remain so. In most of the large universities in that country, the Graduate School is a highly organized institution, with a Dean, a Secretary and a life all its own; the numbers of its students may run into four figures; and lectures and seminars are so numerous that the mere visitor wonders when and where any research is done at all. The student beginning his M.A. course has usually no notion whatever of what research means, and as the M.A. is often given for a pure essay, combined with 'credits' indicating attendances at numerous lecture courses, the student starting his Ph.D. course may not be much wiser. May a Graduate School with these defects, whether it be small or large, never come into being in this country!

Yet there should undoubtedly be a Graduate School in every Faculty – for surely the proper unit is the Faculty rather than the university. There will naturally be a certain uniformity in the regulations for higher degrees, but this should leave each Department with as much freedom as possible. And each Graduate School should be a 'school' in the very best sense: a body with an individuality of its own, of which each member is in the closest personal touch with the senior staff directing it, and inspired by a single aim giving unity to the diversity of its studies. It need not be large: perhaps, if its standards are high, it cannot be. It may include – and it is fortunate if it does – members working for no higher degree at all, but for the work's own sake. But its essential characteristics are unity and closeness of contact. Without these it cannot exist.

Unity. Most of its members will have come up through the corresponding undergraduate School and will have become immersed in the ideals and traditions of that School, which those who enter it from other universities will need to imbibe. Therefore, whenever practicable, its members must meet: if some of them are not full-time students but schoolteachers or employees in business, this may be difficult to arrange, but, without it, individual members will not get the fullness of inspiration which contact with fellow-workers always produces.

Personal contact. By this is meant contact, not so much with fellow-members as with the staff, and, in particular, with the individual's own supervisor. During the undergraduate course, as the next chapter will suggest, all who are able enough to take up original work after graduation will have been gaining an increasing and deepening sense of their closeness, in aims and methods, to their teachers – a growing feeling that they are no longer teacher and student respectively, but are all students at different stages of maturity and progress. If this has been achieved so early, personal contact in the Graduate School will follow as a matter of course; if it has not, it must at all costs be achieved here.

In what condition is graduate study in the Arts Faculties of modern universities to-day? Flexner's judgement is probably not too severe:

The English are ... curiously averse to recognition of graduate students as a group. They are excessively conscientious teachers. 'It is our first business to teach', one hears again and again. They labour under the conviction that, having passed with honours, the student thenceforth needs only occasional contact with the professor.[1]

These generalizations he illustrates by the fact that in forty-seven years Manchester had conferred 2,932 B.A. degrees and only 1,019 M.A.s. This seems to be about the average. Another university of a somewhat different type shows, over the three sessions immediately prior to the outbreak of war in 1939, an average of some 350 undergraduates reading for the B.A. to 150 for the M.A. and Ph.D. If

1. Flexner, p. 254.

we look at the situation departmentally, we shall find among the twenty-five Schools in that university during the last of those sessions seven which had no graduate students at all and three which had only five between them. It is a rare thing for any School in an Arts Faculty to have more than six or eight. And most of these, being graduates of the university concerned, are not required to be literally in residence, nor as a rule is preparation for the M.A. a whole-time job. So the professor hardly ever sees his graduate students all at once: most of them come for supervision on Wednesday afternoons or Saturday mornings; many of them do the bulk of their work by correspondence. There was once a woman student who took an M.A. after three years' study under a professor, yet never set eyes upon him until she met him for the first time at the viva voce. It happened in this way. The professor was appointed between the date of her first graduation and her enrolment as an M.A. student. When she came up for the indispensable interview he had not come into residence and she saw the man who was acting for him, but, as her chosen subject came within the new professor's special field, he took her over when he arrived. Being married, and living at the other end of England, she was anxious to do as much of her work as she could by correspondence, and, as the professor had apparently no particular desire to see her, they remained strangers. This, no doubt, is an extreme and unusual case, but a good deal of the graduate work of a modern university is suspiciously like the tuition given by a 'correspondence college' and some of it is a great deal more like spasmodic private tuition than the work of a Graduate School ought to be.

The so-called 'Doctorate of Philosophy' is a reprehensible institution if taken, as it too often is, as a substitute for the Master's degree – i.e., in two or three years after the B.A. or (more frequently) the B.Sc. In most universities it has the merit of being a whole-time degree and that is about all that can be said for it. In the Science Faculties it is taken entirely as a professional qualification, which in Arts fields it fortunately seldom is. Any university that turns out 'doctors of philosophy' at the age of twenty-three or twenty-four deserves exactly the prestige they bring it. If for the M.A. residence were made compulsory for at least one session and the Ph.D. could be taken only by Masters after a further three years' work under supervision satisfactory to the Faculty, the standard of each degree would be higher.

The M.A., however, in the modern university is quite a praiseworthy degree of its kind. To be sure, it is taken largely for professional reasons, for, though not explicitly demanded by any profession, it is a useful way of covering up a low class in the B.A., or a means of competing with graduates from Scotland or Oxbridge, where, as has already been said, it is equivalent to B.A. or L.S.D. respectively. But, being a pure work of supererogation, it can be taken in a leisurely way, and occasionally it is taken for its own sake alone. Normally, any time between two years and eight may be spent upon it, and, even in two years, which is a minimum seldom found sufficient save by resident students, an able graduate, though untrained in methods of research, can produce an admirable thesis. A few universities, however, such as Birmingham, Leeds and Sheffield, allow Honours graduates to take the M.A. within one year from graduation, a concession disastrous to all students save the most brilliant. Others permit the degree to be taken, in certain circumstances, by examination alone.

It is a question, however, if, even with a two-year minimum, some steps should not be taken during the undergraduate period to mark down students likely to be incapable of doing research and prevent or dissuade them from entering upon an M.A. course at all. It may be said that the efficient professor always knows who such students are – but that can be true only of a small School – and also that facility for research is often latent until long after the age of twenty-one. The last statement I take leave to doubt. Many graduates grow in articulateness until their late twenties, but anyone who, after three years of university training, has shown no originality or initiative is unlikely ever to do so in the future.

A very simple method of separating the sheep from the goats, already in vogue here and there, might be considerably developed if all the universities would agree to give one form or another of it a trial. This is to incorporate a miniature thesis, something like the rather grandiloquently entitled 'Historical Dissertation' prescribed by the History School at Birmingham, into the final year's work for the Honours degree of B.A. To give every Honours candidate a small piece of research to do and report upon during the last year of study, or to include in the final year's requirements an essay of fifty pages or so[1] demanding original investigation or genuinely creative criticism would be to prevent many a young graduate from toiling later on to attain a research degree quite beyond his powers. It might also frequently give the staff of the Schools a very much better idea than they could otherwise have of the particular type of research for which a candidate is or is not fitted.

The most usual argument put forward against this suggestion is that the degree course is already supersaturated; but an exercise of this kind is surely much better suited to university study than a great deal which figures in its programmes and which might very well be deleted from them. A second and more reasonable objection is that not all Honours students are capable of research; and it is no reply to say that they ought to be, for, though this is true enough in theory, one can neither tell, when accepting undergraduates for the Honours School, how their initiative and creative powers are going to develop, nor can one suddenly eject a candidate admitted two sessions previously when his examinations and class work have been satisfactory. Probably the best solution of this difficulty is to make the thesis

1. Birmingham puts the maximum length for its Historical Dissertation at 10,000 words – which would equal about forty pages of double-spaced typing – and deprecates the spending upon it of more than one-third of the final year.

an alternative to an additional paper, the responsibility for the choice to rest with the professor.[1] The most serious argument against the final-year thesis is that, in the midst of a heavy session, on which so much depends, and during which the mental processes brought into play are largely analytical, it is confusing, and will not be productive of the best results, for the undergraduate to be given one single exercise of a synthetic character. It might be better, therefore, if the exercise were done, as far as possible, in his last Long Vacation – i.e., that preceding the Final Year – or, if this is impossible, at the very beginning of his last Michaelmas term, before the shadow of the examination is upon him. Once the preliminary conversations with the supervisor are over, the subject has been approved by him and the plan of attack worked out, the exercise should be entirely the student's own. Quite apart from its main function, it would have the additional advantage of sending down the new graduate with the feeling uppermost in his mind how little, rather than how much, he knows and turning him towards constructive ideals, of which, in university education, all too little is heard.

1. At Leeds, where the Faculty of Arts has a 'dissertation' of this type in its Honours School, some Schools lay down that it 'may' be taken and some (the majority) that it 'shall'. This diversity indicates that the matter is in a very fluid state: the compromise can hardly be considered an ideal solution to the problem.

CHAPTER FIVE

The Twofold Aim: (11) Teaching

I

THE undergraduate (to whom we agreed to confine this chapter) has so many and such insistent problems that, although one may attempt to deal with them all together, they demand consideration as and wherever they occur. Here we shall look chiefly at problems of teaching and study, as they affect the aim and organization of the university course; in the next chapter, we shall consider these and other problems from the specific standpoint of the undergraduate.

The outstanding and the most topical problem to be dealt with here is that of specialization. Everyone, if the word 'instruction' be interpreted in the broadest sense, will agree with a former Head of a modern university that there are three essentials of a true university education: 'efficient instruction; opportunities for deepening and broadening general culture; and full responsible membership of the university society'.[1] Yet it is commonly charged against the modern universities that they give only the first of the three; for nothing has the Redbrick undergraduate been so consistently reproached as for an allegedly excessive, if not exclusive, attention to his subjects of academic study. 'Among those', asserts Aldous Huxley, 'who go through a course of our academic education ... most ... emerge as parrots and specialists. (A good proportion of these return to the schools as teachers and proceed to train up other parrots and specialists.) Minds that delight in what may be called large-scale knowledge ... are rare. Academic education is supposed to impart such knowledge and to infect men and women with the desire to possess it; but in actual fact

1. W. M. Childs, *The Justification of Universities*, Manchester, 1936, pp. 15–16.

few are so infected and few go out into the world possessing it.'[1]

Nor is this type of criticism confined to those outside the universities. 'It astonished me', records Professor Herbert Read, 'to find when I first entered the University of Leeds that the ambitions of ninety out of every hundred of my fellow-undergraduates were crude and calculating. They were interested in one thing only – in getting the best possible degree by the shortest possible method ... Their career was plotted and they were careful not to stray from the thin line which marked an easy path through the world of knowledge.'[2] In an address to the National Union of Students, in 1933, the then Principal of University College, Hull, Dr A. E. Morgan, spoke strongly of the 'deplorably narrow' education of many undergraduates who sink 'deeper and deeper into the narrowing circle of specialization' and emerge with a 'one-track mind'.[3] In the next year he returned to the charge, more weightily if less picturesquely, and denounced what he termed a 'commonplace' of educationists:

The Universities are peopled with men and women deeply schooled in their particular subjects, but in too many cases lamentably ignorant of the learning of their fellows.

This excessive departmentalization of knowledge is more marked in the newer universities, where social contacts are harder to effect; but even in the older universities with their collegiate organization of fellowship it is too prevalent. And it is getting worse, with the result that teaching is excessively specialized and graduates are being turned out of all our universities expert in what they are pleased to call their subjects, but ignorant of much of the knowledge vital not merely to good citizenship but to individual capacity for life.[4]

Though some might demur to Mr Huxley's generalizations, everybody will recognize Professor Read's portrait

1. *Ends and Means*, London, 1937, pp. 197–8.
2. *Annals of Innocence and Experience*, London, 1940, pp. 75–6.
3. *Education in the Modern World: the Function of Universities*, London, 1933, pp. 8–9.
4. *The Listener*, 26 September 1934, p. 516.

and the selected type of Dr Morgan: the only question is how far it is produced by university specialization at all. At least two other possible sources for it exist, which may be mentioned in passing, though to discuss them at length would hardly be relevant. One is the failure of schools of every kind both to arouse and to attempt to satisfy a craving in children for knowledgeableness about things which lie completely outside their curricula. Many schools are less open to that charge than they were twenty years ago, but the prevalent type of children's education is still far too narrow: if freshmen came up with a burning desire for general knowledge, they would find ample means of feeding it even in the universities as they are at present. The second source is in the provision made for children's leisure. Boy scouts and Girl guides have done more to promote 'good citizenship' and 'individual capacity for life' than any changes, effected or contemplated, either in school curricula or in university regulations. But look at the popular magazines that boys and girls read and the types of film that they see. Neither of these all-important influences is in any real sense educative, yet both of them exercise a constant sway over children from perhaps the age of seven to that of nineteen or twenty: the influence of the film, indeed, never ceases.

Were the fault exclusively (for few would deny that it is partially) that of the university, one would expect to find that those who are most lacking in good citizenship and 'capacity for life' are those who specialize most deeply, and that those who take Pass degrees go down with a better general education and a greater sense of their responsibility for the community's welfare. But this is certainly not demonstrable. On the contrary, it will probably be found that nearly all who hold the chief offices in any student community, as well as those whom their fellows would pick out as more than usually knowledgeable, are either studying for Honours degrees or working intensively at one group of subjects to obtain some professional qualification. On the other hand, when I wonder who in my experience has combined

academic brilliance most strikingly with narrowness of
interests, I think at once of a man who, far from taking
Honours in a single School, obtained an Ordinary degree,
and in three out of his four subjects was awarded the mark
of distinction, yet who thought of all four as subjects to be
'swotted' merely for the sake of getting the maximum of
marks in an examination. Such a man, whatever the breadth
of the university programme, would never have been anything but what he was, and the responsibility for him lies at
the door of his home (which was a neat but humble one),
of his school (a large one in a poor area), and of the forces
which provided for his leisure. He is probably typical of a
large class. But typical of another, though of a smaller one,
is a Cambridge undergraduate, who, with precisely the
same type of background, and the same number of hours
in every day, took First Class Honours in one subject, pursued another to a high standard, won two half-blues in
sports, held high office in an undergraduate community,
belonged to half-a-dozen undergraduate societies, and
finally, on going down from the University, immediately
made his mark as a leader of men. And this man, when
congratulated on his all-round undergraduate record,
pushed the congratulations modestly aside.

'There's plenty of time,' he said, 'to get a First and do
all these things as well, if you want to.'

'*If you want to.*' There lies the crux of the matter. The
universities are responsible for providing the wherewithal
for a broad education, but they are not responsible for the
fact that so many boys and girls come up to them with no
desire to gain one. The University Grants Committee apparently thinks that to a large extent they are:

'In this matter the Universities are emphatically their
brother's keeper. It is of vital interest to them that the
human material they receive should reach them unwarped,
and inasmuch as they lay down their own entrance requirements, conduct their own scholarship examinations, and
through their examining boards take a large part in the
conduct of existing School Certificate and Higher School

Certificate examinations, they exercise an immense influence on the schools. The remedy, therefore, if remedy is needed, is to a considerable extent in their own hands.'[1]

There is, of course, truth in this. Blame must be attributed to universities for the narrowness of some of their courses and hence of their entrance and scholarship requirements. Blame must be attributed to examining bodies for making the Higher Certificate too exclusively a pre-university examination. Blame must also be attributed to schools which think too much of examination results, honours boards and future university distinctions and too little of their boys' or girls' personal welfare. But, though these causes explain why children often set out upon a baneful career of specialization before they are sixteen, the real trouble is rooted much more deeply. It goes back to the earlier stages of a child's history over which the university has no control, direct or indirect, whatever. This in no way absolves the university from doing what it can – whether by instituting less specialized courses, or, as will be suggested, by reforming the present specialized courses – but neither does it justify critics in attributing to the university blame for what it is powerless to alter.

In regarding the question of specialization historically, we find ourselves at the mercy of a natural action and reaction, which perhaps will never come to an end, between two separate and distinct ideals of education, the old encyclopaedic ideal, to-day hopelessly impossible of achievement, and a newer ideal which teaches that, as one can no longer hope to learn even a little about everything, one should at least try to learn everything about a little. The exaggerated form of these ideals, which no-one now would seriously defend, is enshrined in the overworked epigram that you must either be a dilettante, and get to know less and less about more and more, or a specialist, and learn more and more about less and less – until, in fact, as some-one capped it by adding, you know everything about nothing.

1. U.G.C., 1936, p. 23.

The newer universities came into being concurrently with the beginning of the reaction from encyclopaedism towards specialization. Men were at last applauding Newman's denunciations, made a generation earlier, of the error of forcing too much upon the student, 'of distracting and enfeebling the mind by an unmeaning profusion of subjects; of implying that a smattering in a dozen branches of study is not shallowness, which it really is, but enlargement, which it is not ... All things now are to be learned at once, not first one thing, then another, not one well, but many badly.'[1]

The reaction was not a purely academic phenomenon, but a result of the increasing mechanization, complication and stress of life which made itself felt at the end of the last century. In mid-Victorian days, a household, aided, if in comfortable circumstances, by numerous manservants and maidservants, would bake its own bread, do the whole of its own cooking, wash its own clothes, and be its own gardener, joiner, plumber and a score of other things besides. Nowadays, servants are harder to get and less efficient when you have got them; father works for longer hours and finds his relaxations away from home; mother and the girls, as often as not, are in paid occupations; while the boys, as has always been the case, are in the City – or in the Colonies – almost before you know they have grown up. The joint family income is larger than would have been dreamed of fifty years ago; against that increase, however, has to be set the cost of the services of a whole bevy of specialists. A laundry washes the clothes; a gardener attends to the garden; a baker bakes the bread; cakes, jams, scones, pastries and sometimes even ready-cooked meats are bought instead of being made at home; and when the smallest thing goes wrong in the house there is always a rush to the telephone for the appropriate specialist to put it right. And if mother sometimes ventures a 'Why ever don't you mow the lawn yourself, dear? You're putting on weight, you know', the answer, in this specialized age, is always an impatient or

1. Newman, p. 142.

longsuffering: 'Because I prefer to be making money, of course: I should hope my time was worth more than half-a-crown an hour; and, when I want to take exercise, I'll take it in my own way'.

It was at the dawn of this kind of world that the Honours degree suddenly acquired a previously unimagined popularity. Who originally planted it appears to be unknown, but it was watered by the newer secondary schools, while the universities, both ancient and modern, nursed it till it throve mightily. Victorian schools had been content to leave the bulk of their instruction in the hands of 'form masters', who taught Scripture, geography, history, Latin, French and English, and could make a show at mathematics, and sometimes even at chemistry, if it were required of them. But this was not good enough for the twentieth century. Geography ceased to stand for lists of capes and bays and become a science; history had to include not only the reigns of the kings of England but the lives of the English people, with a certain amount of information, at least, about the rest of Europe; a teacher of French must have visited France, possess an accent sounding vaguely 'foreign', and be qualified to give instruction in the mysteries of a science called phonetics; even English literature, it was discovered, could not be taught by just anybody. So the old type of form-master was gradually succeeded by the specialist, and the form-master himself, though still such in name, became in fact a specialist too, with the additional duty of adding up all the marks of his class, writing the headings of their reports and – one had almost forgotten the Cinderella subject – teaching them Scripture.

The Honours degree, of course, duly produced the specialist, and he became an accepted sign of the times – not only in secondary education, but in the Civil Service, in industry and nearly everywhere else. Universities founded Honours Schools and new professorships in great numbers, and, until some time after the war of 1914–18, there was a continually increasing flow of students into Honours, while Pass schools came to be looked upon as the resort of the incompetent or lazy. Whatever it may have been in practice, in theory this was ridiculous. In the first place, of those who go to universities a large number have not the power of concentration on intensive study which the Honours curriculum makes essential. And, in any case, for some of the professions the chief need is good pass-men: the parish priest, for example, is of much more use with a Pass degree in three or four subjects than with Third Class Honours – or perhaps any class of Honours – in only one. The undergraduate, too, who takes a degree merely to reach a high standard of general education – a man before going into many forms of business; a woman before taking up home duties – will usually get most out of a Pass course. Yet the majority of these were forced by public opinion into Honours Schools, and the Schools in the subjects generally considered as soft options – History, English Literature, and to a lesser extent French – were choked with Thirds and Low Seconds: out of consideration, in fact, for those who only just missed Firsts, a distinction had to be made in the enormous Second Class by cutting it into an Upper and a Lower division.

Matters were made worse by the fact that at most universities candidates were prohibited from re-presenting themselves for Honours in a subject in which they had failed, and the examiners were therefore very loath to fail anyone at all. At the modern universities candidates who were clearly going to be unsuccessful were transferred to the Pass degree course at the end of their second or third year, but at the older universities, with their looser system of control, this was not always possible, and in any case deterioration often becomes decisive only in the Final year, when the pressure on the undergraduate reaches its maximum. So there was a choice between failing candidates in considerable numbers, lowering the standard of the lowest class in Honours and 'allowing the Pass degree' to the failed-in-Honours, thereby bestowing on them an entirely inappropriate label and to that extent misleading any to whom the label might be of importance.

Not until well into the nineteen-twenties did the reaction against this excessive specialization begin, and it was a good deal less violent than might have been expected, partly because the British reaction to most things is a mild one and partly because the stress of life had made the specialist so indispensable that there could be no question of anything more than adjustment. So a number of universities began to furbish up their Pass degree according to differing recipes. Some endowed it with a moderate amount of specialization, introducing a 'special' or 'intensive' course pursued in greater detail than the rest. Some created alternative ('grouped') Honours courses, involving two main subjects and one subsidiary to them, thus enabling the Pass-man and the Honour-man to meet halfway.[1] Some went farther and altered both the Pass and the Honours degree. The title of the latter they changed to 'Special' (an unfortunate change when one thinks of the Cambridge 'Special'!) and they made it possible to obtain the Special degree with or without 'Honours'. The former they termed the 'General' degree, and by changing the title of what used to be called 'Distinction' to 'Honours', did away with the old opposition between Pass and Honours altogether. Did away with it, that is to say, in theory; for, in spite of their giving great publicity to the new 'General Honours' degree, which, so far as its sound went, left nothing to be desired, it is doubtful if many people have ever preferred it to the Special – whether this be taken with or without Honours. At about the same time, the old, and many thought almost valueless, Intermediate, or First Year examination, which had forced all freshmen to coquet with three or four subjects before entering upon an Honours course, came back into favour, with the result that the latter, curtailed by an entire session,

1. Birmingham, which is the pioneer here, has some very attractive combinations, such as Greek and English with subsidiary Philosophy or Music; Italian and History with Geography or Economics; English and Philosophy with a foreign modern language. The only question is if anything like a genuine Honours standard can be reached on so extensive a syllabus in three years.

degenerated in quality except where the length of the university course was increased by a year to make up for it with the consequent additional strain upon local authorities and far from wealthy homes.

None of these reforms seems to have been particularly successful: it is even arguable that the disease was less undesirable than the remedies. But simultaneously there began a movement, which is still popular, towards broadening university education in quite a different fashion – increasing the number of extra-curricular lectures, debates, vacation courses, travel parties, and the like, which would induce the undergraduate to devote less time to his academic course and to undertake an important part of his own education. No doubt some of the innovations have been beneficial, but their general effect has been to confuse the well-meaning student and turn him into more of a dilettante than an Ordinary degree ever did in the past.

In this connection it is of interest to quote two resolutions passed at a Congress of the National Union of Students in 1938. The Congress first claims that university teaching should

(*a*) train men and women to have specialized information about one or two subjects and general information about a wide range of others;

(*b*) develop a critical faculty and a power to weigh evidence objectively;

(*c*) promote an attitude rising above personal interest.

After recommending greater freedom in the combination of degree subjects and the provision of free lectures on general themes, it goes on to urge:

That no subject, however specialized, should be taught without some reference to

(i)   its historical background;
(ii) its relation to other branches of learning;
(iii) its social implications.

If we pass over the regrettably low conception of the nature of university education here displayed – 'training

men and women *to have ... information'* – the first three things
which the National Union desires are unexceptionable. But
the most striking point about them is that every one can be
obtained through the Honours course, provided always that
the three admirable recommendations as to teaching are
followed also. And that brings us to what may quite possibly
be the solution of the conflict between encyclopaedism and
specialization: *the reform of the Honours course itself.*

Let us see how this course, which admittedly gives
'specialized information about one or two subjects', can be
made to do the other things that are desired of it.

(1) It can, and should, give 'general information about a
wide range of others'. Take two of the Arts subjects most
commonly read for Honours: English Literature and
French. The intensive study of either involves a knowledge
of the history and social conditions of the country concerned
from the earliest times to the present day; and the history
of France is inextricably intertwined with the history of
western Europe. Through English literature we may study
the Authorized Version of the Bible; theology, in Hooker,
Andrewes, Donne and Baxter; philosophy, in Bacon, Hume
and Berkeley; history, in Burke and Macaulay; educational
theory, in Ascham; political science, in Hobbes, Bentham
and Mill; discovery, in Hakluyt and Raleigh. Chapman will
lead the student into Greek mythology; Gibbon, into
Roman History; Carlyle, into France and Germany; Lock-
hart and Southey, into Spain. If he seeks inspiration from
character and ideals, where can he find better and more
varied models than in Shakespeare, Browne, Bunyan, Milton, Herbert and Wordsworth? The French course, apart
from the purely linguistic training which it offers, contains
no less variety, and an equally large number of first-rank
authors lie outside the field of pure literature. Froissart,
Joinville and Commines take us into medieval history;
Rabelais and Fénelon, into education; Fontenelle and
Montesquieu, into science and law; Sainte-Beuve and
Taine, into criticism. An understanding of Descartes lies at
the root of modern philosophy, while neither Pascal nor

Bossuet can have much meaning save for those with some knowledge of theology. Rousseau and Voltaire are in themselves two branches of a complete education. The devoutly minded may drink deeply of Saint François de Sales; worldly wisdom may be gleaned from La Rochefoucauld, La Bruyère and the incomparable Montaigne; while the value of an intensive study of Molière is second only to that of the study of Shakespeare.

It is probably true that, if the National Union of Students were to talk like this to any professor of English or French, his answer would be something as follows:

'Yes, all those things are there, but I can only refer to them in passing and you must dig them out for yourself.'

'Why must I?' the student would reply.

'Because, in the first place, I have only two periods a week for three years – that is, about 120 hours altogether – in which to cover the whole course of English literature: nearly a thousand years. And, though we study a few set books more intensively, the majority of these will always be works of pure imagination, simply because nearly all our greatest works are of that kind.'

'Then why can't we have more lectures?'

'Because on your own showing you are over-lectured-to already.'

There seems no answer to this, and it does in fact bring us to the crux of the question of specialization. The very people who cry out that the universities are over-specialized also contend that there should be fewer lectures and more time for students to think and read. An extraordinary example of this is to be found on pages 53-4 of the National Union of Students' Report on their 1937 Congress. On page 53 they demand 'that lectures should be reduced to a minimum'; on page 54 they propose that over-specialization should be combated by 'courses of lectures, etc., in general cultural subjects. These lectures would be semi-compulsory.' Of course the moment you add these new subjects to the curriculum, you are adding – you cannot avoid adding – new lectures as well. Give effect to one recommendation which is fashionable to-day by making economics, philosophy and social science compulsory for freshmen and you immediately increase their total of fifteen weekly lectures, spread over three subjects – itself a maximum load – to at least twenty-one. Whatever may be the position in Honours Schools, lectures, and good lectures at that, are essential for the introduction of new and difficult subjects to immature minds.

It seems clear that any efficient broadening of the curriculum for Honours students will have to be done through their own subjects rather than through the introduction of other subjects of which they know nothing. And, although the hypothetical professor just quoted entrenches himself securely behind *non possumus* defences which the undergraduate has not knowledge enough to storm, it would be possible to ask him a few shrewd questions which would reveal his weak spots. For instance:

'Are you sure that you put nothing into your lectures on English literature which can be got from books?'

(As a matter of fact, I know the answer to that one; I have seen your students' notebooks crammed with expositions which are little more than summaries.)

'When you lecture on Montaigne, which do you emphasize more – his thought, or the irregularities of his language?'

(I have heard bitter complaints of dreary courses based on Darmesteter et Hatzfeld's *Seizième Siècle* which have dealt almost exclusively with vocabulary and syntax.)

'Is it true that one can take First Class Honours in German without having more knowledge of German history than a few facts and dates and without knowing anything about modern Germany at all?'

I would spare my professor the embarrassment of answering that last question, but before I can go on he retorts that if that is so it is because in *his* School they give the chief place to language: in another University, not a thousand miles away, I could get a First Class without having touched Germanic Philology, and, as the viva voce is separate from the Final (at one university it is '*lawful* [*sic*] for the Examiners to examine orally any candidates for an Honours School'), I need not even be able to speak the language. Isn't that very much worse?

No: considering the condition and the needs of the world to-day, I don't think it is: the one defect is just about as bad as the other. And both are unnecessary. With a rigorous overhauling of the syllabus and the content of lectures, it is possible to plan an English, French or German Honours course which gives due weight to language, literature, history, art, science, thought and social background. At Birmingham, apart from the subsidiary subjects taken by all Honours candidates, candidates for English, French and Philosophy are either 'required' or 'strongly recommended' to attend courses in Fine Arts; some Philosophy courses are prescribed for French Honours; lectures on Greek drama and on History, Fine Arts, Philosophy or Geography for German Honours; History and Geography Honours includes translation from two modern foreign languages. Assuming that these extra courses can be adapted to the candidate's special needs, a graduate with good Honours in such a School has (to quote the National Union of Students) as full a 'realization of the responsibility of citizenship' as anyone else. But let the Union be perfectly clear about this: it is a literal impossibility to plan such a course and at the same time to fill up the undergraduate's time with lectures on half-a-dozen miscellaneous subjects in no way related to his main field of study. It must choose which of the alternatives it will have: a good all-round Honours course or a defective Honours course and Teufelsdrockian lectures on Things in General.

(2) But there are still other demands which the National Union makes on the course of study and which the Honours course already provides. It must 'develop a critical faculty and a power to weigh evidence objectively'. That will never be accomplished by filling the time-table with 'lectures on general subjects'. It is only when one begins to know a subject deeply that this faculty has any real scope at all. At the

end of a course of twelve lectures on Pascal's *Lettres Provin-ciales* the student may not be qualified to express himself critically on the theological questions which it raises, but he will be better educated by the experience than if he spends the same twelve hours in taking a deceptively com-prehensive course on 'Outlines of Theology for Laymen'. Only by seeing that our students' knowledge is sound and deep and at the same time seeking to inspire them with the spirit of adventure and research can we ever develop a critical faculty in them at all. And that is done, primarily through the Honours course, and, to a lesser extent, through a Pass course of not more than three main subjects, of which one at least has close relations with one or both of the others.

(3) As to the promoting of 'an attitude rising above per-sonal interest', that is accomplished far more by example than by precept. The undergraduate is quick to see if his teachers have a disinterested love of learning, and, though he may not realize why, it is for those who have that he will soon develop the greatest respect. Even at school, where to some extent character can be disguised by routine, he has learned to distinguish a few obvious sheep on the staff from the more blatant of the goats; at the University, where greater freedom more fully reveals personality, he will do so, once he feels at home in his new environment, much more successfully. Apart from example, the best way of inculcating disinterestedness is through research, which, in the Arts sphere at least, is a purely disinterested activity. And at bottom scholarship and character are inseparable.

Once we allow that the Honours course, properly handled, can give breadth as well as depth in education, the question arises whether the old 'Intermediate' or 'First Year' examination can any longer be held to justify itself. There is a good case for the view that it cannot.

Its principal weakness is that it is based, not on the Higher Certificate, a good performance in which is the minimum requirement of most Schools for would-be Hon-ours candidates, but on Matriculation, which by most freshmen has been taken two years or more earlier. Except where a School is sufficiently large and well staffed to permit the holding of parallel First-Year courses, one of Intermediate standard and one some way above it, every candidate for Honours is following courses in his Honours subject which are a long way below the standard he has reached at school, and even in other subjects he generally finds them fully easy. So passes this thoroughly demoralizing year, in which the majority of the most able freshmen have definitely deteriorated in their Honours subject, and, unless they have added to it subjects not usually taught at school, such as Philosophy, Economics or Italian, their net academic progress is nil. It may be objected that they have been broadening their minds by attending all kinds of lectures and society meetings at the Union, but surely for any such advantage they may have gained they have paid a higher price than should be necessary.

Another weakness of the system is that it produces a large number of short courses, which in the sense of the word used by the advocates of the Intermediate examination themselves are not educative. Here is a freshman who hopes to read for Honours in one subject, with a second subject as subsidiary, but besides these two he is being forced to read two more, which, at the end of nine months, he hopes to drop – probably for ever. Here is a University of 1,800 students with 79 freshmen of that description in its Faculty of Arts alone, each of them more or less of a drag on at least two courses. Here is a first-year class of nineteen members, only two of whom are certainly going up into the second-year class, though five more may possibly do so. Here is a School of thirty-five undergraduate students, thirteen of whom will have no more to do with it after their first year is over. These are actual examples of what happens. Is this the 'education' at which advocates of the 'Intermediate' are aiming? Does it in fact produce much beyond 'scraps and smatterings'? 'Intermediate classes', writes the critic who uses this last phrase, 'are often burdened with members who have been coerced in this way rather than attracted.'

The sooner we realize that 'a one year's course without sequel or resumption provides too short a period for a new subject to take root',[1] the better.

But that is not the whole of the story. As an Honours course worthy of the name cannot be given in less than three years, and as the first year is, academically speaking, wasted, the full degree course has either to be prolonged to four years or the Honours course to be compressed into two. Either proceeding is bad. A boy intending to become a teacher enters Redbrick University at nineteen. He might have come up a year earlier, but his Headmaster persuaded him to stay and take the Higher Certificate a third time for the glory of the school, and also to try for an Oxbridge scholarship, which he failed to obtain. Redbrick gets him, a year late, and proceeds to make him mark time for a second year, leaving him, at the age of twenty, faced with the choice between compressing two years' study into one (thus making any general self-education all but impossible) and spending three years on the Honours course and then one more on the Teaching Diploma – not earning a penny, in fact, till he is twenty-four. Those who defend the system can take their choice of these alternatives: but is either really defensible?

Let the Honours man, on the other hand, start in at once, while still keen, on his three-year course and the Pass man on the Intermediate course, and each is in his proper place, with work to do just hard enough to act as a stimulus. The Honours candidate can be accepted provisionally for the first term, and, if it be thought desirable to broaden his course (for he will presumably be doing his subsidiary subject as well, or both his Schools if it is a two-School Honours course), he can be made to read and attend lectures in some other subject, such as a new language or some branch of philosophy – as is laid down at Birmingham – with no obligation to sit for any other than a class examination in it. This is surely a first year much more educative than the

1. P. Mansell-Jones, 'Where modern universities are wrong', in *The Universities Review*, October 1932 vol. v, pp. 7–8.

other, and one which can do no undergraduate any harm, as that does.

The fear of premature specialization is a bogy which has haunted educationists far too long – it has not been without its effect even on the urbane and imperturbable Grants Committee. It may be that there is too much specialization somewhere, but it is in some of the subjects in the Higher Certificate examinations that one should look for it rather than at the university. If the two-year Advanced Course in schools were planned on a broader basis than it is, little harm would be done to the principal subject of the under-graduate, since the schools already take this farther than most professors like. If, again, the freshman normally came up at seventeen, and eighteen were considered the upper limit-age for entry, there would be a better case for the broad first-year course than there is now. But the real fault is that we have not developed our conception of what an Honours subject should be and given it all the breadth of which it is capable. Let that remedy, at least, be tried.

II

Neither the Lecture System, then, nor the Honours System, deserves all the destructive criticism that has been showered upon it, and there seems to be but little need of reform in the Pass syllabus. How, if at all, can our treatment of the undergraduate, in the academic sense, be further improved upon?

This book contends that the whole art of educating the undergraduate, in the deeper sense, must be based upon the instilling into him of a true idea of the nature of a university. He comes up, believing that the university is a superior kind of school, and, as we have seen, all the outward and visible signs support that belief. We have to show him that, despite all appearances, the university is not an institution, but a society: that professors and lecturers are not his 'masters' but more experienced fellow-members of the society; that he is the owner, and should therefore be the organizer, of his own time, for good or (if he prefers it) for evil. The sooner he realizes this, the easier it will be to inspire him with the love of initiative and adventure which is one of the essentials of the scholar.

Unfortunately, this is often a lengthy process and its early stages resemble the demolition, brick by brick, of a large building. Here are some of the details of the process.

(1) At most schools, boys and girls, even in the highest forms, are spoon-fed. The instruction to 'learn this for next time' implies the assurance 'and if you persevere in doing that, the school will see that you get through your examination'. The undergraduate, on the other hand, must be made to realize that the organization of his work and the responsibility for covering the syllabus are his, and his alone: professors, dean, library, lectures, are there to help him, but not to usurp his own functions.

(2) At all schools, there is a pathetic confidence in the printed word, natural in the very young, but of course entirely misplaced. Nowhere at school is there any appeal from the grammar and the dictionary; and even in the Sixth – or in most Sixths – 'the book says so' is a complete answer to any doubt, even to a doubt expressed by the teacher. At the university this confidence persists too long: the sooner, and the more rudely, it is broken up by a demonstration of the unreliability of books – especially of text-books – the better.

(3) At school, one believes there is a right and a wrong to everything. Judgements are clear-cut. If one's teacher, or one's text-book, says that Sidney's sonnets are greater than Shakespeare's, then that settles it: they are. The distinction between fact and criticism is blurred, save under an exceptional teacher. At the university, the critical faculty must be developed by a refusal to dogmatize or to accept dogmatic judgements in any question of pure criticism. The teacher, whether in lecture or seminar, must be continually questioning and systematically presenting both sides of every debatable question. It takes a long time to get one's pupils into this habit and many of them never get into it at all:

of these last it must be regretfully said that they have received university instruction but failed to get a university education.

(4) At school, the teacher has to say a great deal about subjects to which he has never devoted any sustained or original thought. (This is less true than in the pre-specialist days, but it is still widely applicable.) The result is that he 'gets up' his lessons in standard authorities, whose ideas he reproduces in simplified form for his pupils' benefit. These ideas the pupil serves back to him, still further diluted, in examinations. At the university, the pupil goes to lectures, and what wonder if he takes copious notes and serves these up at examinations in the same way? To him the university lecture is simply 'the mixture, as before'. If, after graduation, he becomes a teacher, it can be imagined what his teaching will be like – and sometimes, after several generations of this process, the reproduction of authoritative statements is so firmly established a tradition that it seems ineradicable. There are probably many Schools, both in the ancient and in the modern universities, in which it is the only form of instruction ever given.

Here, again, the genuine university teacher will make a clean cut with tradition: it is the only way. 'Accept none of the judgements I give you as more than the expression of my own opinion' will be the keynote of his exhortations. He will explain that, while contact with the mind of any experienced worker is valuable, and the immature student will naturally control any opinions he forms by those of others, his own impressions, opinions and judgements alone are valid for him and it is upon them that he must build his own experience.

This attitude, like the last, takes a long time to establish and precept will no doubt have to be reinforced by practice and even by penalties. It would be well if an essay or an exercise were never accepted when the student had merely reproduced the content of a book or a lecture or uncritically synthesized the opinions of a number of authors. 'Yes, but what do *you* think about it?' is a simple but penetrating question which has lit up the path along which many a student was groping in darkness. For any able pupil it is a great day when he throws off the shackles of the text-book, develops a limited trust in his own judgement and conceives a great longing for the time to come when he can trust it more. That pupil, whatever his defects, has learned the inner meaning of university education.

(5) But the most important, yet most difficult, idea to impart to the undergraduate is that his teachers at the university – his fellow-members – are not so much teachers as collaborators: learners like himself, but in a considerably higher class. Many professors and lecturers would agree that this should be taught, but would say that they have no idea how to teach it. There is no need to try: if a man *is* a worker, the fact imparts itself; and it becomes equally clear if he is not.

Research, as one of the Grants Committee's reports puts it, must 'fertilize' our teaching. We must be readier and more eager to learn than to teach. Our research must not be shut up in a watertight compartment, or taken out and gloated over, like the miser's hoard, at night, and forgotten by day. The spirit of research, rather than the mere fact of research, is what matters. In this sense, where there is no research at the top, there will be no originality, or desire for originality, at the bottom.

It may be (though it certainly is not always) the dab at games, the master of repartee in class, the hail-fellow-well-met out of school who is the success as a schoolmaster. But at the university the essence of success is to have a live mind – to be ready to question, examine, investigate and discover at every turn. Other things – lecturing ability, interest in one's pupils, organizing and administrative skill – are all (as has already been suggested) of great importance. But the other is fundamental. You can lecture with the tongue of men and of angels, but if you reproduce only what is in books your audience will see through you. You can be a second father to your undergraduates, but if they ask for bread and you give them stones you are doing them a paltry

service. And, however great your organizing skill, if it produces something without life it is of little value. Yet, on the
other hand, undergraduates have been known to sit gladly
at the feet of a man whose delivery was atrocious and whose
lectures seldom failed (and this is normally the unforgivable
sin) to overrun the hour, just because he never failed to give
them food for thought. For the ideas which he declaimed
in those monotonous tones were challenging, provocative
ideas, and a page of notes from any one of his lectures immediately set his hearers thinking and turned them back
on their own minds. 'It was life disguised as death', one of
his graduates was heard to remark, reminiscently, 'but how
much better it was than that terrible kind of intellectual
death which simulates vivaciousness and vitality!'

III

The stimulation of thought in undergraduates depends in
great measure upon the University Library. There was a
time, I believe, at Cambridge, when undergraduates were
forbidden the use of the Library in the mornings if they
were men, and in the afternoons if they were women, the
reason apparently being that the tall bookcases in the deep-
set, ill-lit bays might harbour dusty romances. (And why
not? one might ask. Where better could a romance begin?
To-day, one is glad to see, men and women may even sit
next to one another!) In addition to this, no undergraduate
might ever take out a volume. Nor, for that matter, can
he now, though a really determined man who has kept six
terms (why six? Does one learn honesty only at the end of
one's second year?) has for a long time been allowed to
borrow through his tutor.

The 'sister university', as befits its seniority, is still more
austere. No book ever passes out of the sacred precincts of
the Bodleian – and some say that very few Oxford residents
ever pass in. There is a passage in the *Oxford Handbook*
where unconscious humour strives with latent irony, in
which the undergraduate is sternly informed that 'the rules

of the Bodleian do not permit lending'. But, adds the writer, administering triumphant consolation, this is really a great advantage, for 'if it possesses a book, the reader may be sure that that book is in the building'. The undergraduate is now reassured. But not for long. For, continues the *Handbook*, 'he will not search for it himself: the library is not at present arranged for the direct access of the reader to the shelves where most of the books are stored.'[1]

No: our ancient universities cannot be said ('at present') to encourage the free use of a library.

At Redbrick, on the other hand, the undergraduate can at least say of the University Library: 'An ill-favoured thing, but mine own.' The recent date of its foundation means that of old books it can have but few, and its penury precludes it from buying as many new ones as it might, though it buys far more to-day than it did a few years ago;[2] but if it contains only two or three hundred thousand volumes instead of a million and a quarter, all of them, except for a few rare editions, are at every undergraduate's service. He can go at will from floor to floor and from stack to stack, and browse among the books to his heart's content, in any of his free time, for some eight to ten hours daily. And yet, in this respect as in others, he has to be educated. It is astonishing how many students, who have never before been let loose in a library of more than four or five hundred books, are too much overwhelmed by the riches now at their command to make full use of them.

When I have a group of undergraduates to tea, I sometimes ask them playfully: 'Supposing you could have the

1. *Oxford Handbook*, 1932, pp. 188–9.

2. In 1925–6, according to the U.G.C. report (1936, p. 8) 'the total Library expenditure of the University Institutions was £156,000'; in 1934–5, it was £228,000. These figures, of course, include total expenditure – not the cost of books alone. It is worth noting that at Oxford 8.3 per cent of the total expenditure of the University is on the Library; at Cambridge, 5.1 per cent; but that the average for all the universities of Great Britain is only 3.8 per cent. And both Oxford and Cambridge receive under the Copyright Act free copies of every book published in the country.

library without lectures or your lectures without a library, but not both, which would you choose?' I am not quite sure myself what answer the undergraduate ought to give: for one thing, it would depend whether the term 'lectures' includes every kind of tuition, and, for another, whether his subject is one in which books are cheap and numerous. But it is a good question, because it shakes him out of his complacent acceptance of lectures as something (like lessons at school) of which the absence is quite inconceivable and gives him a better idea of the importance of the Library. 'If I were a Dictator of Education,' remarked Sir Charles Grant Robertson, then Vice-Chancellor of Birmingham University, in 1935, 'I should reduce the time taken by lectures to a third of that taken at present, and make attendance in the Library compulsory for three hours a day.' It may be doubted if he would, and also if such compulsory attendance would manufacture bookmen, but again the assertion was well worth making and must have led many an undergraduate to revise his habits.

Besides being a repository of books, the Library is also, to many students, the one place where they can work from morning to night in complete peace. Many of them have their own particular corners in this or that reading-room, where they can leave their own books from one day to another and assemble books from the shelves as they need them. In some of the modern universities, in fact, the Library is the only spot for which many a student has any affection, and it is gratifying to see graduates who have gone down, when they find themselves in Redbrick with time for a little reading, returning to their own favourite haunts to do it.

The deficiencies of the modern university library, as has been hinted, are due to youthfulness and poverty: it will in due time grow out of the one, and also, it is to be hoped, though less quickly, out of the other. Meanwhile the inter-university loan system, greatly improved in its working of recent years, the increasing co-operation with the universities of the National Central Library and the help that can be obtained from the London Library go far to compensate for the inevitable gaps in each university's catalogue. The National Central Library can now obtain for it books on loan from foreign as well as home universities, from municipal libraries and from many private libraries of a specialized character.[1] Another improvement has been in night opening. Not so long ago university libraries used to close when lectures ended, despite the obvious fact that it was precisely then that they were most needed.[2] A few still do; but most, on at least two or three weekdays during term, open till late evening (Sheffield, to its great credit, is open, on five days a week, for eleven hours daily), so that the undergraduate can do nearly the whole of his reading there and both graduates and staff have ideal stretches of time for uninterrupted research.

Besides the University Library, there are two minor sources whence books should be obtainable: the Hostel or Hall of Residence and the University Union.

These are of less importance than the College and the Union libraries were to us in Oxbridge days, for there the lack of hospitality shown by the University Library forced us on to the generally meagre resources of the College and the ample stock of often inferior and much-thumbed editions which could either be taken back to one's rooms or read in the deep arm-chairs of the Union. The function of both is to serve as substitutes for the library which ideally every student should have in his or her home, for, from the educational standpoint, the Hostel is home to the resident student as the Union is to the non-resident. So, rather than text-books and standard works (other than dictionaries and essential books of reference) to be found in the University Library, these libraries should contain wide selections of

1. More information on this subject will be found in U.G.C., 1936, p. 44.

2. Cf. Herklots, p. 50 (written in 1928): 'Not Oxford and Cambridge in the vacation are as desolate of students as the buildings of a modern university at eight o'clock in the evening. University life, as university life, ends at sundown. Midnight oil must be burnt in lodgings, not in the library.'

volumes which will be read for pleasure as well as for instruction: long sets of Scott, Swinburne, Hardy and Kipling; popular works on science; the classics of three or four modern foreign literatures and some quite elementary books in a few more; standard histories on the one hand and the most thought-provoking books of the day on the other. Above all, they should have plenty of good newspapers, together with the best monthly and quarterly periodicals, British, Continental and American. It will take some time to initiate the Redbrick undergraduate into the habit of reading *The Times* and the *Manchester Guardian* – a census taken in one university shortly before 1939 established that of thirteen daily newspapers *The Times* was the least popular, being read by only 6.8 per cent, the *Daily Worker* being favoured by 9.9 per cent and the penny picture-papers by from 11 to 14 per cent. But once the habit is formed it will not be quickly lost and may even last for a lifetime.

Still, even when the University Library is a good one and extends to readers the welcome that it should by means of the principles of continuous opening and unrestricted access to the book-stacks, the student must still be made book-conscious in another way – he must be encouraged to form his own library. Too often, at present, he looks forward to the day when, with his name safely on the Final list, he can take his well-worn text-books to the nearest second-hand dealer and get a few pence for each of them. Ask almost any recent Redbrick graduate to go home and count the number of books he possesses and you will be appalled at his answer. Many a man, after ten years at school and three or four at the University, will have less than fifty; few will have more than a hundred. And this will include school-books, university text-books and books acquired as presents or prizes.

It might be thought that this is a condemnation of the practice of allowing books to be borrowed from the University Library. But that it is not the following consideration will show. In most Schools there are usually a few books which Heads of Departments will not order for the Library because they are essential and inexpensive and they want their students to buy them. But *will* they buy them? Not if they can avoid it! Rather will they sit three in a desk, so that three can share a single book, or copy out long extracts from someone else's, when half a crown would buy a copy for themselves. And yet many of them think nothing of spending half a crown a week on tea-dances at the University Union or on the 'pictures'.

The reason for this is not, as a rule, that they are either too poor or too mean. Granted, their resources are small – but let a Departmental Society have a deficit, or a collection be made for refugees or a subscription be raised for a wreath for a fellow-student who has died, and you would wonder where all the silver came from. It is just that they have never been convinced of the value of book-buying. It is not a subject taught in schools, or, as a rule, in universities. At both their elementary and their secondary school, all necessary textbooks were handed out to them, free of charge; very naturally and properly they were not permitted to mark them; beyond the brown-paper cover which the school insisted on their putting on them for hygienic motives there was not a thing about those books that was their own. So, when they come to the university, and find that they now have either to buy their books or to borrow them, they borrow if they can and buy only as a very last resort. The joy of having a book – a loved tool – continually at hand and by careful and constant use making every page of it a familiar friend is something they have never even imagined.

In no respect is the importance of close personal contact between professor and student so marked as in this. We must teach our pupils, both by example and by precept, what the possession of a library, however small it be, can mean to them.

'Oh, I *could* work *here*!' exclaims the freshman from Lower Back Street, as he enters his professor's spacious and tranquil study, its walls lined, and its tables covered, with books.

'There are five thousand books in this room,' his professor answers; 'but, when I was your age, I had only a hundred and fifty. Books were dearer then than they are now. You can get two Penguin Specials for the price of a seat at the pictures; you can buy an Everyman by playing cricket next Saturday instead of going to the Union tea-dance. Buy a seat's worth and a dance's-worth of books every month and those alone will come to over a hundred by the time you graduate.'

By such unobtrusive dropping of seed here and there, both in regard to this and to other subjects, is the boy or girl from Lower Back Street transformed into a worthy member of a university.

CHAPTER SIX

Students and Student Life

In the Scottish universities, which are, of course, ancient in the extreme by comparison with any English universities save Oxford and Cambridge, all undergraduates, on matriculation, make a solemn promise, known as the *sponsio academica*. It is interesting to compare the form of the declaration made at Edinburgh with that used at Glasgow. Edinburgh inclines to the sentimental: I will be 'dutiful and industrious in my studies' and 'will pay my debt of gratitude and good will on every occasion to the best of my powers, so long as I live'. (Graduands become even more emphatic: 'we ... promise that we will to our latest breath abide in all due loyalty to the University of Edinburgh'.) Contrast the Glasgow formula, which is commendably and rigidly practical:

I will not wilfully damage the fabric or furnishings of the University and will make good, to the satisfaction of the Senatus, any damage caused by me.

Which things are an allegory. Ask any casual group of students what aspects of student life should form the subject of this chapter and you will get the most diverse replies. Some are interested in such problems of curriculum and examination as have already been dealt with; others are anxious for the development of the student body as an organ of opinion; others, again, are preoccupied with such material matters as meals, amenities and facilities for athletics; others look to the future and debate what they will do when they go down. If therefore, student life is to be reflected with any accuracy, the pages which follow will not avoid being somewhat kaleidoscopic. For that, to the detached adult observer, is exactly what the life of a modern university is. The light of publicity plays on one facet after another of adolescent thought, sentiment and emotion; the nature of the impact of current events upon opinion is

unpredictable; one cause, or passion, or craze after another
takes possession of the focus of student-interest. To-day the
trend of opinion is unbelievably materialistic; to-morrow it
will be deflected by some ideal which has caught the undergraduate mind. Now we are severely practical, now gaily
doctrinaire: simply because we are young, free, restless and
eager – or occasionally rather indolent, cynical and old
before our time. No chapter that can be written about us
can capture more than a fraction of the things that occupy
us – but this one is going to do its best.

I

One of the most striking features of questionnaires and
debates on university life and of discussions on the subject
in student newspapers is the desire which the undergraduate
at the modern university seems to feel for a closer relation-
ship with his teachers. If this urge had manifested itself in
the Oxbridge of a generation ago, where college contacts
were easy and fairly natural but university contacts were
rare, one could have understood it, but in a small, compact
world, where staff and students are continually bumping
into each other on staircases and any undergraduate can
ask any lecturer any question at any hour of the working
day, it is less comprehensible. Apparently, however, the
relations desired are not so much academic as personal. It
is undeniable, of course, that the schoolmaster sees much
more of his pupils than does the university teacher. The
out-of-school activities – games, dramatics, concerts, field
clubs, etc. – which in schools are taken part in, and often
organized, by the staff, are run at the university wholly by
students. But it would neither be a popular development
nor a salutary one if the professoriate began to intervene in
these. Already, from time to time, they take part in debates,
contribute to the student magazine, perform at musical
societies, and so on. More it would be unwise for them to do:
undergraduate activities must be entirely in the hands of
undergraduates or they will lose most of their value.

What other relations can be formed? Most professors and lecturers already offer their students such modest hospitality in their homes as modern conditions permit and many of them establish closer relations with graduates who remain in their Schools than would be possible with younger students. Some also meet, and entertain, their students in the Union, or in other buildings where staff-student meeting-rooms are provided. At Bristol University the Guild of Undergraduates has organized series of lunches at which staff and students meet on terms of equality round the same table. About this kind of contact more will be said shortly.

In some universities, professors and lecturers have, entirely on the initiative of the students, been co-opted on committees. In one place the committee is an *ad hoc* standing committee of the Students' Union which exists to promote staff-student contacts: this seems terribly artificial but is at least severely practical, and, if it produces little good, it could hardly do any harm. In another place the committees of societies representing Faculties or subjects studied (e.g. the Engineering Association or the Commerce or Geographical Society) have nominated staff members, apparently on the principle of setting the staff to catch the staff – and to bring them to the societies' meetings. It is a pity that such a drastic measure should be necessary – for drastic it surely is that student societies should be governed by anyone but students alone. To this view an undergraduate critic objected that, if professors and students are really fellow-workers, as this book suggests, the societies ought to belong to them both and therefore be governed by both jointly. Logically, the objection is valid, but it is hardly so in fact, for the two classes of worker are at such different stages of maturity that one can hardly expect the same type of society to appeal equally to both. And as the juniors overwhelmingly outnumber the seniors, it seems fair, besides being good for them, that they should control the organization. The undergraduate just referred to added that they took care to co-opt younger lecturers only – whether because they were more amenable or more likely to attend meetings he was

not sure. But the risk that one of these staff-student committees might become dominated by some masterly senior
member seems quite a formidable one. To that my undergraduate replied that they took care to co-opt the same
lecturer for only a single session. He certainly had an
answer to everything.

Some years ago a little book of great dynamic quality
made the interesting suggestion that all the universities
might have 'outposts in the country' – something, presumably, in the nature of a simple type of country club, to which
'small groups of students, lecturers and ex-students might
repair at week-ends or in the vacation. The undergraduate
there might catch from the professor something of his enthusiasm for his subject; the professor might learn to know
the undergraduate as a man, and not as an object to be
lectured at, or as an examination paper to be corrected: the
man who has been a student but is now engaged in business
might recapture something of an earlier enthusiasm and
temper conversation with a sound knowledge of affairs.'[1]

An interesting scheme this, though much experimentation
might be needed before it became really effective. First,
there would be financial obstacles: not only must the premises be bought but the scheme itself will have to be subsid-
ized if living conditions are to be comfortable enough to
attract the professor and 'ex-student' (barbarous term!)
and yet economical enough to be practicable for the undergraduate. Then it would be necessary to organize parties,
for any professors would not mix with any undergraduates
– nor, for that matter, would the professors want to talk
shop to the extent that the passage suggests. But the real
difficulty would be the apathy of both parties. The desire
for closer contact probably comes from about 10 per cent
of the student body and, less actively, from about 1 per
cent of the staff: because the 10 per cent, like most would-be
reformers, make their voices heard, the proportion is assumed to be greater. When the scheme got to grips with the
majority, it would be found that the 90 per cent would rather

1. Herklots, p. 87.

stay at home any day than spend a week-end – at their own expense, too – anywhere within a mile of a professor, while the 99 per cent would see no reason at all for deserting their families and dragging themselves away from study, garden or golf links to pig it with a horde of students. The question is, could the minority, aided by a sprinkling of 'ex-students' (might we not say 'graduates'?) keep the institution alive until the tradition was created which would do more for the scheme than anything else? If so, there are all kinds of possibilities which would aid it. Membership of the clubs, which could, for example, be located in the Yorkshire dales, North Wales, Somerset and Berkshire, might be offered to the staffs and students of all universities in the country. Visitors from foreign universities could also be invited. Conferences could be held at the clubs. A special club could be set apart (either explicitly or by tradition) for graduates and senior students and another for junior students: the professor who feared that he might be expected to make whoopee could then patronize the former. Yes, there are plenty of possibilities, but the scheme would have to be taken up with vigour and planned on a broad and generous scale without any expectation that it could pay its way for some years.

It is only right to add that, when consulted, neither undergraduates nor professors appear to look upon the scheme with any favour, the general verdict being that it is too unnatural ever to work. In any case it would never be taken up by more than a small proportion either of staff or of students. The real problem is of a far more general kind. It is not so much the creation of occasions for special contact as the bridging of whatever gulf exists all the time. And it is to be doubted if the senior member of the potential partnership can do more than make himself generally and willingly accessible to the junior. The fact is that the value of a university teacher to a student consists not so much in what the former offers as in what the latter asks for and takes. Nearly every professor and lecturer welcomes approaches of any and every kind from his students and many are willing to take immense trouble in helping them. But more harm may be done to the adolescent's sensitiveness and growing desire for independence if the adult gives too much unasked and creates the impression of interfering than if he fails to give because the student is too shy, or too modest, to ask of him. The successful professor is he who can sense when a pupil needs his help and say the right word at the right moment. But to learn to do this takes time and demands gifts not granted to everyone. It becomes easier if and as soon as the undergraduate can meet his professor halfway.

II

The references just made to 'ex-students' tempt us at this point to touch briefly upon the question of post-university employment as it affects the Faculty of Arts. Before the War, both the lack of choice in careers for graduands and the amount of unemployment among them were appalling. Such careers as the Diplomatic and Consular services and higher Civil Service positions generally were ruled out because, in the first place, most Drabtown men of the intellectual calibre which wins them these prizes had preferred Oxbridge to their own Redbrick, and those who had not were so few that it was impracticable to provide them with the necessary specialized classes. There were business appointments, but only of a mediocre kind; for the large firms, which often apply to the Oxford or the Cambridge Appointments Board for promising young graduates, seem to forget that there are ten other English universities as well. What remained? For women, secretaryships and librarianships (generally ill-paid), marriage (which a gratifyingly large number of them achieve early) and – teaching. For men – teaching only.

So, during the two inter-War decades, the Redbrick Arts Faculty became a kind of preparatory school to the Department of Education; and so completely was this taken for granted that quite the usual question for the Dean to ask the freshman was: 'And you're going to teach?' Halfway through this period the phenomenon was remarked upon by Flexner:

An excessive proportion [of undergraduates] become teachers ... A point is soon reached where a university is saturated with prospective teachers ... and the university tends to deteriorate into a teacher-training establishment.'[1]

He was concerned with the effect of the tendency upon the university. In 1937 the National Union of Students, organizing an investigation and a congress upon graduate employment, considered it from the standpoint of the graduate. And they reported disquietingly on the unemployment and misemployment resulting from the crowding of this narrow alley. Unemployment among teachers had begun about 1931 and steadily increased.[2] Of students who left training colleges in July 1934, 20 per cent had not obtained posts at the end of six months. Misemployment (such actual cases as 'a Commerce degree graduate earning 30s. a week as a shorthand-typist, or a Social Science graduate earning £2 9s. a week in a clerical job'[3]) was even worse. University graduates by the hundred were taking posts in elementary schools, and doing less skilled and lower paid work than they had been trained to do, just because it was a choice between doing that and nothing at all. Both Wales and Scotland were worse than England, but England was bad enough:

At Manchester, on the average, 80 per cent of the teaching trainees are Honours graduates, but 60 per cent become placed in elementary schools. At University College, Exeter ... the position is worse, no less than 80 per cent of the teaching students going into elementary schools ... At Sheffield University, out of 56 leaving the Training Department at the end of 1935–6, the position as ascertained after nine months was that 15 were placed in secondary schools.'[4]

And, in anything but a material sense, there was worse to come. Inquiry showed clearly that many students being

1. Flexner, p. 255.   2. N.U.S., 1937, p. 9.
3. Op. cit., pp. 17–18.   4. Op. cit., pp. 18–19.

trained as teachers chose this course with no sense of vocation or even desire for the profession, but simply as the line
of least resistance. Many of them, anxious for a university
career, took advantage of an iniquitous though well-meaning scheme by which they accepted financial help in
advance from the (then) Board of Education, pledging themselves in return to take the training course upon graduation
and to teach for at least two years after it was over. Let
Exeter again provide evidence:

There is a large proportion in our Training Department who
are there not because of their desire or capacity to teach, but
because it was the only possible way of getting a university
education. Only 58 per cent actually wish to teach.[1]

Though conditions are much better now than before the
War, there is still much to be done for the Redbricks of
England as regards employment. Boys and girls must be
induced to decide on their careers while still at school, and,
both there and at the university, must have someone whom
they can consult if their views begin to alter. More careers
must be made possible for students in modern Arts Faculties
and students themselves be encouraged both to think and
to act more adventurously with regard to employment.
Appointments Boards need to be in very much closer touch
with employers as well as with prospective employees: most
of them, for this purpose, would require additional staffs.
Undergraduates should be given much more encouragement
than at present to seek employment abroad. Financial help
should be available for students desiring to be trained for
non-scholastic professions, and the conditions under which
aid is given to intending teachers by the Ministry of
Education should undergo drastic revision. These are mere
indications of developments which we may hope to see in
a new future.

1. Op. cit., p. 19.

III

Let us now, for the remainder of this chapter, return to the university itself and consider its principal 'out of school' activities. We may conveniently follow the traditions of public-school fiction and put athletics first, though at the modern university athletics in even the most popular form come a long way down the scale of interest.

'And every day is a half-holiday!' is said to have been the parting remark of a certain Oxbridge tutor to his freshmen at their first meeting; and the facts that the playing-fields are near the colleges and there are no lectures or classes between one and five mean that anyone can play games who wants to. But at Redbrick, except on Saturdays, and, in some Faculties, Wednesdays, there are continuous lectures from nine to four, and the fact that students would pour into the University daily from all points of the compass made it necessary for the buildings to be reasonably central – i.e., for the athletic grounds to be anything from twenty minutes to an hour away. This means that, although tennis fours can be made up on any afternoon of the week ('if the game is worth the journey'), team-games can never be generally played more than twice a week, puritanical prejudice (which, personally, I deplore) keeping the grounds closed on Sundays. And there are several reasons why not everyone can play as often as that, even if he wants to: undergraduates living in lodgings often go home for weekends; it is precisely after lunch on Wednesdays and Saturdays that trams and buses from the centre of the town to the outskirts are most crowded; on Wednesdays, and sometimes on Saturdays, there are counter-duties and counter-attractions both at the University and elsewhere. Some freshmen were sickened of team-games by their being made compulsory at school: 'Ninety per cent of us hated them!' was the comment of one young graduate on this subject. Another obstacle is that quite a number of freshmen are members of athletic clubs in their own towns before they come up and there may be reasons (powerless, one might think, against *esprit de corps*, which, however, is not always as strong as it might be) why they wish to continue playing for them: a weekly change of environment, the retention of existing friendships, a higher standard of play, the company of their seniors on an equal status, the greater length of time for which they will be able to play for the town club than for the university. And any of these reasons may be reinforced by a natural disinclination to leave an environment in which one is happy. The result is that, as statistics suggest, even the most popular of the Redbrick clubs – Association, Rugby and Hockey – may attract hardly more than 5 per cent of the student community; that disappointingly few play tennis, which of all outdoor games gives perhaps the greatest return in physical benefit for one's time; and that hundreds of undergraduates go through their whole course without once changing into any form of athletic dress whatsoever.

There are many types of exercise, of course, which can be indulged in without a long journey to the suburbs. But at present few of the modern universities are equipped in these respects as fully as they should, and some day will, be. Gymnasia, swimming baths and fives and squash courts cost money, and benefactors too seldom realize their value, or prefer to endow Chairs or scholarships which can be called by their names. Until all urban universities can move to the suburbs or the country a large proportion of undergraduates will have to confine their daily exercise to walks through the streets or take what they can get at home or within the university precincts.

To keep in health and maintain proper physical development, it is quite unnecessary, notwithstanding the beliefs instilled into one at school, to play either cricket or hockey or football. Games like badminton and fives, together with a moderate dose of physical training, are no less beneficial. But physical training, which is sorely needed in the modern universities, has not made much progress there. Once more, it is largely a question of expense. Athletic coaches, however, have not, as in some American colleges, to be paid the salaries of vice-chancellors; and, when one considers the amount of work done by some of the Redbrick professors, and reflects that a full-time instructor could be obtained for one-third of the stipend of any one of them, the problem somehow looks less alarming. Some universities run voluntary 'physical jerks' for both staff and students under part-time instructors, who in a large town are not hard to find. For so long as modern universities remain non-resident, it is doubtful if students' time-tables would ever permit the making of physical training compulsory, and such an edict would certainly meet with violent student opposition. Wider measures, in fact, national in scope, are called for here.

Periodical medical examinations, however, should be both compulsory and free, as they are in most of the larger universities in the United States. When one visits these, one often feels that the palatial buildings, with their luxurious appointments and modern conveniences, need in no sense be objects of envy: scholarship is a hardy plant which may well flourish better in the open ground than in the hothouse. But when one goes round the 'Medical Centre' of one of the large State Universities – the nearest equivalent of Redbrick – and sees the staff of anything from six to twenty physicians and surgeons, not to mention nurses; the up-to-date apparatus; the well-equipped infirmary; the docketed health-records of every student – and there may be as many as ten or twelve thousand of them – one begins to realize what a long way we still have to go. Every one of those students, who receives all his college education free, receives also free medical service, of the very highest quality, from his first day at the university until his last. Incidentally, the whole of the staff, and sometimes even their families, can have it too. We cannot aspire to efficiency on this scale, but at least every freshman should have a medical examination, receive appropriate advice, and be able to consult a university physician at need. Scotland has come nearest to providing this: at Glasgow, for example, every student who so desires can consult a medical officer, free of charge, have his trouble diagnosed and be handed over for treatment to his family physician. There is, however, no compulsion, which is an important element if health standards are to be improved all round. This type of service is a good deal more important than most new buildings, and, benefactors not having been found to provide it, the responsibility for instituting and maintaining it must fall upon the State.

IV

In all modern universities there are two important student institutions, the titles of which differ but slightly. One is the students' association, established under the university Charter or Statutes, recognized by the Senate and the Council as the mouthpiece of student opinion and affiliated to the National Union of Students: this, generally known as the Guild of Undergraduates, will be described in the next chapter. The other is a building,[1] called the Union, the Students' Union or the University Union, which all members of the Guild of Undergraduates have the right to use and members of the staff and resident graduates may join. Some universities have a Women's Union, or a women's section of the Union, as well. As all the social and cultural activities of undergraduates have their centre in the Union, they may be surveyed, in close connection with it, now.

The clubs and societies of any university are legion; and the fact that they all meet in or near the Union enables anyone with a passion for attending meetings to indulge it to the full. One group of societies will include music, folk dancing, drama, chess, photography, philately, poetry reading. Another group caters for the open-air student: horse-

1. At Manchester, the 'Guild' and the 'Union' are combined under the title of 'University Union', which denotes both the association and the building.

manship, motor-cycling, hiking, scouting, mountaineering, botanizing, entomology and other forms of natural history for amateurs. A third group is political, social and international: Conservatives, Liberals, Socialists and Communists are represented nearly everywhere, and there are various societies founded to promote international understanding. Then as soon as any university has any considerable number of undergraduates from some other country – Dominion students, Egyptians, Indians, etc. – they are sure to form a society of their own; nor should one forget the societies which represent Wales, Scotland and the Irish Republic. And even now scarcely more than half the societies have been enumerated, for in most of the universities there are Faculties, Schools and Departments with their own societies – often from a dozen to twenty of them. These are among the most useful of all, and should be appreciated by the teaching body more than they often are. For quite unobtrusively they can do much to combat that narrowing of interests which is such a peril in specialization. They enable students (with or without their teachers) to meet and discuss aspects of their subject which are crowded out from the classroom: the English Literature club discusses recently published books and living authors; the Modern Language Society arranges lectures on the music, painting and architecture of foreign countries or on travel abroad; the Commerce Club and various of the scientific societies arrange visits to factories; the Historical Society debates on current events; the Geographical and Geological Societies organize field-days. All these societies, too, serve as useful links between students and staff; and when some distinguished visitor comes to lecture the society can share in his entertainment.

Clearly, then, there is no lack of outside activity within the Universities, as Oxford and Cambridge people sometimes imagine. On the contrary, there is an *embarras de richesses*, the more bewildering because so much activity is centred in one place and a freshman not too enamoured of study is apt to drop in at one meeting after another just because he is passing a door and sees a crowd going in. If he had to leave his comfortable rooms on a cold evening, and walk to a college at the other end of the town, he might prefer to spend the time at his reading.

Another group of activities is purely social and for the most part consists of dancing, which plays a far more important part in life at Redbrick than at Oxbridge. From the President of the Guild (or Union), who leads off with his opposite number, the Lady President, downwards, all the best people dance, and there are dances in connection with every kind of celebration – even with the most serious conferences. Presumably this is due to the genuinely co-educational basis of Redbrick, which is not, like Oxbridge, a university for men in which a few women are tolerated. Imagine an Oxford Visitors' Debate at the Cambridge Union being followed by a dance, or a serious discussion being held on the ability in that art of candidates for the Presidency. The Redbrick freshman will find three kinds of dance in which he may take part – dance-teas, informal 'hops' and (on special occasions) formal dances at the Union. As a rule, the 'hops' appear to be the most popular, but if I were a student-dictator I should increase the number of the formal dances, for it is these that the undergraduates – at any rate the men – most need. If the truth must be told – and after many years spent among them I am so genuinely attached to them that I hate to tell it – the worst feature of the Redbrick undergraduate is his ignorance of what to do in any sort of company. Even when he has learned not to begin a letter to his lecturer 'Dear Sir' and subscribe himself 'Yours respectfully', he has little idea of the proper way to introduce one person to another and is hopelessly tongue-tied in the presence of ladies. The more often he can be put into evening dress and made to behave formally, the better. But as a rule he dislikes the process and escapes from it whenever he can.

The dance, in some universities, serves one curious and, one would have thought, unnecessary purpose – the bringing together of people from different Faculties. As between the universities, custom varies a good deal, but a semi-segregation seems to be the general rule, to everyone's loss. One of the reasons for this is that the 'subject' societies are distinctly specialist. The Mathematical Society's lecture-placards abound in repulsive-looking notation; the Theological Society is forbiddingly doctrinal; even the meetings of the Geographical Society, despite their attractive announcements, are apt to become highly technical when they get down to it. There is no society for the scientist who likes to dabble in modern poetry or for the philosopher interested in trees and flowers. So inter-Faculty debates, the musical and dramatic societies and the dance-floor are the only common ground. In the first, as the title suggests, the Faculties fight rather than mix. The appeal of the next two is limited. This leaves only the last. Perhaps music is a closer inter-Faculty bond than this enumeration would suggest, however; though it links only few, it links them very closely, and many graduates have testified that they made more friends at the University through the Musical Society than in any other way.

Of the numerous problems of the Union, the most pressing is that of feeding a large number of lunchers in the minimum of time, for five (rarely six) days a week, over stretches of two and a half months. The comparatively stately method of the dining-room with separate or communal tables has as a rule to be supplemented by self-service rooms and a cafeteria. Too many undergraduates, whether from lack of means or lack of time, lunch on a roll and a cup of tea, and it is a pity that the cheap and simple *table d'hôte*, of the 'school dinner' type, which a few of them favour, cannot be supplied, at a lower cost than it generally is, to most or all. If it were, however, such is undergraduate independence that it might easily not pay, especially as the length of the vacations, during which few but medicals and occasional scientists lunch at the university, makes the problem of maintaining a kitchen staff very difficult. In the main dining-hall of some of the modern universities there is a 'high table', on Oxbridge lines, for the staff; at too few of these is it customary for staff to descend from it and lunch with students. At one university a visiting lecturer asked for a table to be reserved for him and the student officers of the society in which he was interested – a proceeding which was thought so eccentric that, both on the entry of the group and during the meal, curious and furtive glances were flashed from all around.

Our undergraduates would hardly be English if they did not grumble frequently and heartily at the Union catering, and about nothing is the suggestion-book in that institution more eloquent than about the kitchen. It may be doubted if one student in a hundred is reasonably satisfied with both the food and the service. But problems are different in different localities and for those which all have in common there may be no complete solution. All the same, one felt, during the War, that when Lord Woolton had finished organizing the British Restaurants for one kind of worker he might have thrown out some hints to the University Unions about more efficient provision for another. It would have been no advertisement for university organization if two thousand undergraduates had turned up outside a British Restaurant one fine lunch-hour and demanded its three courses for tenpence.

V

One of the most interesting accounts in existence of the origin of the associations, one in each university, of which all students are members and to which it will be convenient to refer briefly here as 'Guilds', was given in 1939 by a pioneer of the movement for their establishment, a representative both of an old university and of a new, the late Ramsay Muir.[1] Half a century ago, he said, when he was an undergraduate, first at Liverpool and then at Oxford, the notion that the students should be a corporate body,

1. A summary of this account will be found in N.U.S., 1939, pp. 16–18, from which these quotations are taken: the full text seems not to have been published.

with aims and ideals of their own, would have seemed absurd. At Oxford, 'they just had to submit to be moulded by the powerful traditions of that venerable place: it never occurred to them that they were themselves shaping the traditions of the future or that it was any part of their business to have ideas about what the university ought to be giving to them'. In the modern universities 'they had no common life, no corporate feeling, no kind of organization'.

Their students came in from all quarters of the compass in the morning, and went home at night, carrying with them (at the best) the little conventional packets of orthodox information which they had come to the knowledge-shop to purchase.

Muir himself was one of the founders of what he believed to be 'the first representative student organization to be established in England'. It was the 'deadness of student life' that had inspired him; he had resolved that, 'if fate allowed, he would give up his life to work for the idea of the university, and that, in any case, the first thing he had to do was to try to create a really living student organization'. The body created was modelled – an interesting disclosure, this – upon the Students' Representative Councils of the universities of Scotland.[1] 'Its beginnings were modest, but it had at the outset some healthy conflicts with the academic body which had put life into it.' Out of it grew first one, and then another, of these Guilds, to-day administering, 'without any external control, an income of some thousands a year' – a family of which the parent body is the National Union of Students.

The Guilds have highly democratic constitutions and Councils with a complicated system of representation which it would be of no great interest to describe in detail. Fortunately, the annual subscription, which ranges between £3 and £4 – a heavy one for the student of no great means – is compulsory and charged with the university tuition fees: were it not, there would, it is to be feared, be a large

1. The University of Manchester actually uses the term 'Students' Representative Council'.

proportion of non-starters. For it cannot be denied that there is a very prevalent disease in the newer universities known as 'student apathy' – i.e., apathy to student activities – which causes the keener spirits much preoccupation. Just before the last War it was reported to a committee of the National Union of Students that, in one university 'of about 2,000 students, only about 300 could be said to take a real interest and an active part in student activities. This proportion was generally agreed to reflect the position in most of the universities and colleges in this country.'[1]

It is comparatively easy, as anyone who moves among undergraduates knows, to divide them into the apathetic and the keen; and it is probably not an exaggeration to put the proportions at five to one. There are, of course, cross-currents. In a university, for instance, where general keenness is low, some particular departmental society will register a 90 per cent attendance at its meetings, because it has energetic officers or because the Department concerned has an individuality which can be appreciated by the least sensitive. Similarly, some religious society will attract audiences even outside the bounds of its direct adherence because of the personality of its chaplain. But over the whole area of a university he would indeed be a benevolent observer who challenged these figures as unduly severe.

The disease, however, is not as serious as it sounds, if the contention now to be put forward is justified. This is that the apathetic are themselves divided into one small class and one large one. The small class is composed of the frankly lazy, the well-meaning but incorrigibly indolent, the intellectually myopic, the narrowly bookish and perhaps a very few who, for domestic reasons which one need not particularize, are legitimately unable to do as much as they would like. The large class consists of students who have absorbing hobbies or secondary occupations, who have (as the catch-phrase goes) to 'earn while learning', or who, before coming up to the university, had formed certain ties too strong to break. This is bound to happen in a non-residential

1. N.U.S. 1939, p. 19.

university, and, when one is confronted with individual cases, it is difficult to censure them. Let us take some actual examples. Here is an able mathematician who is also a keen musician and for his last two years at school has been learning the organ: is he to be blamed if in his dinner-hour he goes to practise at a neighbouring church rather than attend meetings of student societies? Another does clerical work on Saturdays to help pay his fees. A third goes home early every day to allow his sister, burdened with the care of an invalid mother, to get some exercise. Still another has become engaged during his university course to a girl living near him: and only those who have never been in love will contend that he ought not to prefer her society to student debates and dances.

But another very large division of this subsection which might be termed the 'otherwise occupied' still remains to be described. It embraces those who have, as it were, thoroughly dug themselves into their own milieu while still at school and have no particular desire to be uprooted. They go to the pictures once a week or to a concert or the tennis-courts on Saturdays, and they frankly prefer spending their time in these ways, with friends of some years' standing, to attending student meetings or playing in student teams and making new friends. Sometimes they are definitely repelled by certain of the less attractive types they meet at the university and can see no comparison between those who now share desks with them and their school friends. The fierily 'keen' have no sympathy whatever with all this. 'Put all freshers on probation,' remarked one such, 'and if they don't pull their weight send them down.' The remedy would be worse than the ill, but it illustrates the extremes of thought that meet in the Guild and at the Union. The fact is that 'student apathy', much less marked at Oxbridge than at Redbrick, is part of the price which a university pays for being non-residential. Change that and you will build up an *esprit de corps* and a tradition of something like 100 per cent student activity; but not before.

Added to that, it can be freely conceded, there is a great

deal of pure slackness in quite petty matters which does argue a lack of team-spirit – and that can be remedied only by another much needed reform, the democratization of the public schools. When in a university of over 2,000 *in statu pupillari* a student newspaper published at a penny weekly has an average sale of only 400 copies, there is something wrong with the undergraduates' sense of corporate responsibility. One university, very little smaller than this, made a special drive to increase its sales, and, in order to stimulate them, placed piles of each issue at strategical points in the University Union, with a money-box labelled 'Please take one and put penny in box'. And yet nearly three-quarters of the students ignored it and the circulation at the end of the term was still well below 500. The reasons commonly given for this lack of interest were diverse: 'nothing in them'; 'badly edited'; 'full of scandal'; 'they get left about and you see them anyway'. Much spadework will be needed, both in training the public and in satisfying it, extending perhaps over generations of student life, before deficiencies of that kind can be overcome.

The university in question was regarded by its sisters elsewhere as particularly daring for having a weekly newspaper at all, for most do not aspire to more than a magazine of dubiously literary quality, published two or three times a term. Yet the weekly newspaper, if less pretentious, is of far greater importance and justifies a brief digression here since it is an obvious method for increasing keenness. It reports all university events and so gives its readers a clearer and more comprehensive picture of the community's activities than they could possibly have without it. Further, it can, if it likes, educate the undergraduate's sense of proportion by giving the things which matter most the greatest prominence. When a speaker of the first rank visits the University, it can make the substance of his address available to a much wider audience than originally heard him. Another of its important functions is to maintain an open forum of opinion, to allow the airing of reasonable grievances, to set out the various points of view on any debatable question, to provide a platform for new ideas and suggestions concerning any facet of the life of the community which it serves. News of graduates of recent date may be included in it, and most graduates should be expected to continue their subscription to it for two or three years after going down. But the cardinal function of the student newspaper is to raise the mental and moral tone of the community. This it will do only if, on the one hand, it is widely read, and, on the other, it is in charge of the right people. Here a quiet and unobtrusive influence can be exercised by the Senate. It is usual for a member of Senate to be invited to act as Censor – or, as it is sometimes put, 'Advisory Editor', principally in order to avoid any clash with authority on the suitability of the material published. If a man is appointed who is on really good terms with the student body, the effect of his collaboration may be enormous.

Just as the apathetic can be divided into a small class and a large one, so can the keen. The majority of these are just thoroughly 'good fellows' – of either sex – with wide interests, ample initiative, super-abundant energy and a sound and broad conception of the nature of education. They are the salt of any community; their influence is much deeper and wider than they ever suspect: happy the university that has them in great number.

But there is a smaller class somewhat more difficult to define. It might be unkind to describe it as composed of politicians, yet in the broad sense of the word this is often how they appear to others. They have, as had the young Ramsay Muir – an excellent example of the type – a very strong sense of their mission: to raise the status of the undergraduate, to defend the 'student class' against the 'ruling class', to ensure to the student certain 'rights' and 'liberties' (not all of which any large proportion of their companions would desire) ; and so on. They are generally efficient organizers, enjoy committees, shine in debates and are mighty in student journalism. So far as my experience of them goes, they do not shine in the Schools. At Oxbridge the nearest

approach to them is what is known as the 'Union man'.
He, too, is a politician, though more usually a party politician, often with an eye on influence and a parliamentary
career. These have more in them of the prophet and the
evangelist; they are sincere and generally single-minded;
but they tend to lack a sense of proportion and to see university, professors and students exclusively from their particular angle.

It is this type which predominates among Guild officials,
and, above all, in the councils of the National Union of
Students and the delegates who attend its annual congresses.
This book is so obviously indebted to the Union and its
congresses that it would be acting churlishly if it referred to
them with any lack of sympathy. Nor has it any desire to do
this. The National Union performs a most valuable service.
It aims at securing a solidarity among undergraduates in
British universities in the service of high ideals. It urges and
inspires university students to realize their responsibility
for the improvement of society and to play their part in this
when and as they are able. It advocates better athletic
facilities, the inauguration of more student health schemes
and the more effective organization of Appointments
Boards. It takes a keen and intelligent interest in the curriculum, in the examination system and in methods of teaching. During the last few years it has done good work in helping to care for political refugees, in furthering international
student contacts, in urging a wider study of foreign affairs
and in endeavouring to deepen social consciousness. And
quite apart from all this, its very seriousness and 'live'-ness
cannot but have a stimulating effect upon any student community.

The congress reports make the most vivid reading and it
is a pity that they are not studied by every professor, lecturer and undergraduate in the country. Organized with the
co-operation of societies representing opposed political
views, of the Student Christian Movement and of a number
of other bodies, it commits none of these by its resolutions,
nor for that matter the National Union of Students itself,

but only the delegates. But that 600 delegates should have attended a six-day congress in 1940 and 1,100 a five-day congress in 1941 is significant of a fixity of purpose surmounting war-time difficulties which will also surmount the greater difficulties of peace.

None the less, one is bound to look critically at some of the congresses' discussions and pronouncements. At Leeds, in 1940, the 600 students, apparently excited by a 'recent encroachment upon student liberties', drew up a document which they termed a 'charter of student rights and responsibilities'. It had five points, each asserting a student's right:

(1) To the free expression of opinion by speech and Press.

(2) To organize meetings, discussion and study on all subjects within the University and College precincts.

(3) To belong to any organization, whether cultural, political or religious.

(4) To participate to the full in all activities outside the universities, and to collaborate with extra-university organizations.

(5) To a share in the government and administration of the universities.

Provided they kept within the law of the land and that of the university of which they voluntarily became members, it would be difficult for any liberal-minded person to deny them the first four rights; very few would ever dream of doing so. The fifth, however, shows an entire misconception of the nature of a university – essentially, as we have seen, a body of mature seekers after knowledge, who have accepted, as part of their work, the training of the immature, some that they may in time join them or other bodies pursuing their aim, some to follow other occupations. If the *discipuli* are to have the privileges of *socii* before they have in fact attained the maturity of *socii*, there seems no reason why schoolboys elected by their fellows should not have full representation on masters' meetings or one child elected by every family should not sit in conclave with Father and Mother to determine the penalty for every breach of nursery discipline.

'Given these rights,' continues the 'Charter', 'we pledge ourselves to fulfil our responsibilities to the community.' But these students have, of their own free will, joined the society known as a university, and it is their clear duty either to fulfil their responsibilities to that society whether any demands they may make are granted or not, or to resign their membership of it. One responsibility of a student, for example, is to apply himself to study during the whole of his course, and acquit himself as well as his ability permits in the examination. Now it is notorious that certain of these student-politicians do very little academic work at all. Such students are clearly not fulfilling their responsibilities to the community – either to the university now training them, or, in most cases, to the State which has educated them free since early childhood. Do they mean that, if they are given a share in the government of the university, they will thenceforth devote themselves to their work? Whether they do or not the counter-question arises: Are students who have failed to fulfil a primary obligation of their membership of the university society fitted, quite apart from their immaturity, to have a voice in its government?

In actual fact, only a very small proportion of students would subscribe to the last demand of the 'Charter' or to such a view of their responsibilities as is indicated by its peroration. Equally they would repudiate the political bias of the congresses. Theoretically, they may work in collaboration with every kind of organization, but in practice the delegates are left-wingers almost to a man and woman. 'They turn everything into a Socialist Society,' remarked one very level-headed undergraduate – 'Student Christian Movement meetings, Poetry Club meetings, even Natural History rambles: their socialism infects them all.' And this impression is certainly confirmed by the Congress reports. At the 1940 meetings, after supporting 'the right of the Indian people to immediate and complete independence' by 382 votes to 26, and asserting that socialism is necessary to any 'new world order' by 375 to 24, the delegates expressed their opinions on the War in a way which their successors will regard in much the same way as do Oxford men of to-day those who in that notorious Union debate declined to fight for their King and country. No less than 281 voted 'that the continuance of the present war is not in the interests of the people of any country' and only 150 supported its continuance till Nazi Germany should be beaten.[1]

Now obviously questions like these are of the first importance. But the point to be made here is rather that any congress of this kind should be representative, not of one pugnacious and clamant section of student opinion, but of student opinion as a whole. If anyone believes either these resolutions or the latter part of the 'Charter' to be so, no figures exist by which the claim can be disproved. But the opinion of one careful observer is that in the main, the student-politicians who feed these congresses with their views are looked upon by the masses as eccentrics, if nothing worse, and that, instead of attracting them, their violent intransigence is merely driving them away.

Before concluding this section it may be worth while contrasting the conception of student life suggested by these congresses with the conception publicized by the Press and popularized by student behaviour during the two decades between the two wars.

How far removed in spirit are the hundreds of passionately earnest young men and maidens queueing up in the pouring rain to sign on for the 1941 congress on 'The Student, his Subject and Society' from the hundreds of undergraduates at Redbrick whom one has seen in olden days rioting in a theatre, marching in fancy dress through the town or fighting pitched battles in the courtyard in front of the main university buildings, pelting each other with flour and soot, even tearing the clothes from each other's backs, in full view of incredulous, head-shaking spectators from the street! Is this, it may be asked, quite another type

1. N.U.S., 1940, pp. 17, 19, 20.

of student, turned temporarily into more useful channels by the War? Or are student 'rags' things of the past, dispelled entirely by a new conception of their responsibility by those *in statu pupillari*?

'Rags', an invention of Oxford or Cambridge – nobody knows of which and neither claims precedence – are in those universities joyful, spontaneous things, sometimes carried by high spirits to excess but nearly always characterized by a deep, sometimes even a subtle, sense of humour. Aping Oxford and Cambridge, in days when they had less individuality than now, the modern universities took over the Rag, of which they appreciated the horseplay but missed the humour, not as an unpremeditated display of pure exuberance, but as a highly organized manifestation of ingenuity and exhibitionism combined. A large proportion of those pressed by public opinion into participation in these humourless performances detested them from beginning to end: in fact, they were probably responsible for more 'student apathy' and estrangement of the individual from the university environment than anything else. Then came a further development. Some ingenious person saw the possibility of directing all this organization into a useful channel. The annual 'Varsity Rag',[1] as the townspeople called it, would still be held early in the New Year, still centre round the pantomime wheezing to its close at the local theatre and still be known as 'Panto Day'. But the *raison d'être* of it would become a giant collection for the local hospitals. The students would have the day off and be allowed to wander about the town in fancy dress all day long provided they rattled collecting-boxes under the noses of everyone they met. The culminating act of this street-collecting would be the procession. The 'panto' would be a gala performance, for seats at which enormous 'voluntary' taxes would be levied for the benefit of the sick. The uproarious 'hop' with which the day had ended would

1. The serious use by students of the vulgarisms 'Varsity' and 'fresher' is a further example of the natural but childish aping of Oxbridge which it is to be hoped may disappear now that Redbrick is growing up.

become a Grand Ball, with guinea tickets, for the same purpose. The free fights in the courtyard would be transformed
into a victory celebration by whichever Faculty had col-
lected the greatest amount of money per head.

The scheme was highly successful. Faculty vied with
Faculty and university with university: the total mounted –
£2,000, £4,000, £5,000: there was no knowing where they
would end. But it was not all gain. Soon there was not merely
a single lectureless day: so greatly was the organization
multiplied that attendances at lectures were thin for weeks
beforehand and the work of both weak and brilliant students was irretrievably ruined. But no-one could object –
it was for charity! Numerous complaints were received of
unseemly, even highly objectionable, conduct on the part
of certain collectors: feeling was roused in the city against
the university. But, after all, boys will be boys – and it was
for charity! No longer was it possible for any undergraduate
to absent himself from 'Panto Day': he would be missed,
and rounded up, and persecuted – it was for charity! Never
had charity covered a greater multitude of sins than here
and now. And the worst of it was that, high as were the
totals received, it was known that many of the larger sums
would, if by less picturesque methods than 'kidnapping'
business men while they were busy making money, have
been given in any case, and that an ordinary Flag Day
would have brought in most of the rest.

Now that the hospitals, taken over by the State, no
longer need support paid for so dearly in a less tangible
currency than money, other causes, no less deserving, have
taken their place. Perhaps it is a pity that advantage was
not taken of the great social change to bring the Organized
Rag, and its official organ the *Rag Mag*, to an end. For,
while the ebullience of youth fully merits the sympathy of
the mature, organized ebullience is merely revolting, not
least to those who feel themselves its victims.

VI

It would be impossible to review the life of a community of young people of both sexes without touching upon sexual morality, and one is quite frequently asked by people outside the universities if the greater freedom and frankness characteristic of life to-day leads to undue licence. Obviously it would be the easiest thing in the world for such licence to find outlets in the life of a modern university.

Looking back over many years studded with numerous revealing incidents, and marked by very few open scandals, I do not hesitate to affirm that the standard reached is a high one. Not having lived for three-quarters of every year in the claustral atmosphere of a public school and spoken to no woman during that time but the house-master's wife and the headmaster's parlourmaid, our men are not carried off their feet by any newly-found freedom to associate with the other sex, which in the Oxbridge of the last generation used to be curtailed by restrictions and safeguards when women took tea in men's rooms or vice versa. As they have been able all their lives to meet their brothers' or sisters' friends, or the friends of those friends, whenever they have wanted to, it seems perfectly natural to them to lunch with companions of the other sex at the Union or to share a desk and look over a book with them at Tutorials. Guild offices are fairly divided between men and women and in debates and committees there is a refreshing lack of sex-consciousness. Less admirable is the tendency in the student newspapers and magazines to print 'gossip paragraphs' about prominent undergraduates and their supposed love affairs which are sometimes only one degree more refined than legends of the 'Bill A— goes with Jessie B—' type which can be seen chalked on walls. But this is only a safety valve for vulgarity and need not be taken as anything worse.

There is too much healthy activity at Redbrick for unhealthy ideas or practices to flourish. About such open scandals and incidents potentially of that type as have come within my experience two very significant facts may be stated. One is that in the large majority of cases, the truth, when revealed by investigation, has nearly always proved to be less reprehensible than the accusation, or suspicion, or whatever caused the investigation to be made. The other is that, where some sordid or tragic story has in fact come to light, there have invariably been some partially or wholly extenuating circumstances. One of the parties has been physically or mentally abnormal, or has laboured under long and serious emotional strain, or has been the victim of a misunderstanding. (The same may be said of most cases of dishonesty, which are, I think, commoner than sexual offences.) This suggests that the normal life of Redbrick students is healthy. They like to hold debates or write letters to the student newspaper on free love and companionate marriage, but in practice they are much-occupied, decent-thinking, clean-living young people, fundamentally sane in mind as in body.

Occasionally, it is true, one sees a boy and a girl lounging in unseemly intimacy in the playing fields, cuddling in some dark corner of the university buildings, or even hurriedly disengaging themselves from a passionate embrace on a Union sofa. But I gather from inquiry among generations of past pupils who can be trusted to speak the truth that this sort of thing is much more generally disapproved of than one might expect and certainly not less so now than twenty years ago. Outside, one seldom sees anything more intimate than a couple with arms lightly linked, and seldom even that. Contrast the scene at southern Universities in the United States, where much younger boys and girls than ours walk about the campus, not merely hand in hand but with arms round each others' necks, lie embracing each other in full view of all, and have been found by professors courting in their private gardens or even on the sofas of their apartments when they have gone out without locking their doors behind them. In one of these Universities what is known as an 'uplift mission' was held a few years back in the hope of eradicating, among other things, the habit euphemistically termed 'petting'. At an afternoon discussion group for women students only, somewhat intimately catechized by a lady missioner, the following explanation of the prevalence of the habit was elicited from an ingenuous sophomore:

'Well, you see, you just cain't get a-hold of those boys unless you go lying around with them!'

It is something to think that our own masculine youth is less exacting.

VII

A much more serious matter in the modern universities than the condition of any form of morality is their neglect of religion, the small part played in their lives by which cannot but cause Christian people much anxiety.

England, nominally at least, is a Christian country, with agelong Christian traditions and an Established Church. The colleges of Oxford, Cambridge and Durham, together with some of the London colleges, are Christian foundations and have obligations with regard to the maintenance of worship and to spiritual education. Most of the modern universities, however, were born in an unhappy era of denominational strife, and, though that is now ended, and the way seems to be opening for a new epoch in which Christian people of every denomination will collaborate against their common enemy, the Charters and Statutes of these universities, with their melancholy legacy of intolerance and suspicion, remain unrevised. Manchester, it is true, while forbidding the imposition on either a teacher or a student of 'any test whatever of religious belief or profession' (*Charter*, X, i), has a Faculty of Theology, with full courses of lectures for degrees in divinity. Leeds also forbids religious tests, and, though creating no Theological Faculty, gives divinity degrees, as well as a 'B.A. in Theological Studies'. Liverpool is more intolerant. A bleak and lengthy clause (26) in its Charter reads (italics mine):

It is a fundamental condition of the constitution of the University that no religious test shall be imposed upon any person ... and *that no Theological teaching shall be given by or under the authority of the University ...* '

No Gospel light, then, may shine officially within the secularized precincts of Liverpool – though the same clause allows the teaching of Semitic languages, Hellenistic Greek and Ecclesiastical History. The curious thing is that for years past Liverpool has had a special lectureship in the Philosophy of Religion, under which, despite the Charter, lectures have been given (and some of them published) by leading divines. Yet the Liverpool Calendar says nothing whatever about this lectureship. Can its Senate be afraid that its Charter may find out?

The remaining universities repudiate religious tests but none of them has sunk to the depths of specifically banning religious instruction. No such instruction, however, appears to be given, as if there were a tacit agreement that neither any one of them as a corporation nor any of its teachers or members in an official capacity shall show any sign of appreciating the fact that the Christian religion exists. Of recent years, some universities have allowed either undenominational or Anglican services held in local churches to be described as University services, and some of them have been attended by officers and teachers – not without a certain amount of opposition, both latent and vocal. There seems, in fact, to be nothing in any of the Charters to forbid this: it may perhaps prove in time to have been the thin end of the wedge. Such services apart, any religious activities that there may be are initiated and organized by the student body: somewhat rarely, a Vice-Chancellor or a professor will preside or give an address at the meeting of a religious society: that is all.

'The universities in the main,' declared the Head of a University College in 1933, 'do not act as if they regarded these questions [*sc.* of students' moral and spiritual needs] ... To a limited extent, more particularly in Oxford and Cambridge colleges, there are those in authority who make it their business to meet students on a footing that encourages inquiry into the difficult problems that beset the questing spirit of youth. Yet ... but a small number get any guidance in this supremely important side of education.[1]

Nor is it merely a question of guidance. The instinct to worship is deeply implanted within us all. Boys and girls to whom worship means a great deal naturally desire, on entering upon a new life, to associate their worship with it: if the university fails to satisfy that need, they are to that extent alienated from the university. Or again, there are boys and girls whom religion interests on its intellectual side, who have learned a little about it at home or at school but would like to attend lectures or study groups and read books upon the subject at the university: to find that the university gives them no help, and may even exclude theological books from its library, is a disillusion to them – they had thought university education was something less narrow.

If there is any doubt that this attitude is a common one, it should be dispelled by a resolution coming from the 1941 Students' Congress – composed of the last people one would have expected to pass it. For this resolution there voted no less than 322; 215 abstained from voting, presumably because they were indifferent; and only 89 were opposed to it. The resolution ran thus:

A lecture or series of lectures in Theology should be provided at all universities and colleges for those students not pursuing theological studies, attendance being voluntary and the lectures being held at a time when no other lectures are being held.[2]

One may hope that such a request, coming from such a source, will in due time induce the universities to change their policy on this vital matter.

At present, the initiative remains entirely with the students. The number of the religious societies is large but few of them can be said to flourish. Generally speaking, the strongest

1. A. E. Morgan, *Education in the Modern World, etc.*, p. 21.
2. N.U.S., 1941, p. 26.

is the Student Christian Movement, whose virility and breadth of outlook make more appeal than do the denominational societies: on the other hand, its directness and methods of approach tend to repel both 'Churchy' people and those who dislike enthusiasm in religious matters. Of the denominational bodies, the Catholic Society, which stands apart from the rest, is usually the most active, and the Jewish Society has also very faithful adherents. The various Anglican societies are supported but poorly: the High Churchmen have their Church Union; the Broad Churchmen prefer the S.C.M.; and the Evangelicals join forces with the Protestant Nonconformists in what is generally known as the 'Christian' or 'Evangelical' Union, corresponding to the famous O.I.C.C.U. and C.I.C.C.U. at Oxford and Cambridge. While it is broadly true to say that these and various other societies of the kind are normally in a sickly condition, one or another of them is occasionally whipped into vitality by some individual enthusiast, and in addition, every two or three years, a breath of life passes through them all when the undergraduates organize a Teaching Mission, which lasts for about a week and is generally conducted by two or three outstanding speakers representing the Anglicans and one or two more of the Free Churches. Roman Catholic students often attend the mission but their organization holds aloof: it has its own methods of instruction, and makes good use of them.

It would probably not be an exaggeration to say that to 50 per cent of the student body the Mission means nothing at all and that of the remainder quite one-third do no more than attend some odd meeting. Statistics have shown that, apart from the Mission, no religious influence whatever organized within the University touches 75 per cent of the students – and this figure is probably an underestimate.

Many of the students comprising this large proportion, of course, are closely connected with religious activities in their own churches. It would be unreasonable to expect a boy who while at school has been a chorister, or a girl social worker or Sunday school teacher, to abandon their work on entering the University; even did it provide alternative activities to occupy their Sundays, they may feel that if they give their Sundays to church work they have done their part. But this consideration touches only students who are actually living with their parents, and perhaps no more than a small proportion of these. Even they would probably be attracted by the idea of corporate university worship if it were widely supported. It does not affect the large majority of students who live in university hostels, in lodgings, in flats shared with friends or in the houses of friends or relatives other than their parents. Few of these have any inducement to go to church on Sundays other than whatever they may get privately, and in most modern universities they will form from 30 to 40 per cent of the total. Apart from the resolution of 1941 quoted above there have been few suggestions that the student body feels any need for religious education, and it is significant that one of the N.U.S. Congresses already referred to, despite its fervent desires for a broadening of the curriculum, seemed not to realize that the best way to 'promote an attitude rising above personal interest' was to teach Christianity.

The remedy for this unfortunate state of affairs is not primarily in the hands of the student body: the first steps must be taken by the Senate and Council of each university.

In the first place, whether or no a separate Faculty be established, Theology should be a subject of study in every university.

No one, surely, be he Christian or pagan, will deny that Theology is a department of learning and as such has an evident claim to figure among the subjects of university study. The arguments of Newman's well-known lecture, 'Theology a branch of knowledge', have never been answered, probably because they are unanswerable. Every one of the terse statements enunciated in his final paragraphs can be substantiated:

I end then as I began: religious doctrine is knowledge. This is the important truth, little entered into at this day, which I wish that all who have honoured me with their presence here would allow me to beg them to take away with them. I am not catching at sharp arguments, but laying down grave principles. Religious doctrine is knowledge in as full a sense as Newton's doctrine is knowledge. University Teaching without theology is simply unphilosophical. Theology has at least as good a right to claim a place there as Astronomy.[1]

The reason why so many of the newer universities reject the study of Theology is that most of them were born into a world soiled with the smoke and dust of acrimonious denominational controversy. Aided as they were by public money, and dependent upon general approval, to say nothing of private generosity, they had at all costs to keep out of the conflict. But all that is now only a memory and it is recognized that we are in sore need of a greater measure of what is common to all forms of Christianity. Even Roman Catholicism has lost much of its old intolerance; the Church of England collaborates freely and maintains the most friendly relations with bodies outside its communion; and each of the Free Churches lays less emphasis upon the characteristics which distinguish it from the rest, and works steadily for greater harmony, if not for reunion. The menace of paganism, which once assailed us in the form of Nazism and Fascism, and still lurks beneath the intolerance of Communism, has compelled the Christian communions to close ranks and face the common foe. Whether or no the universities were justified in excluding or ignoring theological teaching in the past, they can find no good reason for doing so still.

Secondly, there should be Biblical instruction. An undenominational Theological Department would provide each university with a staff of persons qualified to give this instruction to those who desired it, whether within the curriculum or no. We have not been logical about this. Many a schoolboy wonders why he had to take Scripture in the Junior and Senior Oxford or Cambridge Local but is unable to take it in London Matriculation. Is London a secularized

1. Newman, p. 42.

University? No; for it has Divinity degrees. Is Scripture, then, considered as a subject fit only for children and specialists but not for adolescents? Or is it impossible to make it anything more than what it is generally considered – a soft option? It is the last view that generally prevails. After passing the Senior Local, one puts away childish things, which include the pleasant parlour game of 'contexts', analyses of the Sermon on the Mount and the drawing of maps to illustrate Saint Paul's missionary journeys. By the exclusion of Scriptural knowledge from the subjects of university study, we indirectly suggest the same idea. It is ridiculous to pretend that the objection to its introduction is the impossibility of securing that instruction shall be impartial. The things which divide Christians are far less numerous and less fundamental than those which unite them. Where controversial subjects arise, both writers of text-books and teachers can be found who will give the points at issue squarely and leave hearers to judge between them. In any case, there is no question of compulsion. There is far more danger that propaganda will enter the university through the teaching of history than through that of Scripture. Yet no one suggests the elimination of history from the curriculum. Can it really be that we think history more important than religion?

Thirdly, there should be, in an undenominational university chapel, daily and weekly corporate Divine worship. Here there are genuine difficulties as well as imaginary ones: let us take the latter first.

(1) Its institution would constitute an acknowledgement by the university as a whole of belief in God – an acknowledgement already made by the State, to which every member of a university owes allegiance. It would also amount to a declaration by the university that religion is an essential part of a complete and balanced life, and hence of education. But it would in no way imply the introduction of religious tests for membership of the university. No one, either teacher or student, need be present at any service unless he so wished. The services would be conducted by members

of the Theological staff or the denominational chaplains (who already exist and do a great deal of good) with perhaps voluntary assistance from other members of the staff and senior students. If on any occasion the importance of which demanded the attendance of the Chancellor or Vice-Chancellor, both these (which is highly unlikely) had conscientious objections to being present, there are still the Pro-Chancellors (and, in some places, the Pro-Vice-Chancellor), who could as properly perform the functions of their offices then as at any other time. It is pure obstructionism to suggest that the innovation would lead to the introduction of religious tests. Only denominationalism is likely to do that.

(2) Equally baseless is the suggestion that there would be any difficulty in organizing an undenominational service. Certain Nonconformist Public Schools have a form of worship to which no member of the Established Church could take active exception. One thing is essential: that the services be held in no lecture hall but in a chapel built and used expressly for that purpose, the vestry of which, as is the custom at Glasgow, could be used by chaplains for private interviews with undergraduates requiring advice or instruction. The daily service, consisting of one hymn, a few prayers, and, once or twice a week, a five-minute address need average no more than ten minutes or a quarter of an hour. The Sunday service would centre round a first-rate sermon by an able cleric or layman: if to a part of the chapel non-members of the university were admitted this should do much to enhance the prestige of the university and its influence for good.

The real difficulties, however, though none of them is insuperable, would need careful consideration.

(1) The first concerns the Communion service. It is both ironical and tragic that the only service instituted by Christ himself, which should be a bond of union between all Christians, has throughout the ages been a cause of the deepest divisions: the fact that these divisions have arisen from the passionate desire of each section of the Church to

follow, in a matter of such intense importance, what it believes to be the mind of Christ may explain, and even extenuate, but does not make the position less tragic or the future less difficult to plan.

If the Communion were celebrated in the University Chapel according to the Anglican rite, Free Churchmen would be excluded; if according to Free Church rules, very few Anglicans would attend; in either case, controversy would start from the beginning. There seem to be two solu-tions. One is that Anglicans and Free Churchmen should each have their celebration, at quite different hours and possibly in different parts of the building. The hours would arrange themselves naturally, as Anglicans prefer early-morning celebrations and hold them on weekdays as well as on Sundays, while Free Churchmen confine themselves to Sundays, at midday or at night. There is ample precedent for this in London alone: Saint Mary's, Charing Cross Road, for years allowed the Orthodox (who are not in communion with Canterbury) to use its altars and after the destruction of the City Temple by a bomb an Anglican church gave hospitality to its congregation. The other remedy would be to exclude the Communion service from the University Chapel altogether. This is rather a confession of defeat, but it might produce at least one advantage. Among the churches and chapels near the University, some would undoubtedly seize the opportunity to welcome under-graduates to their own Communion services, and might in time become unofficial 'University Churches', affiliated, as it were, to the University Chapel. On the notice-board in-side the Chapel would be announced the services – especi-ally the Communion services – at these churches; and thus the student-communicant would have a bond of union, not with one body alone, but with two. This is a mere outline of the initial possibilities: if one follows them up and devel-ops them, a dazzling panorama of possible service presents itself to which it is hard to see how any who profess and call themselves Christians can be insensible.

(2) A second difficulty, for so long as the modern

University remains largely non-residential, is that of times. If the daily service is held at the most suitable hour – before lectures begin – hundreds, living an hour or more from the University, will find attendance impossible: to get to nine o'clock lectures often means an unholy rush as it is. As lectures end, and students begin to fade away, at different hours, the afternoon is equally impracticable. The lunch-hour, on the other hand, is crammed with political meetings, musical recitals, committees, and so on, besides which lectures overlap so widely that in some places there is barely a quarter of an hour in the middle of the day completely free from them. The only solution – and it is one to which Senates will be unlikely to agree until opinion generally is more favourable – would be to stop all work, as some colleges do, for a quarter of an hour daily, and hold the chapel service then. Where this plan has been adopted, practically all the students, though free to do as they like, attend as a matter of course, while the staff is divided into those who habitually attend also and those who prefer to drink coffee and smoke a pipe in the Common Room. The best time for such a break would be the last quarter of an hour in the ordinary morning's work – from 12.15 to 12.30 or from 12.30 to 12.45. But no law can be laid down on such a matter of detail.

(3) The Sunday problem is rather different. Except perhaps on such special occasions as the Commemoration of Benefactors, one has no wish to draw students away from their own places of worship to the University Chapel if they are happy where they are and especially if they are doing active work there. Yet if the Sunday service is arranged at such an hour as 11 a.m. or 6.30 p.m. that may quite easily be the effect, while if, like the University sermon at Cambridge, it is placed in the middle of the afternoon, very few would attend and some of those few might very well do so by giving up useful work in their own places of worship as Sunday school teachers. Perhaps the least harm would be done by fixing the morning or afternoon in the winter and the late evening – 8.0 or 8.30 p.m. – in the summer.

One important aspect of the Chapel worship should be referred to here. Perhaps the most difficult thing to find in this busy modern world is solitude and quiet; and, as the claims of the world grow more insistent, an increasing number of people are becoming attracted by a type of worship often referred to as the Fellowship of Silence. This is not unlike the worship of the Society of Friends, but, except for a few words pronounced by the leader, it is conducted entirely in silence and thus does not subject the worshippers to the tyranny of the man who may mistake his natural expansiveness for the promptings of the Spirit. Sometimes no word is spoken at all other than the initial commendation of the group by the leader to Divine guidance and a brief prayer with which he closes the meeting. In such a case subjects for prayer are best set out on printed slips placed in the seats. Sometimes each petition is introduced by the leader, after which there is a pause for silent prayer. This kind of meeting might very suitably be held at the beginning or end of the day. It would be advisable for a small room, furnished like a chapel of repose, to be provided for it in the University Chapel, and this might be available for private prayer or reading throughout the day. The number of students taking advantage of this opportunity might very well be much larger than anyone would venture to prophesy.

Needless to say, the provision of these and other aids to religious worship, growth and progress implies the existence of a large and active body of student opinion, which, besides doing its share of organization, would have the supremely important task of building up a tradition for student-generations to come. If past experience goes for anything, this body would be the Student Christian Movement, of which the central organization is strong and efficient and which has undoubtedly won more confidence from the generality of students than any other religious organization. Upon the work of the S.C.M., more than upon any other factor, the success of the University Chapel must depend.

This leads one to inquire what the role of the other societies will be. As so much of what they at present provide would be supplied centrally, it would seem that they should be entirely secondary. The Anglican Society's quiet days and periodical addresses, the Evangelical Union's weekly prayer-meetings and the short daily service of the S.C.M. would now be centralized: the study circle, on the other hand, the celebrations of Holy Communion, and the social work done by each society in its own sphere would naturally remain. There is little doubt that the quickening of religious life in the University, if it can be accomplished, will give a great stimulus to each of the individual societies, and that the surrendering (or, more accurately, the pooling) of part of their work will bring them, not loss, but gain.

CHAPTER SEVEN

Contacts

ONE of the indisputable advantages which the younger university has over the older is that, being situated within a community of natural growth and so large that it does not add noticeably to its size, it is able to establish relations with other bodies which are of benefit to both parties. The chief of these bodies are the schools from which its undergraduates are drawn, and the city, district and county in which it is situated.

I

'I know very little about schools,' wrote an Oxbridge lecturer a good many years ago; 'all I do know is that they send up their undergraduates in a state of atrocious ignorance.' The sentence was typical at that time of all but a very few Oxbridge dons, and of a good many of them it appears to be so still. After all, why should they be interested in their undergraduates' nurseries? What have they to do with them? Herds of freshmen come up, and always will come up, every October, only too eager to adjust themselves to Oxbridge ways and methods. Why should Oxbridge trouble to know anything about the misguided places they may have come from?

There was this much excuse for that attitude – that the schools in question were numerous and scattered, and it would be physically impossible for any college tutor to visit all the places which his pupils in any one year came from. And, in any case, he would gain very little by doing so. For any single tutor may have pupils reading subjects as diverse as Latin, Greek, Philology, Ancient History, Modern History, English, French, German and a number more: he cannot possibly be an expert in the teaching of all these: besides, if he were, he has little or no say in the teaching of any one of them at the University.

At Redbrick the position is quite different. The individual chiefly responsible for teaching and research in Latin is the Professor of Latin, and his responsibility is for that alone. His undergraduates come to him from schools mainly within a radius of four or five miles, and the most distant has no more than half a day's journey. It is therefore both practicable and very desirable for him to be familiar with the teaching of Latin in those schools. From them he can learn better how to deal with freshmen; he can exchange suggestions with the Classical masters, to the mutual benefit of both parties; he can advise intending freshmen as to reading during the Long Vacation before they come up, which, if properly used, can be such a valuable one; and, in a more general way, he can do most useful work by giving the pupils a sense of the continuity between school and university. He can visit the school, not as an examiner – which is the only way that the Oxbridge don ever visits schools – but as a friend. And he will find he is made more than welcome.

By no means all professors work systematically to establish this connection, but many recognize its value by means of occasional visits, by establishing friendly relations with the masters and mistresses who teach their subject, by inviting pupils to special lectures at the University, and so on. At present the good work they thus do is undermined by the influences within the school which are endeavouring to induce the best pupils to go, if they can, not to the University which they should normally regard as their own, but to Oxbridge – a procedure hardly calculated to inspire respect for the man who is trying to build up this connection. But, when Redbrick University is regarded as the natural seat of higher education for pupils in the Redbrick area, such collaboration will become of the very highest utility.

Another way in which the universities might maintain relations with the schools is in providing more refresher courses for teachers.

In the United States, nearly all universities and colleges

have 'summer sessions', which, year after year, are flooded
with teachers, either graduates of the university they are
attending or graduates of some other university who wish
to widen their academic experience and at the same time
increase their paper qualifications by obtaining a higher
degree. About the method by which this can be done there
is little we should wish to imitate. By attendance at numerous lecture courses the candidate piles up 'credits', which,
together with examination, essay or thesis, entitle him to
qualify for the degree, though long before graduating he
may have forgotten every word of his early lectures. Once,
indeed, during a summer session, I entered the office of an
American professor who was being pressed by a teacher
studying for the Master's degree to support her claim to a
credit for a course which she claimed to have attended some
years previously under his predecessor. She had lost the
certificate then given her, and, far from remembering anything about the course, had forgotten even its title; all she
could remember was its date, the name of the professor who
had taken it and the number of the room in which it had
been given.

We who have a different conception of graduate work
can direct teachers, or any other graduates, who wish to
study for a higher degree, without subjecting them to
attendance at lectures at all. But we might consider more
carefully if we have not some responsibility to those of our
graduates who become teachers, and, in teaching others,
need to extend, refurbish and bring up to date their own
knowledge. At present, teachers are almost entirely
dependent for short refresher courses upon those conducted
by the Ministry of Education and others organized by all
kinds of bodies, from Municipal Education Committees to
learned and professional associations. But would it not be
much more appropriate in every way if such courses were
organized by the universities? First, it would bring universities into closer relations with schools, and university
lecturers with their former pupils. Secondly, a teacher
should get more good from a short course given by lecturers

whom he or she knows than by complete strangers. Thirdly, in certain ways the work done could fit neatly into the university course, which would be particularly helpful for the younger graduates. Fourthly, the material resources of the university – library, bookshop, Common Rooms, Students' Unions, etc. – would be available. But it is really unnecessary to go into these advantages further, for they are all summed up in a single phrase: 'It would be coming home.' If the university has been, as it should have been, a real intellectual and spiritual home to its alumni, there is no other place to which they can so fitly come back to 'school'.

Obviously a great many details remain to be filled in before the picture can be even approximately complete. Not every university would necessarily give one annual course in each of its subjects – there would not even be sufficient demand for this at first: the universities could begin by arranging a rota of courses, which would preserve at least some of the advantages referred to. The establishment of a regular Summer or Christmas session (Easter, until its date is fixed, would be an unsuitable time) would necessitate an enlargement of the university staff, but the courses would soon become financially self-supporting, and an enlargement of staff, with vacation duties for some of its members, would facilitate the procedure, already advocated, of granting members of the staff leave of absence in order to devote themselves to original work during the term. Another plan would be to entrust some, though not of course all, of this vacation work to lecturers of the University Extension type; these, besides being university graduates and often members of university staffs, are efficient in technique, and graduates who have taught in schools for some years might be rather more exacting in this respect than they were as university students.

For the scheme to become a complete and permanent success it would need to be taken up by Governing Bodies and Local Authorities, who might well make certificated attendance at a month's university refresher course every two or three years a qualification, if not a *sine qua non*, for promotion. Since there would be no question of obtaining higher degrees, and teachers are only human, some such artificial stimulus would be necessary till the practice became a tradition. And this it surely would in due time. When one comes to think of it, we are an extraordinary people to allow physicians to learn all their medicine, clergymen to learn all their theology and teachers to learn all of whatever subject they teach, before reaching the age of approximately twenty-four. We fondly hope that 'experience' will somehow or other do the rest. But it does not. Experience needs to be supplemented by experiment ere it can reach its fullness. The teacher, to keep alive and fresh, needs from time to time to become the learner. Constant outpouring needs constant intaking. Practice must be reinforced by theory. The old must constantly be tested by the new.

Those whose business it is to harangue freshmen in our universities often remind them that they are entering a society. If they could add that by tradition every graduate who joined a profession returned for a short period to the society every three or four years, it would give a much more vivid impression than anything does at present that they are entering that society ... *for life*.

II

The other important contact which the modern university must make is with the town or city in which its buildings are situated and with the remaining area which the years have marked out as its 'constituency'.

(1) First of all, it has a particular duty to the city which is its home and whence it derives the greatest number of its students. To some extent it recognizes this by the subjects in which it specializes, often as a result of local benefactions: Birmingham's School of Malting and Brewing, Leeds' varied Technology courses, and Hull's Diploma in

Aeronautics are cases in point. But the university should do more for the locality in which it is set than conform to its conditions: it must not merely follow, but lead. As we said in speaking of religion, it should be a genuine 'centre' of learning, and that not merely to a carefully selected group of undergraduates. When some scientific discovery has been made, some little-known country has sprung into the limelight, some book or some theory has become the subject of conversation, the professor whose special study it is should be there to expound it to an audience filling the university's largest lecture-hall. The university, by means of courses dealing as vividly as possible with foreign civilizations and foreign countries, should create a desire for foreign travel, for the learning of foreign languages or for further education of other kinds among those who have travelled in the past. All the social and personal problems which perplex adolescents should be dealt with, for the benefit not only of the few who will one day become graduates but also of the many who will not.

Still greater is the responsibility laid upon the university when the Press is filled with contentious questions the discussion of which it considers to come within its purview. When political or international events take a grave or absorbing turn, or when some momentous social issue is about to become prominent, it should be to the university that serious-minded citizens, whether young or old, turn for a commentary which, humanly speaking, is free from prejudice, or, alternatively, to two commentaries representing opposite standpoints. The professor should be no cloistered academic, oblivious of whatever practical and topical bearing his own subject may have on the life of the day. He has been granted a relatively sheltered existence, not in order that he may hold aloof from life, but that he may view it steadily and whole, with the serenity which comes from study and meditation. He is free, of course, to say what he thinks right – and there is no more glorious aspect of our national heritage than the immemorial freedom of our universities. But speaking, as he will be, *ex cathedra*, he will not use his freedom as a cloak of maliciousness or even as a cloak assumed merely to disguise his own legitimately and conscientiously held political opinions. He will speak with a restraint which comes naturally to him, since he is already wont to weigh his words in the interests of science and of truth, and since he knows by long experience how impossible it is in discussing any subject to attain to anything like certainty. Above all, he will never attempt to make debating points, to strive after effect, or to pervert what he believes to be the truth for the sake of pressing home his arguments. He will never be the advocate, but always, within the limits of his power, the judge.

Some, of course, may misinterpret this self-control as lukewarmness or timidity. It is not everyone who appreciates the measured sobriety of academic exposition, especially in an age when, unhappily, so many of our daily newspapers shriek hysterical hyperboles at each other and at anyone or anything they happen to dislike. But if the exponents are skilfully chosen and are adepts in the technical art of lecturing, opinion will be as surely educated as it has been educated to chamber music by the B.B.C. For, beneath what may at first seem coldness and reserve, or even unwillingness to give a definite pronouncement upon anything, there lie the virtues of the scholar – those same sterling moral qualities as are brought out by the scholar's characteristic activity, research – and when these, which make their appeal to the highest that is in us, are once recognized, they cannot fail to touch all but the unthinking or the perverse. Even the fools, who come at first to scoff, will remain to pray.

This ideal envisages a university with its doors flung open, its lights blazing and its great halls filled on wellnigh every night of the week – yes, and sometimes even on Sundays. If the work were well done, the cost would be small or non-existent, for a nominal fee could be charged either for some of the lectures, or for annual membership of this wide circle, and numbers would do the rest. Nor would it make unusual demands upon the teaching staff, who would share out the labour involved, and, of course, be paid for it: where the demand for lecturers was greater than the supply, it should not be difficult to import others from outside.

It may be objected that the day for this kind of activity came to an end with the popularization of broadcasting. I do not for one moment believe that. The radio has not emptied the concert-hall or killed the lecture society: on the contrary, radio concerts have educated millions in an appreciation of music, and to hear a disembodied voice talking interestingly for twenty minutes whets the appetite for a lecture given by a man of flesh and blood and lasting for an hour. Especially as many lectures are now followed by question periods, whereas the broadcaster is even farther beyond the range of the questioner than was the proverbial parson 'six feet above criticism'.

In any university city which realized this ideal, the best of the university lecturers would become personalities as well known locally as any radio hero. And, quite independently of the additional interest that might be created by means of tutorial classes and study groups in connection with the lectures, there is a thrill about the crowded lecture-hall and the first-rate speaker no less inspiring than that of a crowded concert-room and a first-class artiste. There are many people who prefer hearing a talk broadcast to reading it a few days later in the *Listener*, and this although there is no extraneous excitement about a radio talk and only a very small minority of broadcasters can impress the hearer with their personality. How much more, then, would one not rather hear an authoritative lecture, eloquently or enthusiastically delivered, at first hand, succumb to the mass-emotion of the crowded hall, share the experience with a chosen friend, and discuss it all going home afterwards! As Sir Arthur Quiller-Couch, one of the greatest of modern lecturers, so attractively puts it:

The hearer comes to [a lecture] in a certain state of excitement, which differs from the excitement of opening a book, though it be but the excitement (if the lecturer be known to attract) of finding a good seat ... To a book you can come in your own time ...

Further, this excitement of anticipation is naturally high when the lecturer standing at the desk is a man his audience know to be a man who has fought his fight in life and to be honoured even for his scars. I still recall the thrill, for instance, of listening to Ruskin – cadaverous, his voice attenuated as a ghost's, his reason trembling at the last. But there was the man, and he was speaking; and behind the mask and beneath the neat buttoned frock-coat one divined the noble brain and heart defeated, worshipped the noble wounds.[1]

All of us can recall experiences like Sir Arthur's. One listener will never forget hearing Lord Halifax, speaking as Oxford's Chancellor, to a thronged Sheldonian, of national ideals, at a time of great national tension. Or, long before, to A. C. Benson sitting at the centre of the High Table in Magdalene Hall at Cambridge, the tall shaded candles (there was no other illumination) shining on his silver hair as he lectured in his quiet voice – or rather, had we but known it, read extracts from a book of his, even then passing through the press. Or, earlier still, to the late William Henry Hudson, that prince of Extension lecturers, holding a room packed with artisans spellbound as he spoke of the masters of our literature: how one's heart sank as his voice dropped into the tones which one knew by experience betokened the lecture's approaching close!

I want the city universities to create for hundreds of thousands experiences like these, and greater than these, to be homes of culture both to those who have themselves such homes and to those who have none. I want the streets leading to Redbrick University to be crowded, night after night, with men and women, boys and girls of all classes and types, drawn to it as to a magnet, until it has forged a mighty tradition and is as much the centre of intellectual life in Drabtown as Saint Paul's or Westminster Abbey is the centre of religious life in London and to all who visit it from afar. No 'University extension' is complete which has not

1. *A Lecture on Lectures,* London, 1927, p. 19.

its roots deep in the university itself: like charity, it must begin at home.

(2) To come now to the outer circle of what is commonly known as 'University Extension', one must first pay tribute to the magnificent work done by the Workers' Educational Association and the Tutorial Classes' scheme, work in which university teachers have participated to the full. The modern universities have perhaps done less than one might wish to educate those who would not describe themselves, in the commonly accepted sense, as 'workers' – persons of from fair to comfortable means whose occupations range from clerical work and elementary school teaching to none at all (for the retired and the retiring need and welcome education as much as any) and whose literary reading ranges from *John o' London's Weekly* to *The Times Literary Supplement*.

In certain areas this large and receptive community is catered for by the University Extension movement, or by that part of the movement which derives its being from Oxford and Cambridge. For, long before the modern universities were founded, Oxford and Cambridge, taking the whole country as their parish, marked out for themselves little plots of ground, most of them in the sunniest positions – seaside resorts and inland watering-places were prominent among them – to cultivate for their own. And when other universities arose in those areas, Oxford and Cambridge continued to cultivate them with no less assiduity. So Redbrick, at the outset of its University Extension work, found little *enclaves* of territory of which Oxford or Cambridge was in firm possession. Thus Oxford has centres at Bournemouth and Poole, and Cambridge at Hull, Derby, Wellingborough and Northampton, all of which towns are well within the area of University Colleges. Manchester University found Oxford entrenched at Heaton Chapel, Cheadle and Bolton; Birmingham had it at Hanley, Burslem and Wolverhampton; Liverpool found Oxford at Oswestry and Mold, with Cambridge even nearer, at Southport; and so on. And these two Universities not only retain these old and successful centres but often go so far as to offer them lecturers (their own alumni) resident in the modern universities in whose constituencies they lie, in order to save themselves trouble and the centres heavy bills for travelling expenses.

Were these two Universities thus favoured of the elect to offer to transfer all their centres lying *in partibus infidelium* and to limit their activities to those parts of the Home Counties outside the sphere of other universities and colleges, they would be helping the Extension movement over the country as a whole, and, in particular, those areas where it meets with the greatest difficulty. In the most thickly populated districts, most of the courses are accounted for by the Tutorial Classes and the W.E.A., and single lectures are the order of the day in lecture societies, institutions and schools served by the Extension movement proper. Yet in the suburbs and towns surrounding the university city there is ample scope for courses on all types of subject and for Summer Meetings of the kind held in alternate years by Oxford and Cambridge.

Some university professors who pose as detached observers of the Extension movement but tend in fact to be its not too sympathetic critics, ask if it is really wise for their colleagues to expend so much energy on this form of service. Will not a semi-popular presentation of knowledge, they ask, blunt their scholarly sensibilities, to say nothing of spoiling their academic style of lecturing? If there were a danger of this, the remedy would be to create in all Universities Departments of Adult Education such as already exist in some, and to entrust the majority of the Extension lectures to their members. But there seems no reason why either catastrophe should happen at all. Admittedly, not every scholar by a long way is suited either for semi-popular or for any other type of public lecturing and those who are not should not be asked to undertake it. Those who can do it, and do it well, should find it, not a pursuit deleterious to research or academic teaching, but a refreshing change and recreation, from which they return, none the worse, to their normal round – indeed, very much the better. The objection as to lecturing style is meaningless. There are not two styles – the academic and the popular. It is the material that is different: the style is one and the same. And the rules observed by a successful lecturer apply as well to an audience of three or of three thousand, to a learned discourse or to a popular commentary on the events of the day:

(1) Limit your lecture to a known and exact time and practise keeping to it till you can round it off to the precise minute.

(2) Divide and plan it so carefully that any intelligent hearer, after it is over, can write down the outline of it.

(3) Speak, not merely in front of your students, but *to* them – both literally, through the control and pitch of your voice, and metaphorically, by studying them beforehand and putting yourself in their place.

(4) Aim at making your language concise, vivid, picturesque – but especially concise.

(5) Decide beforehand what impressions you are chiefly aiming at leaving and what effects you want to produce – and lay your plans carefully to that end.

How different university lectures would be if they were built and delivered according to such principles as these! I have often told a young lecturer who mumbles into his book that he should give a few lessons to a good healthy Shell at a public school and watch them throw things at him! It would be almost as effective to suggest his giving a course of lectures to an Extension society audience – and watch its weekly dwindle!

York Powell once said, speaking of literature and the arts, that if you have a library and a printing press, you have all that is necessary for a university. The value of the library is everywhere admitted but not that of the printing press, and it may be thought characteristic of the neglect which we bestow upon it that the subject of a University Press should have been relegated to the very end of this chapter.

The real reason for this, however, is the desire to look upon it, not as a means of publishing purely academic work – though this is an important part of its functions – but as yet another link between the university and the community it serves.

Oxford and Cambridge have built up University Presses which, besides having published some of the most distinguished works, and series of works, ever brought out in this country, are flourishing commercial concerns, producing numerous books which pay handsomely from the word 'Go'. London has also a Press of more recent origin which has produced some excellent work, sometimes showing marked enterprise. By the newer universities little success has been met with except at Manchester, where H. M. McKechnie made a fine job of what in less capable hands might have led only to discouragement and failure.

Every university should put the establishment of a Press in the forefront of its development programme and give it preference in the allotment of money unallocated elsewhere. To start such a venture and put it into the hands of a member of the staff without practical experience of publishing would be, of course, to court failure. A director of ability, however, should not be hard to find, and it may be suspected that there are able men in large publishing houses to-day who would be glad to do pioneer work in a modern university. In its early years, at least, the Press would have to be prepared to lose money, but, if it started from the first to experiment in remunerative lines requiring little outlay, its accounts should soon begin to show signs of vitality. Such lines, all quite proper to a University Press, are: basic textbooks, such as Grammars, Arithmetics and History courses, written by the university's own leading professors, for which their graduates now teaching in schools will do as much as any publisher's traveller; reading texts, of the Pitt Press type, which will be periodically prescribed by examination boards and so be assured of long lives without any effort on the part of the publishers; Anthologies (how much did the English Association make, to its own great surprise, out of *Poems of To-day*?); books of local interest, which the booksellers of Drabtown, whom it costs nothing to canvas, can be trusted to push to the best advantage.

These are only indications: any educational publisher can find many more. In them, until there is capital for the financing of such ventures as the *Cambridge Modern History* and the *Oxford Books of Verse,* must necessarily consist the Press's chief financial interest. Their great advantage is that, small as they are, scarcely one of them will fail to show some profit. The academic interest will be centred in books of two other kinds. One is, of course, scholarly works, including theses worthy of publication, some part at least of the cost of which can be paid by the authors. It is for the dissemination of works of this calibre that the Press chiefly exists. No more need be said about it here since it is implicit in part of an earlier chapter. But it should be among the chief satisfactions of any academic author to have his books appearing over the imprint of his own university and among the chief glories of the university to bring to light the productions of its graduates and teachers.

The University Press, however, should also act as a link with the community. It is difficult in a few lines to suggest in detail how this can best be done. But one obvious way is to join forces with the Extension Board and work with it hand in hand. The Press will print the Board's syllabus. On a table at each of the Board's popular lectures given at the University will be the publications of the Press with someone from the University Bookshop to sell them. Small pamphlets on current events as envisaged by an authority on each, or leaflets of the news-letter type providing background for the lecture being given, should sell at any largely attended lecture like hot cakes. As soon as the Board found that a particular course of lectures, whether held at the University or elsewhere, was drawing large numbers, the Press should be notified and the lecturer approached on the possibility of his writing a small book on the same subject.

Not all these or similar plans would prove successful. Not all of any plans that have ever been made have proved successful. Not all the plans of the great founders of the newer universities proved successful. But when their plans failed, they thought out new ones. They kept on thinking. They kept on experimenting. They kept on believing. Some of their successors seem to be frittering away their initiative in the creating of committees and their time in sitting on them. It is true that they need far more money, principally from the State, than they have ever had before. But they also need insight and vision for wise planning, and common sense, determination and energy for cutting away routine and red tape and getting things done. Will they be content to amble along, hoping that opportunity may come and meet them, or will they venture boldly, risk failure and win the satisfaction and happiness of the pioneer?

PART TWO

CHAPTER ONE

Redbrick in Transition

I SHALL never forget Redbrick in war-time. You should
have seen it on that grey November morning, after our
Great Raid. Out of the hundreds of bombs that fell a couple
of miles away on the centre of the city, we got no more than
two – but what a mess they made! One went clean through
the roof of the Library, though that was a makeshift
building, soon to give place to another: it was for the books
that we grieved. The other turned a wing of the main
building into a heap of rubble – that wing, if you remember,
that houses the overflow from the Administrative Department and the University Press. And almost worse than the
demolition was the damage. Doors off their hinges, windows
gone – and of course the next evening *would* bring the first
snowstorm of the winter!

In a day or two the glass was swept up, the doors were
repaired, the Library was licking its wounds and new
quarters had been found for the two homeless departments.
But no daylight penetrated the boarded windows and we
moved about a building half-lit by low-power bulbs
('Economy in war-time!') like a community of shadows.
How much more eerie it all looked now that the daylight
was gone! A chance visitor must have wondered where he
had come as he groped his way between the columns of
sandbags and through open doors caught glimpses of rows
of beds – the dormitories of the fire-watchers. And out of
the dim distance would emerge, not normal undergraduates, but shadowy figures in the uniform of Army, Navy or
Air Force; only when they came near enough to let one see

the books they were carrying did the place begin to look like a university after all.

Yet for all the devastation, and the dimness, and the depletion, Redbrick never once gave you the impression of being dead. Except on that Black Monday after the fall of France, when we all crept about, speaking in low voices, as if someone in our midst had died, the buildings had always an air of suppressed activity. The undergraduate societies still went on; Union elections were held with an uncanny normality; the University magazine contained the same old weary jests; the same notices appeared, exhorting the greatly reduced body of freshmen to do their duty by a not so greatly reduced number of meetings. There was a rather noticeable atmosphere around us of 'Business as usual'; and one felt that, if on some fine day in 1943 the War had suddenly collapsed and demobilization had been accomplished with an impossible celerity, life at Redbrick would instantly have swung into its wonted rhythm and the War would have been – well, almost! – forgotten. Even in the days of our lowest vitality, when we had not quite recovered from the shock and disorganization of the bombing, one thought of Redbrick as a wounded soldier, limping and swathed in bandages, but looking around him eagerly to discover how he could best 'carry on'.

That much for the outside view: and what of the University's internal functioning? Well, during the first year – the 'phoney' year – some of us who have a vivid recollection of how the universities were depopulated in 1914 could never get over our amazement that the second World War should see us with 70 per cent of our normal attendance. And, even to the bitter end, there were many ways in which things were surprisingly near-normal. Comparatively few professors went on war service; many lecturers remained with us whom we might have expected to lose; the undergraduates' military education was planned so skilfully that it disorganized lectures considerably less than the pre-war preparations for Panto Day. Most graduate work came to an end, but both research funds and direction were still at the disposal of those who were able to use them, and the learned reviews which Redbrick publishes went on appearing, though in a queerly shrunken form. Some of the Faculties, such as Medicine and Engineering, which the Government considered of national importance, actually 'registered students' (to use Redbrick's unlovely language) in greater numbers than ever before. The chief casualty was the Faculty of Arts.

Not for about two years after the War began was it put out of action. Arts men, like Science men, could at first go before the Joint Recruiting Board, and, if approved for the purpose, could stay at the University until they were nineteen with a guaranteed minimum of three terms' attendance. But, when the calling-up age was lowered to eighteen and a half, the Joint Board machinery was scrapped, except for scientists, and the schools were notified that deferment would no longer be possible for fit men of military age who were studying, or had intended to study, in the Faculty of Arts.

'Does it really matter?' asked the man in the street. 'How much does it all amount to?'

One of the finest short pieces of academic writing, in my view, which came out of the War is the script of a broadcast by Professor V. H. Galbraith which appeared at a time when we in the Arts Faculties were at our most depressed as a result of the latest and unkindest cut in our student body, which denuded our classrooms of all fit men above the age of eighteen. The broadcast was a simple yet eloquent description of what the Arts Faculty stands for – dealing 'not with this or that aspect of knowledge, but with man in the round: with man as he really is with a life to lead and a soul to save'.

The arts faculty, I believe, is the most practical of all the faculties, just because it studies the big questions and studies them in a non-specialized, non-technical way. It is the one that affects the life of the citizen. Every man has to make decisions of vital importance for his own life. He has, for example, to decide what church he will attend, or stay away from. He has to decide what woman he will marry, what school he will send his children to, which political party he will belong to. The fact that you are a physicist, a chemist, or an expert electrician will not, as such, give you the slightest help in answering any one of these questions. Why not? Because they are not scientific: they are human. Now, the sort of thinking a man does when he chooses a church, or a wife, or a political party, is precisely the sort of thinking which an arts faculty seeks to develop. Here the right decision is as much a matter of feeling as a matter of thought ... The arts student pursuing at his university, perhaps rather abstractly, the truth about great matters is simply acquiring a true sense of values. It is this which makes all the difference between good and bad decisions.[1]

That was how we all felt about the waste in the early months of 1943. The education of young men in judgement, the training of them in the lessons of the past, had almost ceased. Our universities were becoming 'specialized technical schools'. And we Arts teachers, who sincerely believe that French is as important as physics and refuse to admit that history is bunk, felt very keenly the depreciatory attitude taken up towards Arts subjects both by the man.in the street, who is the product of our imperfect education of the past, and can only be pitied, and by the Government, who ought to know better. 'Do you seriously mean to tell me', remarked a Drabtown business man who buttonholed me on the tram one day in the summer of 1940, 'that 70 per cent of your boys and girls are still at school? Learning Latin and Geography and Literature and – and all that sort of thing, when we're engaged in the greatest life-and-death struggle that the world has ever known? What in the world do Latin and Geography matter now? Close all the universities, I say, and get down to the War. That sort of thing's all right for peace time.'

Is that attitude, ridiculous and deplorable as it sounds to the academic mind, so very different from the official attitude which was taken up by the Ministry of Labour and National Service? Every attempt was made by enlightened people to alter it. *The Times* protested strongly against what

1. 'The Lost Years.' In *The Listener*, 13 May 1943, p. 567.

it hardly exaggerated in terming 'the wholesale suppression of the arts courses' as being 'gravely prejudicial to the national interest both now and after the war'.[1] 'The grave effects of this do not appear at the moment,' wrote Sir Richard Livingstone, 'but they will be increasingly felt in the future. ... It is ... fatal not to provide the trained intellects necessary for the world of peace; and graduates take longer to produce than aeroplanes or guns.'[2] 'In bleeding the arts faculties white,' concluded Professor Galbraith, 'I fear we may be lowering the general standard of intellectual life in every university in the country.'[3]

Let us look at some of the ways in which this policy worked out in practice. Here was a History Honours man, in his second session, hoping to take a brilliant degree in two years' time and then to spend the rest of his life teaching the subject to our neglect of which we chiefly owe the two world wars. He was in a low medical class, though not in the lowest of all, so, after being refused deferment and forced into uniform, he was excused the usual course of physical training and put into the office to add up figures and act as what his somewhat elementally minded sergeant termed a 'clurk'. Here were two linguists snatched from the University only six months before taking their degrees. One was a bespectacled youth of amazing fluency in German: he was accepted for 'Intelligence', and, after nearly killing himself in the endeavour to become a motor-cyclist, for which, as one glance at him would have shown, Providence had never intended him, was posted to a certain port where for two and a half years he performed routine duties, occasionally speaking a few words of French. The other, a fine athlete, of half-Russian parentage, who speaks four languages, was told that 'Intelligence' was 'full', and so went through the mill of an infantry regiment, in company with youths from London slums, eventually rising to the rank of corporal, and speaking no word of any language but his own. A well-meaning chaplain told him that it was a wonderful thing

1. *The Times*, 10 February 1942; 22 December 1942.
2. T.E.S., 8 July 1944.   3. *The Listener*, loc. cit.

for his character and that he would emerge from the Army like gold tried in the fire. Quite possibly he did – but one might suppose that he would have been of more use to his country in Russia.

These are typical cases of misfits and misjudgements: very much more flagrant ones would be easy to find. I am not complaining, however, of the pushing of historians and linguists into the infantry so much as of the removal of them from the universities. If they had numbered hundreds of thousands, it would have been a different matter, but probably all the hard cases combined would not have exceeded a total of two thousand a year, and the influence of these men and women on the post-war world would have been incalculably more potent than anything they ever did to promote the defeat of Hitler.

Consider what happened. For four years very few women, and, except for a few crocks, hardly any men, graduated in the Humanities. The men raised the most serious problem, for from them several key professions, such as the Church, the Bar and the highest rank of the Civil Service, are almost exclusively recruited. These men were cut off, first at nineteen, then at eighteen and a half and at eighteen, from a continuous course of study. Some of them, who had kept sufficient terms before being called up, were awarded 'war degrees', so that, if they wished to, they could call themselves 'B.A. (War)'. Others had to put in a further year of desultory study before gaining the same distinction. But neither class, in any sense, had a university education. The best, of course, overcame the impediment by educating themselves. The remainder were disabled for life as literally as if they had lost an arm or a leg – only they received no pension. The tragic thing was that they contracted this disability because their studies were the constructive ones of peace and not the destructive ones of war. Had they been engaged in sciences which would enable them to build bombers or manufacture poison gases, they would have been left to finish their courses undisturbed. Because their studies were in languages, history, economics, foreign civilizations – the only studies which will teach the nations how to live together in peace – they were ruthlessly truncated. And yet our politicians were continually reminding us how unprepared we were for the post-war world in 1918 and exhorting us not to think we had won the War of 1939 unless we also won the Peace that followed it. How was that going to be done when so many of the potential leaders among our peace-winners were being deprived of their training?

The worst effects of this short-sighted and unintelligent policy are now manifest in the schools. The Ministry of Labour, fortunately, was able to adopt a policy of keeping women teachers in the schools and dissuading any who might wish to do so from joining the Auxiliary Services. Girls at school, too, were allowed to enter upon teachers' training courses and women undergraduates to graduate, even in Arts subjects, provided they were going on to take a course of professional training. But these provisions were insufficient even to maintain an adequate supply of teachers within the schools already in being. During the very years when men preparing to teach – and this includes men outside the A1 health category – were being sent into the Army, vast plans for educational expansion were receiving a welcome tempered only by the criticism that they failed to go far enough. The school-leaving age was to be raised to fifteen: that meant more teachers. New types of Secondary school were to be created and new schools in large numbers were to be built: that meant more teachers. Institutions for compulsory part-time education were to be set up: that meant more teachers. Classes all over the country were to be reduced in size: that meant more teachers. Every young person capable of profiting by a university education was to have one: that meant more teachers. In the shortest possible time after the end of the War the leaving age was to be raised to sixteen: and that would mean more teachers still. And on top of all this, here was Sir Malcolm Robertson, Chairman of the British Council, calling for 'teachers by the thousand' – 'a national service', as a critic put it, 'an army of teachers ready to go anywhere in the world in order to disseminate the British character and outlook'.[1]

Where were the teachers to come from? Where *are* they to come from? It takes a man or woman three, four, five years after leaving school to qualify for a post. Many of the smaller departments at Redbrick, for the last four years of the War, produced not a single Honours graduate intending to teach. Only now, six years after the cease-fire, are they beginning to produce them again in appreciable quantity.

Was it necessary to hamstring ten thousand careers and to sabotage the post-war effort in order to beat Hitler? If it was, then there could have been no alternative, but many of us wonder – !

II

Back to Redbrick now, back to memories of the war-years; and let us record what effect this wholesale removal of undergraduates had upon the Arts Faculties.

In my own experience, the worst effect was depression. That is not apparently the experience of everyone and the other side of the picture ought to be shown. 'Realizing', wrote Mr H. C. Dent, for example, 'that they had at best little more than a year of university life before them, freshmen everywhere cast aside their traditional irresponsibility and devoted themselves to their studies with an earnestness which surprised everyone save themselves.'[2] I can only say that I saw nothing of this. The freshman generally considers, rightly or wrongly, that he is entitled to spread his net wide during his first year, to join a vast number of societies, try out various games, take part in all kinds of Union activities, and so on, before settling down to two or three years of concentrated specialization when the Inter-

1. T.E.S., 14 August 1943 (letter) and 28 August 1943 ('Teachers and National Service').
2. *Education in Transition*, London, 1944, p. 138.

mediate — often little more formidable than the Higher
School Certificate, which he has already passed — is over.
The effect of the knowledge that he would be called up at
the end of his first year, or early in his second, was merely
to make him feel the uselessness of doing any work at all.
Whether for this or for other reasons, first-year examination
results in Arts subjects were worse than they had ever
previously been in Redbrick's history.

This means more than it may seem to. It means the destruction of traditions and standards which have taken a
long time to build up. People outside the universities do not
always realize the enormous differences in tone and efficiency that exist between one School and another. The remark
one sometimes hears, that X— is a 'better university'
than Y—, is quite meaningless. The only comparisons
possible are between individual Schools at X— and
Y—. A first-rate professor, a devoted and hard-working
staff, will take twenty years to create what a bad appointment to the Chair, when the professor retires, can destroy
in no more than a couple of sessions. A series of poor years
as regards entrants will produce the same result, only more
slowly. And that is what the Second World War did to
nearly all the Arts Schools of the universities. There were
few graduate students — perhaps none — to stand for the
Schools' tradition and to look after the younger people as
only graduates of the same School can. There were men
in the third and fourth years to set a high standard for the
first and second; and the women, their work sadly impeded
by the strain of air-raids and the claims of National Service,
were too closely intent on scraping through their examinations to have thought for much else. Few schools, again, did
not lose some inspiring lecturer to the Forces, and many,
through the operation of the retiring age or for other reasons, saw the departure of their Head. All these causes produced a weakening of traditions, and a lowering of standards,
which has not even now been set right.

A third effect of the War was upon the age of entry. As
soon as the call-up age was fixed at nineteen, boys and girls

naturally began to come up at seventeen instead of at eighteen, and, when it was lowered to eighteen, a substantial number attempted to register at sixteen, so as to have two years' study, and, in some universities, to qualify for a 'B.A.(War)', without returning when the War was over. Redbrick had never had any statutory downward limit of age for entry, but, when admittance was sought by children of sixteen – and, in a few instances, not even quite of that – a resolution had to be hurried through the Senate fixing the minimum age for registration at seventeen and a half.

But the most disastrous effect of the call-up upon the university Arts Faculties was the Long Vacation Term – where this was brought into being. In Science, where much of the undergraduates' time is spent in laboratory work which cannot be done at home, there may be strong arguments for a Fourth Term: in Arts, there are none. Even with three ten-week terms it is hard for the intelligent but lecture-ridden undergraduate to get through all his necessary reading – let alone his thinking – but with four terms it is absolutely impossible. In order that four-term students may be pushed safely through their examinations they have to be given prefabricated material and pre-digested reading: the lecturer, that is to say, must present his pupils with summaries of original and critical works and of portions of text-books which they have not the time to read, and these they must assimilate and serve up to the examiners as though they had read the originals themselves. Unless one is to leave whole sections of the syllabus uncovered, there is no other way. Therefore, when the Ministry of Labour coyly suggested to the Universities that it would be in the national interest for their young people to graduate more rapidly, the wise ones replied: 'No: even in war-time we must not lose sight of the meaning of education.' Others, however, reflected that, when the War ended and ex-Service men and women began pouring in, they would be glad to have as few war-time students left ungraduated as possible. And so they fell to the suggestion of the Fourth Term – some of

them almost eagerly. This innovation will have an adverse
influence on traditions and standards for years to come.

It is perfectly true, on the other hand, that full educational use has not been made of the Long Vacation in peace-
time, and a remark on this may justify a brief digression.
There can be no question of the Vacation's being shortened:
if anything is to be shortened, it should be the ten-week
term. Both staff and students need the Long Vacation badly.
The passage-at-arms between the Oxford professor and the
Oxford college tutor:

P. 'You College Tutors don't know what it is to stare into the
fire and think.'
C.T. 'Ah, that's what we call the Long Vacation!'[1]

is something more than a veiled attack on our English
climate. Nor is it only at Oxford that at the end of the session 'everyone, whether don or undergraduate, professes to
be dead beat and is'.[2] The problem that both Redbrick and
Oxbridge have to solve is how to make the Vacation of
greater value to the undergraduate. But the harder solution
to find is Redbrick's.

'Most of our students', observes the Association of University Teachers, in a recent report,

come from homes where they have no private room or library,
where they are continually called upon to help with housework,
where they are continually distracted by calls to take part in the
amusements of family and friends. Some of them take employment
for a considerable part of the vacation, because of financial
stringency. Very few belong to homes where study is understood
and really encouraged. It cannot be said that the Long Vacation
fulfils the function that would justify its existence.[3]

The report then advocates the institution (except, it would
appear, for students of languages, social science and other
subjects where work outside the university is essential) of a
Long Vacation Term of 'say six weeks'. This would be utilized, not 'for the extension of formal lectures and teaching'

1. R. R. Marett, *A Jerseyman at Oxford,* Oxford, 1941, p. 124.
2. Ibid.   3. A.U.T., April 1943, par. 3 (d) iii.

but 'as a period for the stimulation of private reading and discussion, organized mainly to this end. We can confidently expect', it adds, 'that much more and better work will be accomplished in such conditions than in the students' homes. The demands on the staff would be relatively small and the private work of the staff would be extremely little interfered with.'[1]

For myself, I should deprecate the institution of such a Term, otherwise than by departmental initiative. Undergraduates, who live in Drabtown, or have friends there with whom they can stay, enjoy the full use of the University Library, with access to the book-stacks and ample space to work in. Ample, indeed! Walking in August through the Library of a University which has some eight hundred students resident in its locality, it is rarely that I find more than thirty or forty there at any one time. Hostel accommodation should be open during the Long Vacation to any students who give good notice of their intention to reside and financial help for this purpose should be available for any who can show both merit and need. In most progressive departments programmes of vacation work are already provided: if here and there a professor can conveniently hold weekly seminars or discussion groups for his pupils this seems a wholly admirable thing. But to make this compulsory might often lay too heavy a burden on any staff engaged in research – nor, though it may sometimes be desirable, does it ever (given library and hostel facilities) seem to me necessary.

III

On the question of university numbers in the post-war world very little argument is possible. We shall probably all agree that, with Secondary education compulsory till fifteen or sixteen, and Part-time education till eighteen, full-time Higher education should be denied to none who are fitted for it. This principle, though not specifically

1. Ibid.

stated, seemed to be in the mind of the then Minister of
Education when he observed in 1943: 'The aim of a national
policy must be to ensure that high ability is not handicapped
by the accidents of place of residence or lack of means in
securing a university education.'[1] All who can pass an
entrance test which must not be lower than at present should
be admitted to the university; and those whose parents cannot afford to pay for them should be admitted without fee,
and, if necessary, with a maintenance allowance large
enough not only to keep them in reasonable comfort but to
compensate their parents for the loss of their earnings. Some
think that university fees should be abolished altogether,
but for my own part I do not. I support the abolition of fees
in Secondary schools because, Secondary education being
now compulsory, it is as illogical to charge for it as for the
registration of births. But since Higher education is voluntary, it seems to me that those who can afford to pay for it
should do so, proportionately to their means, and should
regard this, not as an imposition, but as a privilege.

University education for all who are fitted for it, then,
but not, in the strictest sense, for 'all who can profit thereby'.[2] For most boys and girls of 'Grammar School' type
can profit, to some extent at least, by university life. We
need a more stringent test than that. And the test must be
twofold in character. First, a certain standard must have
been reached in general knowledge and breadth of interest
in order to do away with that academic narrowness to which
further reference will be made later and which is so largely
a question for the schools. Secondly, the candidate must
qualify in the special subject or subjects which he proposes
to read, and, in doing so, should be required to give evidence
of sufficient scholarliness of mind to make him a suitable
recipient of academic teaching. To take one example of
what I mean by this, I would rather admit a candidate in
English literature who gave signs of a critical and independent mind and of some capacity for literary appreciation than

---

1. *Educational Reconstruction*, London, 1943, par. 98.
2. A.U.T., May 1944, par. 4, p. 53.

one with an encyclopaedic knowledge of dates and facts who could write or repeat pages of poetry, but whose intelligence appeared not to surpass that of the proverbial parrot.

Such should be the entrance test, supported, if thought desirable, by a school report and an interview, and planned by all the universities in conjunction in such a way that any one university, or associated group of universities, would accept the examination conducted by any other. But, once this type of test was established, and expense was no longer a bar to entry, would the numbers in the universities be so very much greater than at present? The National Union of Students, which habitually goes to enthusiastic extremes, would like to see the university population, during the next ten to twenty years, increase from its pre-war 50,000 to 200,000 or even 250,000. It is quite common to hear or read the view that university numbers ought to be doubled.[1] The A.U.T. calculates 'on roughly a 50 per cent increase of our student population',[2] and speaks with commendable caution about even this. For myself, I would go lower still: from 30 to 40 per cent would be an outside estimate; and I should not be surprised if, after a period of dubiously successful experiment, the figures were stabilized at no more than an additional 10,000. No such estimate, of course, can be more than a guess, but it might be worth while setting down the facts on which my own guess is based.

1. Of my own pupils, and of the undergraduates whom I examine at other universities, quite 10 per cent, and in some years 20 per cent or more, are unfitted for university study. Most of these are the non-scholarship pupils who have scraped through an entrance examination which at present comes too early and is not very suitable for its purpose; a few of them, however, hold scholarships and were considered 'clever' at school, but find they have neither taste nor ability for higher studies. The majority of these, on a more

1. E.g., Simon, p. 14; R. E. Priestley, in *The Listener*, 11 November 1943.

2. A.U.T., May 1944, par 11, pp. 53-4.

adequate type of test, would fail to get through. Assuming
the numbers to be reduced in this way from 50,000 to 40,000,
can there really be 60,000 more who at present are kept out
of the universities solely because of the cost? Forty years
ago, yes: I know of many boys of that time who wasted their
undoubted gifts through lack of opportunity. But to-day I
seldom find among Higher School Certificate candidates
boys and girls who would do well in a university but fail to
go to one; and several correspondents who are inspectors of
Evening School classes say that to find the academic type
of mind among these young people in business is very rare.
All this suggests that, if more suitable and efficient entrance
tests are applied, our numbers will not rise so far above their
pre-war level.

2. It seems very unlikely that, except in teaching, the
outlet for university graduates will be appreciably wider
than heretofore. If this proves to be the case, any undue
swelling of numbers will before long subside. A boy may be
anxious to go to the university if this will fit him for his
trade or profession, but if, on leaving it, he is going to line
up in competition with rivals three years younger, he will
hardly recommend his little brother to follow his example.

3. I believe – and certainly I hope – that we shall never
as a people send our sons and daughters to universities solely
because is it 'done'. England is often compared unfavour-
ably with the United States because that country sends
nearly ten times as many young people to universities as we
do. But, leaving aside the fact that a large proportion of the
institutions to which those young people go would not be
described by us as universities at all, there can be no question in the mind of anyone who knows them that a majority,
and perhaps a large majority, of American undergraduates
ought never to be where they are. The university population
of a country furnishes absolutely no guide to its relative
intelligence. Compare even the weakest of our universities
with the universities of a country where tuition and maintenance are free, entrance is merely by letter of good character
from school, degrees are awarded mainly for attendance at

lectures and examinations are largely a formality. What basis of comparison is there? I hope, before I die, to see a better educated Britain, but I expect it to come, not by an increase of 300, or even 100, per cent in the university population, but by improvements in, and extensions of, Primary and Secondary education, together with the provision of numerous types of Higher college, alternative with the university, above the Secondary leaving stage. Some of these might be affiliated to the universities, but most would not. Polytechnics, technological institutions, schools of domestic science, advanced language schools, institutes of social science and international relations – these would help to make us a better educated, and a *more appropriately* educated, people than a policy of large increases in the number or the size of our universities.

The foregoing considerations have reference only to boys and girls entering the universities through the normal channels. A good deal has been said recently about the possibilities of admitting persons of mature years, few of whom, at present, chiefly for financial reasons, take advantage of the methods which examining bodies have adopted to smooth their path to matriculation. The McNair Committee, in its search after new sources for recruits to the teaching profession, came to the conclusion that 'there are intelligent men and women still comparatively young who, after a spell in some other occupation, ... would adopt teaching as a profession if a clear way into the profession were available and made known', the Committee recommended that 'the Board of Education should offer a maintenance allowance (with adequate additions where appropriate for wife and children) to men and women of maturer years who desire to be trained for the teaching profession and are judged fit for such training'.

By no means all such candidates would pass through a university, and there are several other professions, notably the Church, which would gain by having more recruits of this kind. The A.U.T. considers that the presence of adult students, particularly those who come with the help of Trade

Union and similar grants, is of great value to the universities as well as to society in general.[1] No-one with any experience of such students would question this. The younger undergraduates are impressed, and sometimes influenced, by their earnestness and industry, as well as by the very fact that they have thought a university education of sufficient worth to justify their making sacrifices and taking risks in order to obtain it. They will also, I think, benefit by their greater experience of life: the opportunity of mingling, on equal terms, with persons considerably older than themselves is not one given to many adolescents.

The chief difficulty about admitting adult students arises in the organization of the teaching. When only one or two are found in a department, and these have come at their own expense, impelled by an overwhelming conviction that they can stay the course, they will probably have sufficient ability to adapt themselves to the absorption of material in a form designed for less mature minds – though that does not mean that they will derive the maximum of benefit from it. But, when the doors are thrown open more widely, two things will happen: first, the standard of the entrants will decline, and secondly, they will come in greater numbers. In that case, there would seem to be no expedient other than separate classes for them, probably of the seminar type, and this arrangement has in turn two great disadvantages – that they would then mix far less with their younger fellow-students and that the expense of admitting them, already heavy, because of maintenance and family allowances, would be still further raised. As the A.U.T. also remarks, 'the pre-university educational facilities available to such would-be students need to be overhauled so that they are well prepared for a university entrance test.'[2] This could probably be effectively organized through the University Extension Board and the Workers' Educational Association, but it would involve still further expense and labour, and some critics might doubt if these would be compensated for by the results. Personally, I am inclined to think that

1. A.U.T., April 1943, par. 3 (v).   2. Ibid.

they would and I am eager to see experiments made as soon
as is practicable.

It is right to point out that, bold as such experiments will
seem to-day, we may, in a decade or two, look back with
positive amusement at a time when we thought them so.
Every university teacher is familiar with the phenomenon
of late development: the callow, listless, or otherwise sub-
normal undergraduate suddenly becomes alert and mature
in the course of a session, or even during a Long Vacation.
With the establishment of compulsory part-time education
to eighteen there may be very much more of this, and a
consequent large-scale transference of part-timers to universities, which in turn will demand special pre-entrance
legislation and entrance tests. Again, so much better educated will our young people between eighteen and twenty-
five be than in the past that many of them may discover
vocations for a university career during this period. And,
finally, continued part-time instruction must stimulate all
forms of adult education: for that reason alone, the present
trickle of adults towards the universities may become a substantial stream.

What is the optimum number for a university? That is a
question now a good deal under discussion, but it is not,
perhaps, a very important one. The A.U.T. suggestion of
from 2,000 to 5,000, provided that residence is possible for
a large proportion of these,[1] seems reasonable. But it is not
always realized that the answer depends as much on Faculties as on Hostels. The academic life of the university must
centre in the Faculty and the Department, just as its more
intimate 'home' life will centre in the Hostel or College.
Most Faculties − certainly all Arts Faculties − will need
between twelve and twenty Departments in order to com-
prehend all branches of knowledge for which there will be
students. A Department, 'to deserve the name, must have a
staff large enough to undertake teaching and research and
to embody some corporate experience'.[2] The fulfilment of

1. A.U.T., May 1944, pars. 72–3; pp. 61–2.
2. Op. cit., par. 70, p. 61.

this condition would involve a Faculty of Arts of from 500 to 700 students. And no university, if it is to serve both national and local needs, and also to provide its undergraduates with breadth of experience, should have fewer than three Faculties: a more usual number is four or five. Thus we arrive at a minimum of approximately 2,000: the maximum, once the principle of general residence is agreed upon, will ultimately be determined by the amount of hostel accommodation that can be provided.

The late Warden of All Souls, who from his Oxford home looked out complacently upon the 'wide variety' of English university life and found it very good, would like to see an 'additional provision of universities, particularly in our great provincial centres'.[1] Not, I hope, while those there are still have inadequate buildings, disabling deficits and a skim-milk *clientèle* well creamed by Oxbridge. I can see no need for the creation of new universities, except that Charters should be given, within a reasonable period, to the University Colleges of Southampton, Exeter, Hull and Leicester, following the granting of a Charter to Nottingham. If England, instead of twelve universities totalling (before the War) 35,000 students, had sixteen with an average of 3,000 each, all reasonable demands would be met for a long time to come.

IV

What changes in staffing do the present numbers in our Arts Faculties necessitate? My own answer is: Very few. In an earlier chapter I cited the case of a Faculty with 324 weekly lectures (some of which are 'offered' but not 'taken') and a staff of seventy-eight:[2] this means an average of about three and a half hours' lecturing a week. How the Vice-Chancellor of Birmingham University can say 'We must double our staffs to deal more adequately with our present

1. W. G. S. Adams, 'The Modern Idea of a University,' in *Education Handbook*, Norwich, 1943, p. 21.
2. See page 159, above.

numbers'[1] passes my comprehension unless he is referring
to the proposal that formal lectures should give place to
expositions and discussions among small groups, and for
that the present staffs would have to be multiplied by much
more than two. With this question I have already dealt in
some detail; and, so far as I know, no critic has challenged
my estimate that a completely tutorial system of instruction
would, in a small university, involve additional expenditure
of something like £160,000 a year. The change-over, if it
came, would of course be effected gradually, so that it
would be some time before the full cost was incurred.
Nothing but this, I think, could justify our increasing the
pre-war staff-student ratio, which, for our pre-war kind of
programme, was quite adequate.

Another of the topics dealt with in an earlier chapter
which has been discussed a good deal of late is the Sabbatical Year. 'Periodic release from teaching duties', claims the
A.U.T., 'is a burning necessity if minds are to be refreshed
by sustained and undistracted intellectual effort.[2] But a
Long Vacation is free from teaching duties and it lasts for
about thirteen weeks. If salaries are raised, so that lecturers
no longer have to devote so much of their time to hack work,
it should give ample time for sustained intellectual effort.
Beyond this, Sabbatical leave should be allowed, as a privilege and not as a right, to professors and lecturers who can
show that they need it, and, what is more, whose original
work is of a quality and a quantity that suggest they would
make good use of it. In too many cases a Sabbatical Year
automatically granted would be devoted to a combination
of gainful employment and pure relaxation. Let the principle be established that Sabbatical leave can be obtained
for purposes of genuine research only, and that the researcher's full salary will be paid him (less any part advanced to
cover his necessary expenses) on his production of evidence
that it has been used for this purpose, and a blow will have
been struck for the cause of scholarship. But the automatic

1. *The Listener*, 11 November 1943, p. 553.
2. A.U.T., April 1943, par. 3 (*e*).

system will produce only further demoralization and a lowering of our already low standards.

None of the reports and discussions which have appeared say very much about the need for care in the making of permanent post-war appointments. During the 1914 War – which provided the modern universities with their first experience of large-scale disorganization – a good many mediocre lecturers were appointed for lack of better, and some of them, unfortunately, were retained when the War was over, partly because this seemed the simplest way of coping with the flood of ex-Service students and partly because they had been for five or six years long on the staff and there was a reluctance to get rid of them. Further problems arose where the ex-Service flood was so copious as to necessitate a large addition to a Department's peace-time establishment. Nobody wanted a post-war appointment which was only temporary, for, when it came to an end, all the best permanent posts elsewhere would be filled. On the other hand, the universities knew that the numbers in the Departments when the flood had subsided might not justify the retention of the lecturers appointed to stem it. So some Departments took a chance and appointed to permanent posts people who should only have been temporary; others made temporary appointments and took the best men they could get; while others made do with the staff they had and grossly overworked them.

The same problem has now arisen again, and in a heightened form. The post-war influx, representing six years instead of four, has been much greater than in 1918-20; but there is this important difference – that almost anyone who accepts a temporary university post can, on its termination, find work in a Grammar School. It was therefore, I think, a mistake not to have made all post-war Arts appointments temporary except those to positions in existence before the War began. All permanent appointments should, of course, be made by a Committee, but in elections to lectureships the Head of the Department concerned should have the right of veto, for he alone knows the type of person who can do the job he needs done, and yet he cannot always give a reason – or, at any rate, a reason intelligible to the non-specialist – for disapproving of the Committee's choice. The best Committee for appointments other than to Chairs and Readerships is one of three: the Dean of the Faculty, the Head of the Department concerned and a senior member of the Faculty Board who has some detailed knowledge of the subject which the successful candidate is to teach.

The question nowadays most often being discussed is that of salaries. I have already suggested that the pre-War salaries in the lower grades were (by 1939 standards of living) fairly reasonable, but that Grade I Lectureships, Associate Professorships and full Professorships all needed to be raised. The figures I gave were all based on pre-war costs of living, and, if appropriate additions are made, to meet increased costs, together with family allowances and grants in aid of research or travel for purposes connected with university work, they still seem to me adequate.

The salary now usually paid in Grade III (£400 to £475)[1] is surely as high as is desirable, provided that an exceptionally good candidate can begin near the top of the scale and exceptionally good work bring more rapid promotion. I am sure that it is a great mistake in any profession to give young people large salaries. We want to attract into university life, not those who dream of easy money and ample leisure, but those who are willing, and indeed eager, to make sacrifices for the sake of an ideal. In particular, it would be wise to keep the Grade III salary somewhat below the corresponding stipend of the Secondary School teacher, so that migrations from university to school by those found not to have the qualities for academic work might not be without compensation. Since the university teacher is so highly paid in time he can hardly resent a slight compensatory disparity in money.

That Grade III should be a probationary grade is most important. Nobody can possibly tell beforehand if a candidate, however brilliant his academic record, is going to be

1. See p. 100, n. 1, above.

successful in a university lectureship. So many qualities are involved: scholarship, initiative and staying power for research; technical excellence as a lecturer, and also (a very different thing) as a teacher; friendliness combined with firmness, together with patience, tact and judgement in dealing with undergraduates; industry, perseverance and punctiliousness, despite freedom from any such external control as obtains in a school – all these, and, as well as all these, the qualities needed by every professional man and woman. I am not convinced that what are in effect life appointments should be made even in Grade II, but I am certain that it should be possible to terminate a lecturer's first appointment at the end of five years without attaching any kind of stigma to him or giving him cause for grievance. His research should not suffer from any uncertainty that he may feel as to his future, for during these early years anything that he writes will be brief and limited in scope, his chief work being to learn his job as a teacher and to prepare himself, by reading, for more substantial research at a later date. Most Grade III lecturers, of course, will know long before five years are over that they are to be promoted into Grade II, so that the plea so often made that their research is impeded by uncertainty is seldom of much substance.

If Grade III ends at £475, and Grade I runs from £900 to £1,100, that leaves an adequate range of £425 for Grade II. Taking twenty-seven to thirty as the normal age for entry into that grade, annual increments of £25 would mean that the lecturer was approaching Grade I at the age of forty-five. It is during these intervening years that the more brilliant man will get his Chair at another university; but, as I have said before, it is most important that the man who does not should never, even in moments of depression, feel that he has nothing more to look forward to. A man who has either not applied for Chairs (disliking, perhaps, organization) or who has consistently failed to get one for nearly twenty years, is still in a reasonably good position, though it does not – and it should not – compare with a long-established Professor's. The Professor must be among the leading men in his field, and that type of man, in academic life as elsewhere, deserves a high salary.

The proposals adopted by the Council of the A.U.T. in December 1943 are now out of date, but there are some points in them fundamental enough to merit consideration.

The Council's first proposal is to abolish the probationary grade altogether. 'Some universities', they remark, use it 'in order to maintain a set of inadequately paid lower posts, and, except in these, nearly all Grade III teachers are found to deserve promotion to full lectureships.' This is a surprising statement, and quite contrary to my own experience, but presumably it could be supported by convincing evidence. They propose further to create a probationary period, within the lowest grade (which they would call Grade II), of only two years. This, I think, is hardly long enough. In any case, if the probationary principle is admitted, it would surely be in the interests of all to describe the status as 'Probationary Grade', or Grade III. For, if a young man is appointed for two years to a Grade which normally belongs to the permanent staff, and is then dismissed, he has a more legitimate grievance, and possibly develops a more justifiable inferiority complex, than if he had been appointed to a lower Grade which all the world knows to be probationary.

The Council's allocation to professors – '£1,500 as basic salary' – is too low. Not necessarily at the beginning; for, as I have said, there is a case for paying a brilliant young professor, lacking in experience, no more than the top figure for an Associate Professor, who will be over fifty, and have had at least the experience of a quarter of a century. The magic title 'Professor' should not necessarily at first carry with it a salary higher than anyone else's. But the professor should be on a scale too, and rise by at least £50 annually, so that, as his administrative duties become more onerous (and they always do) and his research becomes of greater value and importance, he has less reason to be troubled about money.

The principle of a salary scale for the professor is one of

vital importance and it is disappointing that this has not been fully admitted by the A.U.T. Council. They have, apparently, some idea of the unsatisfactoriness of the present position. 'In certain subjects', they say, 'the demands of industry, etc., make it necessary to offer particularly high salaries for professors. It is important, however, not to keep professorial salaries low in some subjects in order to be able to compete for professors in others.'[1] But that is precisely the effect of the 'basic' salary, without fixed increments. In many universities the professor, appointed at forty or thereabouts, waits some six, eight, ten years before receiving one morning a note from the Treasurer to say that he is to have an increase of salary. And the next increase may come in another six, eight or ten years – or not at all. It is a most unsatisfactory situation, often affecting those who have given the university the longest service. At fifty-five, the professor in question, elected fifteen years before at £1,450, is earning £1,550 or £1,600, and he cannot possibly base any plans for the future on the certainty that he will ever earn any more. Meanwhile he and his wife are growing older and need the amenities of life more than in the past; his children are proving very expensive at college; he is saving little or nothing. On the other side of the balance sheet is the book he has been writing for the last ten years – a completely unremunerative piece of research, for which he will have to pay if he is to get it published, and which is making greater and greater demands upon his time and energy: he cannot possibly put it aside to engage in journalism or mark cartloads of examination papers. ...

Or can he? Or does he? Has he in fact any real choice? That is the position in which the 'basic' policy places him, and, being only a Professor of Modern History, he can do nothing about it. Were he a Professor of Pathology, or Industrial Chemistry, he could do a great deal, because in the respective fields of private practice and industry a far larger income and not less interesting work awaits him. For which reason the university is more lavish with its invisible

1. A.U.T., May 1944, par. 85, p. 64.

increments in Science and Medicine than in Arts. It is surely time that the Arts professor was treated better.

Fortunately one voice has been raised on his behalf more effectively than that of his own association. The British Association's Committee on Post-war Education recognizes the need for universities to have, and to keep, professors of the highest quality:

> The reputation of our universities depends more on the quality of their professoriate than on any other single factor. For the sake of university teaching and research we should make it more easy to retain our very best men, and to attract outstanding men back from the outside world when they are still at the height of their powers.[1]

While recognizing that in Medicine, and some other subjects, higher salaries will have to be paid, this Committee avers that it would be 'bad policy' to 'consider only outside competition' and thus 'make a considerable saving on the classics'. 'The existing organization of our society being what it is, all wholetime professors in all English universities should be increased to at least £1,500 a year at 1938 prices'.[1]

This means, on the basis of a 20 per cent increase in costs, £1,800 – a considerably higher assessment of the professor's worth than that of the A.U.T.

1. B.A.C., p. 42.

CHAPTER TWO

Redbrick Looks Ahead

SATISFACTORILY high among the problems with which Redbrick is now preparing to cope is the problem of residence.

There is no matter concerning university education on which opinion has moved forward more rapidly than on this. In an earlier chapter I remarked how, in 1930, the University Grants Committee had 'disclaimed any intention of suggesting that the modern universities "are expecting to transform themselves into institutions mainly residential in character" ',[1] and went on to put forward what I thought the rather bold view 'that every university must have sufficient hostels to accommodate a very large proportion of its undergraduates and every student should be compelled to reside, either within one of these hostels, or in lodgings affiliated, as it were, with the hostels, and under strict university control'.[2] No-one has been more surprised than I to find that, since those words were written, this ideal has become accepted as that which all universities should attain at the first possible moment.

In an interim report presented to the British Association in September 1942, that Association's Post-War University Education Committee laid it down that 'at least one year's residence in college or in a university hostel should be required of every internal candidate for a first degree' and added that, according to figures supplied to it, 'the cost of making this change (without so adding to the expense of a university education as to exclude any student however poor) would be far from prohibitive'.[3] Ten months later, another report by the same Committee, remarking that there was a 'general call' for better residential facilities at the modern universities, spoke rather more soberly of the cost:

1. Cf. p. 57, above.   2. Cf. p. 58, above.   3. B.A.C., p. 4.

To implement this recommendation would involve ... not only capital expenditure on sites, buildings and equipment, but also considerable annual expenditure ... Hostels with the right standard of amenities, including rooms for resident tutors, adequate and well-furnished common rooms and study rooms, libraries and single bed-sitting rooms, cannot be run cheaply. At the prices ruling in 1938-9 the average annual cost per place, including both capital and maintenance, will not fall far short of £100 a year.[1]

This sum is considerably larger than was charged for board and lodging in Drabtown before the War, so that, even if the undergraduates required to reside in hostels were such as would normally have gone into lodgings, an extra charge would fall due for maintenance. Actually most of them live at home, which makes the charge higher still. If in addition all undergraduates – or all who were given free places with maintenance – were required to reside for a year, most people accustomed to our present scale of expenditure on education would certainly term it 'prohibitive', even though no university would spend more annually on this than the cost of a few minutes of war.

The A.U.T. also advocates the one-year residential principle – only, however, 'as an immediate objective'. 'We would aim ultimately', it continues, 'at a residential system of university education' – there we have the measure of the revolution of opinion since 1930 – 'but since this is a long-term objective, we suggest that meanwhile universities should make arrangements to allow non-residents to "dine in" at a hall of residence, if they so desire'.[2]

So much for theory. What is going to be done in practice?

The lead, not for the first time, has been taken by the University of Manchester. In May 1944, the Press reported its Vice-Chancellor, Sir John Stopford, as saying that the University was anxious, as early as possible, to accommodate all students in hostels for one year – probably the first – an innovation which would require six new halls,

1. B.A.C., pp. 40-1.   2. A.U.T., May 1944, par. 87, p. 64.

each taking from 150 to 250 students. The cost of this, on pre-war values, would be some £700,000; and, pending the time when it would become possible to build, they hoped to get temporary accommodation.

On the heels of Manchester came Leeds, which, in a 'Report on Post-war Developments,' submitted to the University Grants Committee, set as 'an ultimate aim ... for all students residence in a hall for at least three out of the four years which will normally be required for a degree course.'[1]

It may be, however, that we shall have to take bolder measures than any of these if we are to solve the problem of residence. I was interested recently to read in *The Times Educational Supplement* (and I hope we are all conscious of our debt to that journal – so vital is it in these vital days, so broad in its sympathies and so alert for action) of an experiment in community student life that has been going on for the past nine years in the University of Toronto. In 1936, twelve students rented a house at a low figure from Victoria College, and 'with a minimum of furniture and equipment they went into residence and started housekeeping on a co-operative basis'. Six years later, there were one hundred students in five houses, one for women and four for men.[2]

The government of each house was in the hands of its members, who also provided the necessary capital in the form of ten-dollar loans. The management was undertaken by an elected committee of five. Profits were distributed once a year according to the amount paid for room and board. Dons (one of them with a wife and child) as well as students lived in these houses on a basis of strict equality, though they found that in fact they were frequently called upon to act as advisers. 'The actual planning and running of each residence thus remained almost entirely in the hands of its student members.'

There are several reasons why such a venture should be

1. T.E.S., 1 July 1944.
2. 'Community Residence for Students.' In T.E.S., 25 March 1944.

more successful in Canada than here. For one thing, staff-student contacts are closer in a country less affected by long authoritarian tradition. Mr Herklots' idea of staff-student hostels, which I examined in *Red Brick University*, has, I see, been revived by the A.U.T.:

> Simple hostels should be established in the country, where staff and students of particular departments can work together for a few days or weeks. In a work-fellowship of this kind a new attitude to work is engendered.[1]

But such fellowship, I fear, is still very much in the region of wishful thinking. Another impediment to our adoption of the Toronto plan would be that there is no tradition here of 'earning while learning' – or, in the transatlantic idiom, 'working one's way through college'. The author of *The Times* article himself suggested that the responsibilities might be 'too exacting and time-consuming for students at the undergraduate stage'. But they would consume time in a healthier way than do many undergraduate activities and they should be at least as beneficial and fruitful as those of office-holders in the Students' Union. The danger is not that the idea would prove unworkable if it were put into practice, but rather that it would not be put into practice lest it should prove unworkable.

But for this, and any similar, experiment the present period is just the right time. First of all, it is unconventional – and in the War years, during which we all did unusual jobs and were thoroughly mixed up with each other, convention went by the board. Next, it is better suited to students of some maturity than to the boy or girl coming straight from school, and the demands of National Service are providing the universities with a large number of mature students still. Then, during the war years, we became used to community life. Boys and girls, not to say men and women, who had never so much as shared a bedroom with anyone, were herded together, by night and by day, in the Forces, in the Women's Services, as evacuees, in air-raid

1. A.U.T., May 1944, par. 88, p. 65.

shelters, as fire-watchers. Even boys and girls coming to the universities from day-schools had learned something of community life, and had their rough edges smoothed down, through having been transferred to camp schools. Lastly, a long and exhausting war emphasizes the importance of the essentials of life and the triviality of its trimmings. At any other time those who believe in the residential university might be inclined to wait until the State or some private benefactor presented them with sets of brand-new hostels each standing in its own extensive grounds and equipped with the latest thing in study-bedrooms. The post-war mentality is much more likely to favour the rough-and-ready solution – even a rougher, and a readier, one than that of Manchester.

I hope, then, that the Toronto experiment will be emulated over here, with all the variants that our different and diverse conditions may suggest to us. At the same time, it is only right to point out that nothing of the kind can ever solve our large-scale problems. For nothing less is aimed at than to convert non-residential universities, in which some 150 students out of (say) 2,000 at present reside, into residential universities in which barely 150 will *not* reside. This can be done only by the erection of many halls of residence, housing sufficient numbers to provide a community life which shall be really broad and varied. And, from the first, these halls should have a diversity and character which will aid them in building up their own traditions. People say they can never become colleges, like those of Oxford and Cambridge, because the latter colleges grew up, for the most part, as independent foundations, and were never in any sense mere hostels. That is how it seems to us to-day. But I should like to call them colleges, so that they may strive to become what as yet they are not, but what I for my part believe they are capable of becoming in the future. They can create and develop traditions, they can receive gifts and endowments, they can inspire patriotism and affection. And once there are not just one or two, but ten or twelve, healthy rivalry will aid their development.

No sign of the educational times is more significant and more encouraging than the simultaneous realization in the minds of so many that a residential Redbrick is on the way.

II

A second question with which Redbrick is becoming increasingly preoccupied is how far specialization is leading to narrowness of outlook.

This is no new question: during the last twenty years it has been raised again and again. I have discussed it in an earlier chapter, quoting some typical criticisms of university education as over-narrow, showing that the increasing tendency to specialization is a social, rather than an academic, phenomenon, and finally examining the much-attacked Honours course, which, as I see it, stands less in need of supersession than of reform. 'The real fault is that we have not developed our conception of what an Honours subject should be and given it all the breadth of which it is capable. Let that remedy, at least, be tried.'[1]

Two interesting contributions to this discussion have been made by Cambridge men – one a teacher in his own University and one a migrant in the north. In a brilliant lecture of which more will be said later, Professor Bonamy Dobrée relates the alleged excess of specialization in the newer universities to the demands made upon them, at their foundation, by society.

Society, at the time most of us came into being, lacked technicians and school teachers, as once it lacked clerics; and just as the older universities were founded to meet the earlier need, so the newer were brought into being to satisfy the later.[2]

This is not to say, continues the author, either that the newer universities should not have produced what society asked of them or that they 'did not from the start, from the moment that their charters (in some instances) transformed them from science colleges into universities, cherish

1. Cf. p. 188, above.   2. *The Universities and Regional Life*, 1943, p. 7.

wider ideals or seek to embody more dynamic aspirations'. But, he adds, 'the plain fact of the matter is that they still in the main turn out technicians and teachers narrowly trained in their tasks, largely because that is all that the societies which they serve ask of them'. His remedy is, therefore, that 'the societies must be induced to demand more'.

Now I think we have to make a clear distinction between narrowness in the curriculum and narrowness in university life. Let us consider each in turn.

Narrowness of curriculum is too often assumed to be inseparable from specialization. It is true that specialization was forced upon the universities by the demands of society – though not only by those of provincial society: there is even more specialization at Oxbridge than at Redbrick. But society has never demanded that the curriculum should be narrow. To take, for convenience, some of the examples given above, the newer universities got their charters at just about the time when the schools were demanding that teachers of English and French should have a deeper knowledge of their subjects and a more thorough training in the teaching of them, and therefore undergraduates hoping to teach English literature began to devote at least two years of their university course mainly to English literature instead of giving one-third of their time to mathematics and one-third to history. So much was imposed from without. Where the university, the department and the undergraduate were still perfectly free was in determining exactly how the special subject should be studied. Here you have an undergraduate who, without neglecting set books and periods, uses his special studies to delve into philosophy, theology, educational theory, political science, and so on; who reads widely in contemporary literature; who gets into touch with, and keeps abreast of, modern literary movements and modern thought. That is the best type of specialization, the 'broad way'. Here, however, you have an equally industrious undergraduate who for an equal number of hours daily mugs up set books and periods, and anything else which he deems 'likely to be set', learning by heart yards of verse in the hope that he may get a chance to reproduce them 'in the exam.' and committing to memory strings of dates – the births and deaths of leading authors and the years of publication of their principal writings. That is the 'narrow way', the way of the student in blinkers, which has brought upon specialization quite undeserved obloquy.

If narrowness, as opposed to specialization, is in no sense imposed upon the university by society, still less is narrowness in university life. One of the advantages of the internal university degree not perhaps sufficiently realized is that, save for rare exceptions, a degree candidate gets the class he deserves. A man with a first-class mind and first-class application gets a First; a man with a second-class mind and second-class application gets a Second; and so on. Where the second-class mind is combined with first-class application, or vice versa, the result is more often a Second than a First – the large number of students of that description is in fact responsible for filling the class known as 'Two-one'. It is a very rare thing, that is to say, for a student to get a First by pure 'swotting' to the exclusion of interests outside the examination syllabus. Even from the restricted 'class-list' standpoint, quality of mind comes out as well where interests are wide as where they are narrow. If our students fail to reach out as widely as they should it is partly because they do not realize this, partly because school training has led them to think of the degree as the be-all and end-all of existence, and partly because, with the best will in the world, they just *have* to catch the four-fifteen train home. None of these reasons seems to have anything to do with the demands of society ...

My second quotation, from Dr F. R. Leavis, expresses only an individual opinion, but gives considerable food for thought:

A distinguished war-time migrant remarked to me recently that he found Cambridge, with all its advantages, surprisingly content to be an agglomeration of departments and special studies. In spite of the unsurpassed opportunities for intercourse across the departmental and specialist frontiers, and in spite of its being so much urged in favour of the college system that it favours such intercourse, he found little evidence that the use made of these opportunities amounted to much.[1]

The first comment upon that observation of those of us who are not Cambridge men would probably be that, if it is justified, Cambridge is evidently going the way of Redbrick, with less excuse for it. But on consideration I am disposed to think that the distinguished war-time migrant had been unfortunate in seeing Cambridge under what were temporary and abnormal conditions or had failed to penetrate very deeply into its spirit and life. Outwardly, of course, any efficiently organized university in this specialist age will appear an agglomeration of departments and the fact that Cambridge has of late become more departmentalized means only that it has been increasing in efficiency. But as to intercourse across the departmental frontiers, that *must* take place where intelligent people, whether dons or undergraduates, are thrown together as they are at Cambridge. Except to the extent that everyone was preoccupied in 1943 with the War, with the cramming necessitated by shortened courses, with the demands of National Service, and so on, neither undergraduates nor dons can possibly fail to educate themselves, as the latter class habitually do in the Combination Room during the hour after Hall and the former class round the fire during the small hours of the morning.

The problems, then, which Redbrick has to face are how to broaden curricula which must of necessity continue to be specialized and how to provide undergraduates with more facilities for educating each other – i.e., for residence.

To judge from the A.U.T. Report, a composite solution of the specialization problem is to be attempted.[2] First, the

1. *Education and the University*, London, 1943, p. 31.
2. A.U.T., May 1944, pp. 56–8. The quotations in the text are from these pages, except where the contrary is stated.

number of Honours students will be reduced. Secondly, both Pass and Honours courses will be remodelled. Thirdly, the normal course for the first degree will extend over four years.

These proposed solutions have all been discussed in an earlier chapter; and, except for the attempts being made to equate the prestige of 'General Honours' (formerly the Pass Degree with the mark of distinction) with that of 'Special Honours' (formerly known as the Honours Degree) they seem wholly commendable. However much one may applaud the intention (to quote Leeds University) of 'improving the status and character of the General courses and "divorcing the implication of excellence and mediocrity from Honours and Ordinary",' [1] it is impossible to blink the fact that the Special Course, whatever name be given to it, does demand higher qualities of mind and mental activity than the General Course, and that First Class Special Honours will always win higher esteem than First Class General Honours, especially if the content and the treatment of the Special Course are to be broadened. At present some of the advocates of General Honours are protesting too much, and, unless they recover a sense of proportion, they will find that they are doing their cause more harm than good.

In other respects the A.U.T. recommendations are unexceptionable. The Honours degree course has quite wrongly become 'the normal course for all students; while the more general course required by the Pass Degree tends to be looked upon as waste land'. Many who enter upon an Honours Course, merely for reasons of prestige (or, one might add, because of the demand for specialist teachers), are 'ill-fitted for specialization'. The present Honours Courses (to be termed 'Special' Courses) should therefore be remodelled so as to 'link up the specialist with other spheres of study', while the present Pass Courses (to be termed 'General' Courses) will 'continue general education on a higher level and from a different angle' from that of

1. T.E.S., 1 July 1944.

school. Either type of degree should be awarded with or without Honours.

Thus far the A.U.T. If its recommendations are adopted, the Dean, in interviewing the freshman, will consider (i) if his school record, examination results and performance at the interview seem to fit him for a Special or a General degree; (ii) if the profession which he proposes to enter demands a specialist or a general type of qualification. He will record the information and impressions thus gained upon a card and dismiss the freshman to his courses of study, which, according to the A.U.T., are for one year, or even for two years, to be of a general character for all, providing 'instruction in a group of correlated subjects'. At the end of this period, the undergraduate will return to the Dean, who will add to his card particulars of his performance in the courses and examinations which he has taken since his entry, and, after a period of meditation, will assign him to the Special or the General Course, sending him, if the former be his goal, to consult Professor Blank, who is in charge of it. No-one will deny that this procedure is a great improvement on the present state of things, which may be illustrated by the following scene in any Deanery on one of the first days of any October.

[Dean or Dean's assistant sitting at table, C. Enter, L, girl at head of queue. She has been waiting in the queue for an hour and a half and is showing signs of strain.]

DEAN. Pass or Honours?

GIRL. Honours.

DEAN. Subject?

GIRL. English Language.

DEAN. Other first-year subjects?

GIRL (*hesitatingly*). Latin and – I think – either French or ...

DEAN (*decisively*). Latin and French. Thank you. For French you take Courses 101 and 102. For Latin – let me see – Courses 102 and 104. For English Language, go and see Professor Crusty, second floor, first door on left. Sign this form. Thank you ... Send in the next, please ...

Yes, the new method is infinitely better. So much more

human! But, when one reflects that the Dean of an Arts Faculty at the beginning of a session frequently has 200 freshmen, to say nothing of shoals of problem-cases from higher years, masses of routine, piles of correspondence, and a Faculty Board meeting, with its accumulation of vacation business, on the following Monday, one is tempted to write it down as a counsel of perfection. Certainly a posse of Deans, or Directors of Studies, would be needed, and even then registration would take several times its present number of days before the Deanery (or Deaneries) would be empty.

> 'If seven maids with seven mops
>   Swept it for half a year,
> Do you suppose,' the Walrus said,
>   'That they could get it clear?'
> 'I doubt it,' said the Carpenter,
>   And shed a bitter tear.

Any such reform as this, as the A.U.T. has clearly seen, presupposes a degree course of four years, and even this would allow for only one year of general instruction – which in fact is, I think, quite sufficient. A full three years' study is essential for any Honours Course worthy of the name. But I hope that the maximum of pains will be spent on the reform of the content of the Honours Course, for I am sure that we have not even begun to realize how very much better it is capable of becoming than it is at present. Specimen detailed syllabuses should be sent to the A.U.T. by Heads of Departments who are experimenting in this direction and published for the benefit of others. 'Each subject', as the Report says, 'has its own lines of development, which should be the subject of consultation between experts from the universities.' What a pity, and what an astonishing thing, that in a country where no university is more than a few hours' journey from any other, the experts in each subject do not meet regularly for several days' consultation – say at the end of September, when the new session is about to begin!

III

A third group of problems concerns representation – of the non-professorial staff on the Senate, and of the academic staff, whether professorial or not, on the Council.

The academic government of a university by a Senate consisting of professors alone is nowadays generally felt to be a mistake. Because there happens, for example, to be an endowed Chair in Modern History and only a lectureship or a readership in Ancient History, it seems hardly fair that one of these Departments should have its interests represented on the Senate and not the other, especially in universities where the Faculty Board, on which every Department is represented, has not a great deal of power. Again, there are often men of experience who are not even departmental Heads, yet who are far better administrators, and have a much profounder knowledge of university business, than the average professor, and have also, as a rule, considerably more time. The A.U.T. Report lays it down that 'the Senate should include all heads of academic departments, the librarian, and an adequate number of representatives of the rest of the academic staff'[1], leaving individual universities to experiment as to non-professorial representation and in due course to pool their experiences. This is a matter which, now that it has been well ventilated, may safely be left to take care of itself. Within a short time we shall certainly reach a satisfactory solution.

Academic representation on the Council is a thornier subject and at the same time a more important one. For, as I have already explained, the Council at Redbrick is supreme. At the worst, an obstructive or intransigent Council could reject every resolution which the Senate submitted to it; and, at the very best, no decision which the Council makes can be seriously affected by the minute academic representation which is all that it allows. In practice, it is true, the Senate is permitted, with rare

1. A.U.T., May 1944, par. 58, p. 60.

exceptions, to have the controlling voice in all academic matters which involve no expenditure, while the Council controls everything else. It is often said that this arrangement works quite smoothly. So does a dictatorship – on the surface. But, in the era that is just beginning, dictators are going to disappear, and so, let us hope, is the dictatorship of Big Business, however benevolent, over education.

I believe that within the next ten or twenty years there will be as complete a revolution in opinion on this subject as there has been over residence. To-day, no doubt, most academic persons would demur to the view that 'in the ideal university a Senate or Council composed of graduates and teachers would be completely autonomous',[1] but by 1960, unless I am much mistaken, they will be proclaiming it far and wide, if in fact that ideal has not in many places been achieved. The A.U.T. is politic – and a little timid. It believes that 'the present representative character of University Courts and Councils is appropriate to the present situation and stage of development of the regional universities',[2] but considers that the academic members of Councils should be more numerous and 'have the unquestioned right of participating in all decisions affecting the university ... , including questions of finance'.[3] 'The Council', too, 'should not have the right of veto over purely academic matters, in which decisions can be taken only on the basis of professional knowledge and experience': among these matters is explicitly mentioned one of the most usual subjects of controversy between Councils and Senates – viz., elections to Chairs.

All that is paving the way to something better and is probably as much as can be said by an academic association in public or on paper. But one may perhaps be allowed to inquire how a lay body came to have this all but complete control over an academic society and by what right it retains it.

Reasoned out from first principles, the position is

1. See p. 84, above.   2. A.U.T., May 1944, par. 55, p. 59.
3. Op. cit., par. 56, p. 60.

absurd. The university is a society of seekers after, and dis-
seminators of, knowledge. It should therefore be governed
either by the whole of its mature members – that is to say,
its graduates, who do, in fact, exist as a joint body, known
as Convocation – or by such of them as are still actively
working with and in the society. In practice, a smaller body
elected by one or other of those classes of graduate would be
more practicable. Below this Council, truly representative
of the society which it governs, would come the body whose
composition has just been discussed, the Senate. Every
member of the Council would, under this scheme, be a
graduate of the society; or, if the State and the local
authorities which contribute to its maintenance should
demand representation upon it, the voice of the society
would still be predominant.

How does this compare with the Council of (say) thirty-
two members which dominates a typical modern university
to-day? The Chancellor and the Pro-Chancellor are
members of the society only because they were made so at
some Honorary Degree ceremony. Of the other thirty,
seven are members of the Senate, elected by that body or
by the Faculties, and two are members of Convocation,
which elected them. That leaves twenty-one, out of
thirty-two, in whose choice the society has had no part,
and eleven of whom, besides not being members of it,
are members of no university at all. Most of them have
been elected, either by that miscellaneous body known as
the Court of Governors, whose eventual abolition I have
made bold to prophesy, or by the various local authorities
who make contributions of differing value to the University's maintenance. And, looking at the names of these
worthies, anyone knowledgeable in local politics will
suspect that this one has been nominated by a Socialist
Town Council to 'uphold the principles of democracy' and
that that one has been nominated by a Tory Town Council
to 'keep the place from going Red'.

Those are the people who from time to time may veto
the long-thought-out decision of an academic body,

advised by the relevant experts, upon the most suitable candidate for a newly endowed Chair, or who may refuse a professor, struggling to keep his department up to date, some small amount of money needed for its development. Surely it is time that we recognized such conditions as anachronistic.

It was natural, of course, that Redbrick's founders and first benefactors should have wished to have a large share in its government: during the years of its immaturity and slow development, no-one would have grudged them that, though, despite the fine work they did, they would sometimes have gained had they been more closely associated with academic interests. But they have all gone, and many of their descendants have other and very different interests, while the University is now fully mature and quite capable of self-government. Let it govern itself, then, with such intervention only as logic and reason dictate.

The other day I heard two members of the Redbrick Council declaiming against a so-called 'Socialist' newspaper editor who had said that our civic universities should be controlled by the State. Redbrick, they said, must at all costs remain autonomous. The actual consideration of that question demands a fresh section, but in this context I venture to draw attention to their adjective. Autonomous! And both these men were nominees of the Drabtown Borough Council, one of them the father of two Redbrick graduates, but neither of them a university graduate himself.

As State aid for the modern universities increases by leaps and bounds, which it must, their government will become a question of great moment. I think we may be prepared for some considerable changes.

IV

Autonomy, like so much else in Redbrick politics, is closely bound up with finance.

Since the end of the 1914 War, all the universities have

been receiving public money, on what must be termed a
very small scale, through a body, academic in composition,
already referred to, the University Grants Committee. It
is quite clear that, if even a fraction of the reforms which are
being demanded on all sides are to be carried out, State
aid will have to be given to an extent hitherto undreamed
of. For where else is the money to come from? Not from
local authorities, which to-day are contributing barely
one-quarter even of the meagre amount given by the
Treasury. Not from private benefactors, crippled by
Income Tax, Surtax, Excess Profits Tax, Capital Levy,
and Death Duties. Not from fees; for, even if those who
wish university education to be free fail to get their way,
there is certain to be an increase of freely placed, as against
paying, students. Only State aid is left; and only the State
has aid available on the scale that is needed.

How much money shall we require? Estimates vary.
The British Association Report, remarking that the present
annual Treasury Grant is equal only to the cost of four
hours' war, opined (in italics, for greater emphasis) that it
'should be at once *doubled*'.[1] The Vice-Chancellor of
Birmingham University bids higher: 'If the subsidy were
trebled it would not be as big a proportion of the national income as our chief colleagues in the United Nations pay
for the education of their best minds'.[2] Lord Simon, while
willing to accept a doubled grant for the first year, wants
the present grant to be *quadrupled* at the end of five years.[3]
I will bid a great deal higher than that – and within a
decade I believe that even the figures which follow will be
considered modest ones. For residential developments
alone each of the newer universities should be promised a
non-recurrent sum, varying slightly according to its needs
and potentialities, of about one million pounds. For open
scholarships, research and tutorial posts, new buildings,
travel grants and various other facilities which they must
have before they can begin to compete with Oxford and

1. B.A.C., p. 40.   2. *The Listener*, 11 November 1943.
3. Simon, p. 5.

Cambridge, the same universities should have a recurrent annual grant of about half a million. On top of that should come the regular annual grant made to all the universities, a substantial part of it to be devoted to repairing the devastation wrought by the War in the Arts Faculties. This grant might at first total ten million pounds yearly: of what it would eventually rise to I have not the faintest conception. Those figures represent perhaps the cost of a battleship down and an annual sum which alternatively, if we preferred it, would buy us a day of war. Only the equivalent of the battleship would be unsinkable and between a day of destructive war and a year of constructive peace the choice should not be in doubt.

Do let us start to think on this sort of scale and not in terms of doubling or quadrupling a miserable yearly pittance of two millions. The only thing I apologize for in my estimate is its inadequacy. But it is merely the thin end of the wedge. It does at least enable reforms in Higher education to be looked at together with those in Primary and Secondary education without the need to take up a magnifying glass when one passes from the latter to the former.

All this leads up to the question of State control of the universities, and to-day, as thirty years ago, some of us are regarding such a possibility with trepidation. The first two points I shall make will meet with general agreement. One is the principle that the granting of public money carries with it the right to exert an appropriate degree of public control. The State cannot simply distribute two million pounds a year to the universities and then forget about it. On the other hand, there is no doubt that university autonomy in this country has produced good results – and anyone inclined to doubt that should spend a year in one of the American State universities, or in certain Continental countries where university teachers change with changing governments, and research, teaching, scholarship and everything else are dependent upon the vicissitudes of party politics. I would rather the universities continued exactly as they are than suffer that.

From the standpoint of the universities the present arrangement works admirably. The University Grants Committee, even in its pre-war form, was a well-meaning, and, as a rule, an understanding body, which made periodical visits to the places that its recommendations were to benefit, heard all available evidence and inspected conditions for itself. Although (or should the word be 'because'?) its members were not politicians but academic experts, the recommendations, in the words of its Chairman, have been 'invariably accepted', and because to them 'the principle of university autonomy has been as sacred ... as to the representatives of the universities themselves, there is probably no country in which the universities have 'been more free from any kind of State interference'.[1]

They have enjoyed freedom of teaching and public utterance and freedom to determine the lines of their own development. Their staff have been subject to no kind of test, political, religious or racial. This unusual combination of State support with full autonomy has been brought about by a method peculiarly British, in that it is indirect and is nowhere clearly formulated.[2]

But can this desirable state of things continue if State aid is vastly increased? In theory, yes, for an increase in the amount of a grant does not affect the principle according to which it is given. There may, however, develop a demand for control, and, should this come from any considerable section of the tax-paying community, it cannot be entirely disregarded.

One consideration that may prompt such a demand will arise if Redbrick is given proportionately more substantial aid than Oxford or Cambridge. For, although both types of university have debts to the community, that of Redbrick, which draws upon a sharply defined constituency, is the more obvious and the more easily assessable. 'There is a growing feeling that the life and work of the universities should be more closely related to the life and work of the

1. Sir Walter Moberly, 'The University Grants Committee'. In *Communication*, No. 1, January 1944, p. 7.
2. Ibid.

nation as a whole, and that there should be stronger links
between the universities and other institutions of society,
particularly the public services of education and social
welfare and organized industry.'[1] One might suppose that
more effective *local* control would better advance these
aims than a tighter State control; but there are many
somewhat vocal critics who see in State control a remedy
for every ill, and it is by these that the demand would be
led. Nor would they be satisfied with a quite excellent
suggestion already made, that the University Grants
Committee should become a committee of the Privy
Council and be supported by subsidiary committees to
advise on the various departments of university activity.[2]
'Direct control' would be the cry. And it would only swell
in volume when met with pleas like Dr Priestley's that 'if
the State is wise, having provided the tools, it will leave the
universities to get on with the job without dictation'.[3]

Direct control would presumably mean, for one thing,
regular inspection of organization, administration and
lectures by a new division of that service to which the
Norwood Committee proposed to give some such high-
sounding name as 'His Majesty's Educational Advisory
Service'. I cannot speak for the administrators, but I should
myself have not the slightest objection to discussing departmental organization with an Educational Adviser or to
giving him the run of my lecture-rooms. In fact, such an
innovation, if it were practicable, would probably do all
our teaching a world of good. It would keep professors and
senior lecturers up to scratch, for their lectures are never
criticized – to their faces – from one end of their career to
the other. It would strengthen one's hand in recommending
the dismissal of unsatisfactory probationary lecturers,
which one always rather hesitates to do at present just
because the recommendation has to be made on one's
own responsibility and 'there's always the chance that

1. Ibid.
2. For further discussion on this subject, see Simon, pp. 11–12.
3. *The Listener*, loc. cit.

he may improve'. It would perhaps do something towards
the establishment of a training course for young lecturers –
a reform which I have already advocated, and which,
despite critics who argue wishfully, is perfectly practicable.
It would have a salutary effect upon students, who would
think, as boys and girls at school always think, that it was
they, not their teachers, who were being inspected. And if
life appointments were abolished, as I think, for all save
the most proved and experienced teachers, they should be,
it is not only probationary lecturers who would be on
their mettle.

But *is* university inspection practicable? In any effective
sense, I very much doubt it. To take teaching alone, the
work of every year above the first is so highly specialized
that an inspector would be needed for almost every Department and more than one for a good many. This would
mean, in addition to district inspectors advising on administration, a very large number of peripatetic part-time
specialists each of whom would inspect the whole of the
universities in which his particular subject was taught. At
once a number of objections arise. Where are the specialists
who have the practical knowledge of teaching, save in the
universities themselves? If they were not in the universities, how would they use the rest of their time? – for the
small amount of work that many of them would have to
do would bring them very little remuneration. If they
were in the universities, how could one avoid the personal
clashes consequent upon the setting up of colleagues as
inspectors? And then what about the cost of this new
inspectorate? Would it not altogether exceed whatever
benefits it brought? Would not the money be very much
better spent on the tutorial system?

The farther we proceed along these lines, the more
objections we encounter. And when we come to consider
the inspection of research, the proposal breaks down altogether. For on most research projects there are only a handful of people who are competent to speak at all, and only
one or two, here and there, who can speak with real

authority. The idea of a university branch of the inspectorate may therefore be dismissed altogether.

A more practicable, if less desirable, form of control is State representation on the Council. Provided the representatives chosen are in close touch with university affairs I can see no inherent disadvantage in this whatsoever, and a great deal of benefit. The difficulties arise when we come down to details. Returning to our Council of thirty-two, we find that five members are nominated annually by the local authorities which make contributions to the University funds, but that the total annual amount of their contribution is less than one-fifth of even the pre-war Treasury grant. Assuming a comparative representation, then, proportionate to contributions, the five local authorities would only have one member between them, whereas the State would have five representatives to itself. This would no doubt cause regional heart-searchings and possibly open strife, yet, on the other hand, once the principle of State representation on the Council was conceded there would be no peace until it was commensurate with the proportion of State aid. For myself, provided the Council is predominantly composed of the University's graduates and teachers, I should be content to let the other interests fight out their representation: twenty-four graduates and teachers, six State nominees and two local authority nominees would be a reasonable compromise, both the University and the State being represented on the Finance Committee. The danger, of course, lies in a gradual encroachment by the State: it would be as disastrous to have a Council controlled by bureaucrats and politicians as by directors of commercial houses and indifferent or half-educated aldermen. Once more, the *status quo*, even if as anomalous and illogical as many other British institutions, seems on the whole preferable to any innovation that can be envisaged at the present time.

Until we discover what are to be the shape and the extent of future State aid it is perhaps difficult to carry either speculation or suggestion any farther. Unless public opinion changes in a way that there is no reason to expect, there is little risk of what would be a major disaster – the transformation of the universities into State institutions and of their teachers into Civil Servants. The only possible reply to that move would be the foundation of new and independent societies which would have to fight Redbrick's early battles all over again.

But lesser disasters are not inconceivable. What is there, for example, to prevent future appointments to the University Grants Committee 'being confined to persons politically acceptable to the Government of the day? What is to restrain a future Committee from putting irresistible financial pressure on the Universities to adopt particular policies? In the allocations of grants to particular Universities, what is to restrain members of the Committee from favouring unduly those Universities with which they have most intimate personal connection? On the other hand, what is to prevent particular Universities, secure in the enjoyment of their block grants, from going their own way regardless of any national policy and of any sort of co-ordination? The answer to these questions is that there is no legal safeguard, but none is needed. The real safeguard lies in a very strong convention and tradition and in the determination of all concerned to make the system work.'[1]

These are pointed questions, asked and answered by the President of the Committee himself. I share the implied optimism of his answer. The very slight extent to which benefactors have been able in the past to interfere with university policy emboldens me to believe, with the British Association Committee, that 'the universities will be strong enough to resist any harmful requirements which the Government might be tempted to couple with substantial increases in State grants'.[2] The growing authority of the University Grants Committee ('moral rather than official, since it resembles that of the scholar and scientist rather than of Government')[3] convinces me that no further control is likely to be needed. But the British Association

1. Moberly, loc. cit., p. 8.   2. B.A.C., p. 43.   3. Moberly, loc. cit., p. 8.

Committee adds a caution which I should also endorse: 'While the universities safeguard their autonomy, they must get over their fear of government influence in university affairs.' We must be prepared for changes – and not only for the changes that we desire. If we proclaim aloud, as many of us are doing, that the new era brings with it new needs and new responsibilities for the nation, we must not forget that it also involves new obligations for ourselves. And chief among these is the obligation to examine any question afresh in the light of changed conditions – even principles which we had considered axiomatic and privileges to which we were so accustomed that we had come to claim them for ourselves as rights.

CHAPTER THREE

Problems of the Future

BESIDES the problems with which Redbrick is already at grips and others which she is preparing to attack in the immediate future, there are many that will have to be left until these are disposed of or that will be created by conditions not yet in existence. Some of them are concerned with regional activities, which seem of sufficient importance to justify treatment in a separate chapter. Others may be dealt with here.

I

The problem of inter-university co-ordination seems as yet hardly to have occurred to the Universities, so ready are we always as a nation to leave things to chance while we can rub along as we are. I often reflect what a magnificent thing would be made of university education by that eminently co-operative nation, the United States, had it both our deeply rooted traditions, which dollars unfortunately will not buy, and also a territory as small as Great Britain, where the Universities, by comparison with its own, are almost at one another's doors. No-one wants the organization of the British Universities to be uniform, or their curricula identical, but there is room for a higher degree of uniformity than we have at present, and in addition for close and valuable co-operation in matters where it is advisable, or inevitable, that there should be divergence.

To some of the anomalies arising from our uncooperative spirit I have already drawn attention. An attempt should be made to standardize degrees, especially the misleading degree of M.A. Critics have said that this could not be accomplished without coercion from above, so deeply engrained is academic individualism. But I believe that, with a little good will and a strong infusion of the co-operative spirit, the obstacles to it should not be insuperable. There ought to be no great objection, for example, to making the M.A. either the first degree in Arts or a degree taken automatically (or at least without examination or thesis) at any time after two years from graduation, and to instituting a B.Litt. or an M.Litt. as the first Arts research degree everywhere. To make the doctorates of different universities more nearly equal in merit (nobody wants them to be exactly the same, but some of the present inequalities are ludicrous) would be a harder and a more delicate matter, but it might at least be attempted. Graduates reading for a research degree should be able to migrate freely for part or the whole of their course, going where they can get the best facilities and the most expert direction. Professors and lecturers should 'exchange pulpits' for short periods, so that other universities than a man's own might have the benefit of his specialized knowledge. Scholars coming here from abroad should as a matter of course register their impending visits with a central academic agency, which would then notify all the universities in the country: at present a distinguished man of letters or science may come and go before one hears of it. Co-operation between university libraries, already in existence, should be extended. Universities with special problems of any kind, or with special developments in view, should communicate them to the rest. These are only examples set down at random: the number of opportunities is legion; the use we make of them only too small.

Then we should all combine to enter into closer relations with the universities of other countries. Here good pioneer work has been done by the British Association Committee, which would like to see a World Council of Universities, and also, 'as one of the organs of any post-war Society of States (or other international authority) an International Education Organization representative of teachers (including university teachers), governing bodies, local education

authorities, and governments. This body should make inquiries, offer suggestions, issue reports, encourage experiments and give, where needed, grants in aid of education
in its international aspects.'[1] This idea, says the Committee,
has already taken root. Not only has the State Department
at Washington shown interest in it, but 'a Conference of
the Ministers of Education of the Allied Governments and
of the French National Committee is now meeting regularly
in London under the chairmanship of the President of the
Board of Education'[2] – a 'living nucleus' out of which the
post-war organization ought to grow. In April 1944, in
fact, this conference 'accepted the tentative draft constitution for a United Nations Organization for Educational and
Cultural Reconstruction', to be open 'to all the United and
Associated Nations and to such other nations as shall be
accepted by the assembly of the organization after the war.
The Conference decided to forward the draft constitution
to the Allied and Associated Governments.'[3]

Such a body will study, in greater detail than has been
done heretofore, such fundamental questions as the best
auxiliary language for international communication, mutual recognition of university qualifications, international
student exchange, the entry of British students into foreign
universities and reciprocity between professors and lecturers
of different countries.

Though on the practical side many of the details of this
scheme remain to be worked out, it is undoubtedly based
upon broad and worthy conceptions and embodies a vision
which we must not lose. Yet before we British can co-operate
efficiently with other countries we must learn to do so
among ourselves. During the latter part of the 1939 War
a body was created with the somewhat cumbrous title of the
Association of University Professors and Lecturers of the
Allied Countries in Great Britain. At one of its early meetings a Belgian professor referred to the 'insularity' of the
British Universities, which before the War made it very
difficult to create contacts with them. 'Whenever we wished

1. B.A.C., p. 44.   2. Ibid.   3. Ibid.

to establish relations with the British Universities,' he declared, 'we were obliged to approach each one separately.'[1] It would be a curious anomaly to have an association coordinating, in so far as this is possible, the Universities in the leading countries of the world and yet no means of coordination among our own. It is stranger still that the excellent work done by the Universities' Bureau of the British Empire should not have pointed the way to a Universities' Bureau of Great Britain.

Apart from the University Grants Committee, which, though chiefly concerned with finance, issues a valuable quinquennial report going into many academic problems by no means wholly financial, the only co-ordinating body in existence is the Committee of Vice-Chancellors and Principals. This body, whose composition is strictly that indicated by its title, meets informally from time to time and its members communicate to their Senates such particulars of its proceedings as they may think proper. Only to this extent has the world, outside the limited circle of Vice-Chancellors and Principals, any knowledge of its proceedings. 'It is understood,' says Lord Simon, 'that the Vice-Chancellors' Committee does not normally attempt to consider long-range university problems.'[2] It issues no reports, possesses no secretarial staff and no income and cannot of course commit the Universities which it represents in any way whatever. None the less, it is, by reason of its very composition, a body of great weight, and during the War it 'has come to be recognized by the Government Departments as the normal channel for dealing with the universities as a whole on administrative questions'.[3]

If the money to be spent, and the progress to be made, in the future now dawning is to be for the greatest good of the greatest number, a much more intimate and detailed co-operation between the Universities is essential. The A.U.T. Report proposes the creation of an 'Academic Council', 'large and representative enough to be competent to

1. *Communication*, No. 3, 15 May 1944.   2. Simon, p. 8.
3. Simon, p. 8.

discuss the work of the universities from all sides, and empowered to send recommendations to the University Grants Committee. It should include a certain number of members of the academic staffs elected from each University.'[1] The British Association supports a similar recommendation, made by the Parliamentary and Scientific Committee,[2] that a Universities' Advisory Council, entirely free from government control, should be set up by the Universities 'to consider the whole range of university policy and to effect co-ordination and eliminate any unnecessary or wasteful overlapping'. It would include 'the Vice-Chancellors of the universities and the Principals of the university colleges, teachers of various grades in the universities and persons of distinction in other walks of life, e.g. industry, agriculture, medicine, education and government services'.[3] Such a Council, it would seem, could not fail to be extremely large; it is hard to elect two or three 'persons of distinction' without thinking of a dozen more with even better claims. I would rather see the present Vice-Chancellors' Committee enlarged by the addition of one member from each University elected by its Senate: the Pro-Vice-Chancellor or a senior Professor or a senior Dean would be the obvious kind of choice. This Committee, or Council, would meet at regular intervals, with power to make recommendations either to the Universities or to the Grants Committee or to any Government Department.[4]

To the committees of this body, which would be small but numerous – Finance, Research, Students' problems, Foreign relations, University extension, and so on – professors

1. A.U.T., May 1944, par. 76, p. 62.

2. An unofficial group of members of both Houses of Parliament and representatives of certain scientific and technical institutions which has recently published a report on 'Scientific Research and the Universities in Post-War Britain.'

3. B.A.C., p. 43.

4. Both the British Association Committee (op. cit., p. 43) and Lord Simon (p. 12) suggest that the Grants Committee might later function as a Committee of the Privy Council, the Lord President speaking for it in Parliament.

or lecturers should be freely co-opted, the aim being to get together, on any one subject, the half-dozen people most competent to deal with it in the country. There is to-day in a certain university one man of outstanding experience on the subject of adult education; there is another who has had extraordinary success in organizing staff-student contacts; a third has spent many years in the universities of Canada and South Africa; a fourth has an unusually good business head and in his own Senate and Council is on every Finance Committee. Yet, unless they happen to be active for a time in the Association of University Teachers, not one of these ever has the opportunity to use his natural gifts of special knowledge or long experience *in the service of university education as a whole.* That is where we are at fault. Anyone would suppose that universities were, not colleagues, but rivals. We must get it into our heads that what matters primarily is not the interest of any one of us but the interest of the whole. And until we are working among ourselves on that basis we cannot expect to get far in co-operation with other countries.

II

We have said a good deal about the freedom of the university from the tyranny of bureaucracy or party politics; we now come to a no less important subject – the freedom of the academic individual from a possible tyranny on the part of the university.

The worst forms of enslavement, if we preserve for our society a reasonable degree of autonomy, are never likely to come to us. We are in no danger of being made to conform to religious tests; of being forbidden to make known our political opinions; of being arrested for having opposed the Government of the day; of being dismissed from our posts for having proclaimed liberal views. Such things happen continually in certain countries less favoured than our own; but if occasionally anything of the kind has happened here the case has been an extreme one on which opinions have been divided. And in these respects our freedom is likely to increase rather than not. The freedom now to be alluded to is on a lower level, but none the less it is one that we should do all in our power to preserve.

Both at Oxbridge and at Redbrick, the academic person, who for convenience may be described in this section as the professor, has enjoyed professional liberty of a very high order. At Oxbridge, because his statutory duties have always been extremely light: one can give thirty, or even sixty, lectures in two and a half eight-week terms and yet have considerable leisure for branching out in other directions. At Redbrick, because although teaching and administration have generally been heavier that at Oxbridge, the University would never have established itself within its special community had not the professor been allowed, enabled and encouraged to go about its constituency and make as many contacts as he could. So, wherever he may be, he is free to interpret his duties as he likes. He may be primarily a research worker – an old-style professor, who sees little of the world outside his study: if so, no one will attempt to induce him to change his habits. He may be by temperament an administrator: in that case, without contravening the terms of his appointment, he can devote comparatively little of his time to teaching and research. He may believe that the best service he can render to the subject he professes is to survey and supervise its teaching in schools and thus strengthen the links between school and university: if he does, he can examine for the School and Higher Certificates, be an Occasional Inspector under the Ministry of Education, develop contacts with local Education Committees, sit on the Governing Bodies of local schools and visit as many schools in his own locality, or outside it, as may invite him. He may feel that his subject is studied too insularly and spend his spare term-time in corresponding with foreign universities and his vacations in visiting them. These are only a few of the prospects which open before a professor in a British university on his appointment. He is free, and provided he neglects neither his research nor his teaching he ought to be free, to mark out for himself the particular sphere of service in which he feels he can labour to the best advantage. Some of Redbrick's most distinguished early professors, the men who have been instrumental in carrying it to a level which fifty years ago no one would even have imagined, have struck out for themselves in most original and unconventional ways, as they could not have done had the University not shown itself to be wisely liberal. In passing, their activities have not been without influence upon Oxbridge.

Of recent years, however, there has been a tendency, showing itself in various directions, for the newer universities to define and delimit the activities of their staffs in a way which may in time become harmful and even dangerous. I am not referring to research and teaching: these must take precedence of everything else, and if a professor does nothing to add to knowledge or neglects to conduct or provide for the lectures and classes prescribed by his Faculty Board and by the Senate, it is the clear duty of the Senate to bring him to book. What I have in mind is the large margin of leisure which every professor has when he has complied with the minimum requirements of research and teaching and which he can fill either by doing more research and teaching or in such other ways as those just described. In the staff of any Faculty there is a tremendous amount of potential energy, often highly imaginative and constructive in character, which can and should be used for the benefit of the Faculty, of the University and of education and learning as a whole. Sometimes the maximum of good will be done if the energy of a particular professor is used in the service of the Faculty; often, however, his parish is the world and his vocation is such a wide one that the Faculty, and even the University, will profit by it only to a secondary degree, the primary beneficiary being Secondary or Adult education, or the country as a whole, or some part of the learned world, or even posterity.

It has been the glory of our universities that they have allowed those of their teachers who feel called to use their leisure in one of these ways to do so freely; and not the least attractive feature of academic life, which to many people more than compensates for its material shortcomings, is precisely this freedom. But there are signs that a change is coming which, wherever it puts in an appearance, academic persons must resist with all their strength. In one University, let us say, there is a Council whose lay members feel that 'these professors have altogether too much holiday', so they endeavour to lengthen terms or to impose hours of attendance in the University buildings. They are defeated, of course, but they will return to the charge till they score an initial victory, as, unless we are vigilant, they sooner or later may. Or here is a Vice-Chancellor, coming to his post, in middle life, from some other sphere, with little experience of university administration, who sees professors as civil servants and tries to work upon his Senate and Council to treat them as such.

The other day, a promising young lecturer was attracted by the advertisement of a Chair then vacant in a modern University, wrote for particulars of it, and was shocked to receive a leaflet which referred him to a regulation in the University Calendar limiting the freedom of full-time professors as follows:

A Professor shall devote himself to the work of the University and shall not undertake any continuous teaching or continuous professional engagement during the Session outside the University without the special consent of the Council; and if he accepts an external examinership or other office involving temporary absence from University work, he shall send the earliest possible intimation thereof in writing to the Vice-Chancellor.

Such a regulation, in his view (and in mine), is gravely reactionary. To begin with, a professor should devote himself primarily to the cause of scholarship, and only secondarily to the particular University which he serves, since that University is itself the servant of scholarship. And only he, or someone closely associated with, and expert in, his particular field of study, can judge if he is doing so. No other person can act as the keeper of his conscience – not even an academic person, and certainly not a heterogeneous body composed largely of business men and representatives of City Councils.

That opening clause of the regulation is bad enough, but the next clause, which translates principle into practice, is worse. Let us take an imaginary example or two to see how it would work.

Fifty miles from Redbrick there is one of the new County Colleges, which, under an unconventional and energetic principal, has won extraordinary success and is anxious to get Professor Active to give a sessional course of lectures within his special field of International Relations, promising him a crowded house and a substantial number of weekly essays to reward his labours. Professor Active has no mind for twenty-five journeys of fifty miles each way and he foresees that acceptance will take a great deal of his time and energy and probably entail his dropping some other piece of work which is more directly concerned with the University, though it can be done equally well by one of his staff. On the other hand, he knows of no one else as easily accessible who can give this course, he recognizes in the County College a vital centre of intellectual life, and, weighing the matter with much care, he decides to accept.

In a liberal society that would settle the matter, but at Redbrick University it has now to be brought before the Council. (Not, it will be observed, before the Senate.) At the next meeting of this body Professor Active's academic colleagues support him and on everybody's lips is forming the word 'Agreed' when up rises an ungrammatical Alderman, who has been a disease on the Council for the past two years, but, being a political light in the city, can always be relied upon to rally a few supporters. The Alderman draws attention to the number of applications this particular professor has of late been making. Does he belong to the University or does he not? Here he is, gadding about all over the country – and abroad, in fact: how long is it since he got that leave of absence to lecture in South Africa? – instead of going about his duties and teaching in his own

classroom. What did we appoint him for? Are we paying
Redbrick professors to spend all their time out of the city?
The Alderman moves that the permission be not granted,
and further suggests that the Vice-Chancellor drop a hint
to Professor Active that these continued applications are
causing the Council displeasure.

A discussion follows. The Council has only five academic
members against twenty-four laymen, including six nominees of municipalities. The voting is fifteen to six, the remainder abstaining; Professor Active is refused his permission; and the Vice-Chancellor duly has a few words with
him, though not perhaps precisely on lines which would
have been approved by the obstructive Alderman.

An illustration of another kind brings the narrow and the
liberal viewpoints into even more obvious conflict. Let us
suppose that something has happened which fortunately is
never likely to happen – that the energetic and deservedly
prosperous English Association has fallen on evil days and
its branches are dying out everywhere. The Council of the
Association, meeting to discuss the position, decides that
there is only one remedy: it must persuade some man of
ability, personality and enthusiasm to give as much of his
time as he can for a couple of years to travelling about the
country, resuscitating old branches, founding new ones,
addressing meetings in the universities, keeping in touch
with local correspondents – and all this without remuneration other than a small allowance for secretarial help and
out-of-pocket expenses. Except for idealistic motives the
proposition is not an alluring one and the choice of a suitable person is a serious problem. Only a man of standing
has any chance of success – and men of standing are seldom
willing to take service with moribund associations as unpaid
publicity agents. Eventually the Council decides to aim
high and risk a rebuff. The best man the meeting can think
of is Professor Livewire, who holds the Chair of English
Literature at Redbrick, and to him a delegation accordingly
goes. At first he turns down the suggestion on the spot. Redbrick is not far from London, and yet is on main lines to

the north, so that he is well placed for travelling facilities. But the Fridays and Saturdays which, with an occasional Monday morning, are the only days he could give the Association, are just the days he needs for his forthcoming edition of Dekker, which has been on the stocks for many years and is approaching completion. Then the delegation puts the matter to him again as one of extreme gravity and urgency, affecting the study of English, not merely at Redbrick and other universities, but in schools and other institutions throughout the country and even in the Dominions and the Colonies. He is the only man they can think of who combines prestige with enthusiasm and scholarship with the power of popular appeal. Will he not come?

Professor Livewire asks for further time to consider the proposal, and eventually decides – with some regret, it must be admitted – that he will be fulfilling his vocation better by devoting those two and a half days a week to the English Association than to his own research. So he accepts the invitation for an initial period of twelve months.

And then he has to ask permission from the University Council. I do not know if the irrepressible Alderman grows vocal again and I do not greatly care. What I am protesting against is the parochialism which defines service to a university as work done within its precincts or within the normal sphere of its extra-mural activities and the illiberal and illogical system which elects a man to a position of trust and then refuses to trust him. Professor Livewire was presumably appointed to do three things – research, teaching and organization in his special subject. Very well: by all means let the University see that he does them. If, at the end of any session, or term of years, it is found that he has failed to do them, let him state his case, and, should he be adjudged guilty of dereliction, let him be warned, reprimanded or even dismissed. But at least give him freedom of judgement over whatever the period is for which he is appointed, and, if he is to be appointed for life, let him be trusted for life.

Perhaps it will be said that such permissions as have been specified are in fact always given and that such clauses as that in the calendar referred to are intended only to restrain professors from becoming company directors, or from holding two posts at once in different universities. That may be the custom at the present day, but there is a very serious risk that it may not continue. In any case, the principle is as abhorrent as the further regulation about external examinerships is futile. If 'temporary absence from University work' has to be notified to the Vice-Chancellor, what about the professor whose week-ends in his country cottage last from Thursday to Tuesday, the professor who attends the university throughout the session in the afternoons only, and the professor whose only research is done in his garden?

There is another direction in which a cloud like a man's hand is appearing, to be a future menace to academic freedom, and that is in the attempts being made in some quarters to interfere with Heads of Departments.

The Senate has, of course, a perfect right to give as much or as little liberty to these Heads as it thinks advisable, just as a County Education Committee is justified, from a legal standpoint, in exercising strict control over the headmasters and headmistresses of its Secondary schools. But in both cases the wisest policy is to give as much latitude to your Head as you can. It is true that in the university, where the Heads are in closer touch with each other than in the schools of a district, a greater uniformity is necessary, but if all proper care is exercised in making appointments the proportion of capable Heads should be higher, the fields being smaller, the contacts of professors and lecturers being closer than that of headmasters and their staffs, and detailed, confidential information from expert advisers much easier to obtain.

The development which threatens to endanger the freedom of departmental Heads, and to hamper their activity, is the rapidly growing tendency to multiply the number of committees. To some extent this is due to the universities' growth in size, for a Senate of twenty can debate in a way that a Senate of sixty cannot. But it is attributable much more frequently to the increasing tendency to trust a committee of five more than a single professor and to the growing belief that the single professor is likely to be prejudiced, whereas a committee cannot be.

There are many questions, needless to say, which can best be settled by committees – questions, for example, in which several interests are involved, varied information has to be sought and diverse points of view have to be reconciled. But it is hardly too much to say that if a question *can* be decided by an individual, it *should* be. For an individual has normally a much greater sense of responsibility than a committee: everybody knows how, when each member is undecided on some matter, one prominent personality, anxious to get off to another engagement, says: 'Well, I propose so-and-so' and all the rest (subconsciously remarking 'Well, if he thinks so, it's probably all right') fall into line without demur. Now, if that is so in business of a general character, how much more so is it in business that affects one particular Department! Take such a matter as a junior appointment on the staff, a modification of the scheme of lectures or a change in the regulations of the Faculty which chiefly affects a single Department. If the departmental Head can be reasonably confident that, provided he has first talked it over with the Dean, any recommendation that he may make will be passed by the Faculty Board and the Senate without discussion, he feels the maximum of responsibility, and, if he is efficient and conscientious, he will go to any pains to ensure that his decision will be the best one. But if the same decision is left to a committee of five – and many such needless committees, alas, are far larger than that – the result is very different. Sometimes the Head, having very definite views about the matter, makes a strong recommendation to the Committee, which, as none of its members has any special knowledge of the subject, it is not rash enough to reject. In that case, precisely the same result is reached as if there had been no committee at all, at the additional cost of the waste of some hours of several people's time. Sometimes a similar recommendation is made, and, either because its members think they know better than the expert or because there are general considerations which seem to them to override the expert's special considerations, is rejected. In that case there is a chance that the decision may be a better one, though it is also probable that the Dean would have persuaded the expert of this when they discussed it together. But, assuming that the Head is unconvinced of it, his defeat engenders in him a feeling of frustration, which leaves its mark, even if it eventually disappears, and which grows to an alarming extent if the committee's decision proves to have been mistaken. And so we come to the worst of the possible results of this over-confidence in committees. After a Head has been defeated in a number of departmental issues, whether through the obstructiveness of committees or through the unfortunate chance that several such may have happened, for different reasons, to disagree with him, his sense of frustration becomes permanent, and either he leaves the University for another in which conditions are better or he remains and gives up the attempt to develop his Department any further. Possibly he may still do good work, devoting his leisure to research, or Extension work, or contact with the schools. But the University has lost something which no committee can ever give it – the imagination, energy and enthusiasm of a specialist. In a minority of instances, of course, the departmental Head may himself be incompetent, pernickety or prejudiced, and the Committee has then saved the Department from too steep a decline and held it in a state of moderate efficiency until he can be got rid of. But experience and inquiry would suggest that this is very seldom the case. Departmental Heads are generally chosen with great care; and when, as infrequently happens, they prove incompetent, their incompetence is still more infrequently accompanied by such energy and conscientiousness as has been described: it usually grows out of the demoralization produced by having a secure position until the attainment of whatever age is fixed for compulsory retirement.

I would plead, then, with great earnestness, that all academic persons, and in particular all departmental Heads, be appointed only after the most careful inquiry, and, once chosen, be treated like persons in positions of trust, and given as much freedom as possible. The risk of their making an occasionally faulty decision, which, in such matters as the appointment of a probationary lecturer or the modification of a syllabus, is not irreparable, is far less harmful than the much greater risk of blunting the keen edge of an imaginative mind and an energetic disposition, which, in a Department under a comparatively young man, may not be rectifiable for a quarter of a century. Besides which, there is no more soul-killing or time-wasting experience than the setting up of unnecessarily numerous or unnecessarily large committees. And neither with time nor with living souls can Redbrick, facing its huge programme of development, afford to dispense. It has already too little of the first and too few of the second. It needs more of both.

III

If, in the first part of this book, I said nothing about Redbrick's treatment of women, the reason was certainly not indifference. The subject was never absent from my mind: it is one of the few, indeed, on which I hold really strong views. It was left out merely because there was not space to treat it at any length and it deserved more than passing consideration. This it shall have now.

The problem is confined to the staff. Undergraduates, whether men or women, are treated with perfect equity. Women attend the same lectures as men, have their own Common Rooms at the Union, elect their own officers (there are normally two Presidents yearly, one of either sex), queue with men for meals, debate with them and dance with them to their hearts' content. It is only when a woman becomes a lecturer that she begins to wonder if she is really wanted.

One amenity, it is true, she does enjoy, and it is a substantial one: Redbrick gives equal pay to men and women for equal work. Let us hope that it may soon be nobody's amenity, but everybody's right. If two men do the same piece of work, for the same party, and do it with equal efficiency, no one would dream of refusing them equal payment. There is therefore no *moral* justification for denying it to a woman and a man. If the woman works for seven hours a day and the man for eight, or if the woman demonstrably achieves less than a man in the same period of time, the case is different. But for the headmaster of a school of 450 boys to be paid £850 a year and the headmistress of the girls' school of 450 to be paid £700 is ridiculous. Equally so would it be if Redbrick advertised a History lectureship at £400 for a man or £350 for a woman. Fortunately Redbrick does not.

None of the arguments used by the defenders of this inequality will hold water. There is no shadow of evidence for the theory that women work less, or achieve less, in education than men. The average schoolmistress works quite as hard, and gets quite as good results, as the average schoolmaster. The girls at a County School are as well turned out, in every respect, as the boys at the neighbouring Grammar School. The headmaster may be more of a public figure in the town than the headmistress, but the headmistress, as a rule, devotes more time to the details of school organization, and I would risk any money on her being at least equally efficient.

Another and a very unworthy argument used against equal pay for equal work is that women should be paid less because they can live on less. If they can live on less, it is only because they have learned to make and repair their own clothes, cook their own meals and do much of their own housework when their day's teaching is over and their men colleagues are sitting at ease with the newspaper before the fire. But both man and woman have twenty-four hours to the day; and if the woman chooses to spend her leisure in saving money, the man is perfectly free to spend his in earning money. To penalize a woman for her own thriftiness is hardly justice.

A more specious argument is that men have to keep families on their pay – or at least should be enabled to do so if they have any – whereas women do not. Disregarding, for the sake of brevity, a whole group of exceptions to this generalization which have sprung up during the past difficult years, we have first to observe that, if there were any force in the argument, there should be a graded rate of pay for men, according to the size of their families, another graded rate for women with dependants, a lower rate for bachelors without dependants and a lower rate still for spinsters. If work is to be fairly remunerated on a basis of the worker's circumstances, an even more complicated scheme than this would be necessary; but it would seem very much fairer to give equal pay for the same work and to compensate workers with dependants by means of income-tax relief and of family allowances substantial enough to solve the problem of child maintenance.

The only reason for the perpetuation of this inequality which has any general relevance is the economic one. In commerce and industry there are fewer openings for women, who are therefore in greater supply than men, and this fact operates in a natural way to lower their wages. If all employers have to pay women at the same rate as men, it is said, they will (for several fairly obvious reasons, such as the higher sickness rate in women) prefer men, and women will be worse off than at present. If the rates are equalized in some types of employment and not in others, men will tend to prefer the latter to the former. In either case, we are told, there will be a social dislocation consequent upon the disregarding of an economic law.

These considerations might well apply to universities, in which men and women are competing all the time for the same jobs. No one, so far as I know, has observed that men tend to leave university work, where women and men are paid equally, for school work, where they are not: perhaps that is because university work is in other respects more desirable. But my point is that these economic arguments are not, except quite directly, applicable to the schools, for in the large majority of cases men alone teach in boys' schools and women alone in girls' schools. One might expect that, under present conditions, the boys' schools would be full of women – but other than economic considerations prevail in education. For that reason there need be no fear that if the rates are equalized, as it is to be hoped that in time they will be, men would leave teaching for other occupations where women are paid proportionately less. Teaching is still, to a great extent, a vocation, and those to whom it is not remain in it because of various non-financial advantages which it has over other occupations. And, quite apart from all this, ought not the remuneration of a profession so often entered for high moral and idealistic motives to be governed by standards of equity and justice rather than by economic laws which treat it as an occupation on a level with industry and commerce? For my own part, I think it should, and I am glad that in this respect Redbrick has led the way.

But, although the woman leaving school work for a university has certainly the advantage of no longer being paid at a lower rate than her male colleague, she encounters other disabilities which she had not previously known.

Most modern universities, having very few women on their staffs, make quite inadequate provision for their accommodation and comfort. In one, there is no women's Common Room, and women are excluded from the Men's Common Room on the ostensible ground that there is no room for them. In another, a woman departmental Head has to share a private room with her staff, whereas every male Head has a room to himself. Another gives no women private rooms, but only a single Common Room, so that they can never interview students privately. Still another has one single cloak-room for the women of several

Faculties. There can be few modern universities, if there are any, in which the women lecturers have not some grievance of this type.

Until recently, again, some of the modern universities made the position of married women extremely difficult: unless they resigned on marriage they risked being asked to do so in a not distant future. Since university work is less physically exhausting than school work, there was always a case for the more generous treatment of married women here. Now that the principle of retaining them in schools seems likely to be established – principally because of the prospective dearth of teachers – for some time to come, little more need be said about this here, but it is perhaps a suitable point at which to draw attention to the wise and enlightened treatment of the question of resignation on marriage to be found in paragraphs 89 to 95 of the McNair Report, to which it may yet be necessary some day to call the attention of the Redbrick Council. The Report stigmatizes the requirement, where it exists, that women teachers shall resign on marriage, as tending to stamp the profession as one for celibates.

This deters young women, most of whom naturally look forward to marriage, from spending the time and money required to prepare themselves for teaching. They seek other occupations, though many of them may be gifted as potential teachers. In short, the marriage bar depresses recruitment.

Quite apart from the question of supply, it continues, there are good reasons for having married women in schools. Children of all ages 'benefit from the care and training of teachers with experience of home responsibilities, including the experience of marriage and, perhaps, the care of children of their own. The influence of a wise married woman on adolescent boys and girls and on her colleagues, both men and women, is an advantage which the schools ought not to have to forgo.' The Committee ends by recommending that teachers in grant-aided schools be not required to resign solely on the ground of marriage and that arrangements be made by which married women who wish to do so may return to school work after long absences.

A graver disability than either of the two foregoing still awaits women who enter upon university work – namely, their meagre prospects of promotion. The position is that practically all Chairs in Great Britain, except a few in modern languages (e.g. at London, Birmingham and Manchester) are held by men, and, so far as my information and experience go, it is unusual for any woman to be considered for a Chair by a selection committee, with the natural result that very few will apply for one.[1] Nor is it much more usual for a woman to be appointed to a Grade I lectureship or to the Headship of a Department. Yet, where a woman is second-in-command, and her chief resigns, no hesitation is shown in appointing her, for however long a period, as *chargée d'affaires*, nor is there often any evidence that she fulfils this trust any less ably than a man. Once a new Head is appointed, she fades out of the picture and as a rule returns to her subordinate position, often without any improvement in salary or status. It never occurs to anybody that she might have been the new Head herself. A man, under such conditions, would very probably, and properly, go elsewhere, but a woman cannot, so slender is her chance of getting one of the few minor posts available to her.

One hesitates then, before recommending a woman, however brilliant (and in the Arts faculties of modern universities the best students are generally women), to embrace a university career.

'What are my prospects?' inquires a First Class woman graduand after beating all the men of her year.

'Well,' one replies, 'you *may* get a post; though, other things being equal, a man will probably be preferred to you. If you do get one, you will have about £8 per week, with microscopical increments, and, at the end of five or six years (assuming that you keep your post) you will have reached about £10 per week. By the time you are forty, you

1. Several more women have been appointed to Chairs since these lines were written, but opinion is changing only very slowly.

should be earning £800 a year, but it is most unlikely that you will go farther. There is little chance of your moving from one university to another or of your ever becoming a departmental Head. So, if you have any material ambitions, apply for some other sort of job: women are better elsewhere unless they have private means, love the work for the work's sake alone or intend to seek an early escape in marriage.'

Now why should women be penalized in this way? Not because they are unpleasant or undesirable colleagues: everyone with experience of a mixed Common Room knows how much the women contribute to it – and besides, any university could afford the luxury of two Common Rooms if it so wished. Not because they fail in research: most learned reviews in the Humanities will have a greater number of women contributors than of men in proportion to the numbers of each working in universities. No: the reason seems to be a prejudice against women, partly as being unsuited to teach men and partly as lacking talent for organization.

As far as organization goes, one might hesitate to make a woman managing director of a large business house: women have not the tradition of big business behind them. In the United States the same view is sometimes taken as regards academic organization and men are not infrequently appointed as presidents of large women's colleges. But in our own country, where for a century women of unusual gifts have ruled, not only colleges, but large girls' schools, and made them famous, it is hardly logical to close to them the headships of university Departments in very few of which there is as much organization as in one small Secondary school. As to teaching, few would recommend that boys of between eleven and sixteen should be taught by women, for when the immature mental processes of the child begin to develop they are best understood by a man, and as the boy is influenced by predominantly masculine ideals he needs men to look up to. Even so, there are many co-educational schools in which boys are taught by women, as well as men, throughout. But, after about the age of sixteen, and increasingly in late adolescent and adult life, the readiness with which a youth or a man learns from a man or from a woman has nothing to do with their sex. In both the last two Wars, the success of women with Sixth Forms in boys' schools was very marked. And, in the higher world of scholarship, the sexes are less differentiated than in any other.

It is disappointing, not only that women have been so poorly treated in universities, but that they have made no efforts to get themselves treated better. Even more than prejudice, it is thoughtlessness that has barred their way to promotion; for few university men would attach much importance to the arguments just put forward. A determined and unanimous series of attacks by the combined body of university women teachers would probably win a comparatively easy victory.

After World War I, women became enfranchised simply because the signal services they had rendered their country established their claim to equality with men in this respect more firmly than any number of speeches could do. There can be no university in which, during the recent War, women did not render services equally notable by stepping into responsible positions vacated by their male colleagues. Let them demand as their reward – and they will surely obtain it – that universities advertising posts in teaching or research shall henceforth state: 'Women are eligible for this post equally with men.' A new and more enlightened tradition than that of the past would not be long in building.

CHAPTER FOUR

The Leisured Professor at Bay

IF, out of a sense of its great importance, and the conviction that this has not been generally realized, I return now to the subject of Arts Faculty research and the professor, it is not with the intention of merely repeating what has been said above, and what I have written elsewhere. I wish rather to correct some misconceptions, to comment upon the discussion which has followed the breaking of the conspiracy of academic silence and to go into further detail regarding my suggested remedies for an abuse the existence of which seems to be generally admitted.

I

First of all must be reiterated the axiom that research – that is to say, the pursuit of knowledge, together with the obligations that this involves – is absolutely essential to the idea of a university, and that, if there is any conflict between research and teaching, research should come first. Since *Red Brick University* was written the British Association Committee has come out with a dictum that has a genuine ring all too seldom heard:

> Research ... is an essential part of the work of every university. ... Apart from research, university education of the right kind is impossible.[1]

It will not do to say, as the former Warden of All Souls says, that the 'central function' of a university is to provide a liberal education, and its 'main practical work' to 'train people for the various professions', putting the obligation 'to advance research and to increase the sum of knowledge' second.[2] It is perfectly true that 'research, which is the

---

1. B.A.C., p. 29.
2. 'The Modern Idea of a University'. In *Education Handbook*, Norwich, 1943, pp. 14–15.

highest form of specialization, should have the foundations
not only of a thorough scientific training in the field in
which the researcher is working, but also as a basis of
liberal culture which widens the mind and helps to relate
the piece of special research to kindred problems and wider
issues'.[1] But a liberal or a professional education, though
many pursue the one or the other for its own sake alone,
should always be, in the mind of the university, activities
at once subsidiary and complementary to the pursuit of
knowledge.

The general reaction to this position seems to have been
that of *The Times:* 'This is perhaps an extreme view, but all
opinion emphasizes the importance of research.'[2] Unfortunately, as far as Faculties of Arts are concerned,
opinion seems to 'admit', rather than to 'emphasize' it,
and little is done towards the translation of principle into
practice. But at least it is conceded that research is, and
must always be, one of the aims of a university, and many of
my readers, both in letters to me and in articles and reviews,
have been emboldened to come out on the side of scholarship with a decisiveness which must surely produce an
effect on Faculty Boards throughout the country. What is
more, many of them show a perfectly clear realization of,
and a deep shame at, the parlous state of Arts research
to-day. 'We feel that all university teachers and students
are deeply indebted to you for your outspoken words,'
wrote two lecturers with experience both of Oxbridge and of
Redbrick, 'recalling them to their true vocation. If they do
not return to it, productive scholarship will be entirely in
the hands of scholars who do not hold university appointments.' And reviewers, who necessarily write with caution,
have taken the same line:

Such is our plight now that one of the best things he [Truscot]
has said is that a university exists in order to seek truth and ensue
it. It might be thought beyond belief that this required to be said

1. Op. cit., p. 15.
2. 'Universities after the War.' In *The Times*, 3 April 1944.

about universities with a thousand years of liberal tradition behind them ... But we cannot be sure that this is so.[1]

Yet, satisfactory as this may be so far as it goes, it certainly does not go far enough. And, weighing these and other opinions expressed in reviews and articles, I am certain that too many of the writers are, perhaps unconsciously, obsessed by a narrow and unworthy idea of research, which somehow or other must be got rid of before we can make very much progress. Could we only abolish the word, it might help a good deal, but what are the alternatives? 'Investigation' sounds pompous; 'original work' might refer to novel-writing; 'higher study' (a word sometimes employed by universities in association with 'research') suggests absorption rather than dissemination. I have noticed that some of our most distinguished researchers in Arts subjects never use the word at all: they merely refer to their 'work' or their 'writing'. But unhappily the 'work' or 'writing' of so many other people would mean something so very different! No, the word, it is to be feared, has come to stay: all we can do is to try to marry it to some worthier ideal and so make an honest woman of it.

A few months since, I read in the late Dr T. R. Glover's *Cambridge Retrospect* a passage which admirably illustrates the harm which this unfortunate misconception can do:

> Long ago A. E. H. Love, who left St. John's to be professor at Oxford, made the criticism that Cambridge after all was devoting herself chiefly to the production of professors. The newer ideal for a professor was devotion to 'research', which is very well in scientific studies, but less obviously useful in literature. Broadly speaking, in literature the less a professor 'researches' in the modern sense of the term the more likely he is to understand what he is doing. Manuscripts and antecedents are of little help to the real understanding of literature.[2]

Now this passage can safely be cited because Dr Glover was an eminent researcher in a broad, yet entirely

1. D. G. James, 'New Notions about Universities.' In *The Universities Review*, November 1943, p. 10.

2. *Cambridge Retrospect*, Cambridge, 1943, pp. 110–11.

admissible acceptation of that word, whose work all scholars regard with admiration. He clearly takes the 'modern sense' as equivalent to factual research and the making of 'discoveries', and it is perfectly correct to say that too much stress has been laid upon by this comparison with re-interpretation, scholarly appreciation and creative criticism. Selection committees have often preferred a young man who has made some lucky 'discovery' to a maturer man and a more experienced teacher whose output has been honest and steady but has rather tended to the textual or the expository. Learned reviews have been known to reject very competent critical articles in favour of contributions by less mature and gifted writers which were supposed to contain something 'new' and thus to 'add to knowledge' (i.e., of facts). At the same time, it seems most unfortunate that so respected a scholar as Dr Glover should have thrown off this somewhat irresponsible paragraph, since any effect it may have can only be to diminish respect for research in the good sense as well as in the bad. Still more must one regret the implied approval of the word 'useful' as a desideratum for research work. If only one learned book in a hundred, and one learned article in a thousand, can be said to have added to the welfare or happiness of man (which I take it is what 'usefulness' means), there are few pieces of honest investigation which do not carve out one more step on the ladder leading somewhere. Even our old friend, the graduate's thesis on 'Jones in France',[1] will tell us something about Jones and something about France, and, if conscientiously done, it may save some less callow worker much routine labour and become a brick in the edifice which all will recognize as 'useful' – perhaps 'epoch-making' and 'alone of its kind'. And, quite apart from this, who can estimate the 'usefulness' of the most immature piece of factual investigation to the investigator himself? Research of any kind is a training in method. And one must learn to design a four-roomed house before attempting a cathedral.

1. See p. 148, above.

With Dr Glover's paragraph may be contrasted a few lines from the biography of another eminent Cambridge scholar, Sir J. J. Thomson – lines which will strike an echo in all who both value and practise research and train others in it:

The special value which he attached to research as a means of education was that it necessarily took the learner away from that reliance on teachers to which all set teaching was subject. A man who was attempting even the most modest piece of research had to find out what others had done on the same lines, and he had to find it out for himself in the largely uncharted country of original literature, instead of having it presented to him in a cut and dried form by a lecturer ... [He] maintained that he always saw the minds of those attempting research strengthen and mature under the process. It gave independence of view, self-reliance, initiative, and training in judgement: and the very disheartening phases through which a research worker generally goes before light begins to emerge was in itself a valuable training for the battle of life.[1]

It will be observed, of course, that this last passage, which, though written of Science, is equally applicable to Arts, refers, not to mature scholars, but to the young, while the preceding passage has to do with the research of 'professors'. This raises another point which seems not to be generally realized – that, in most Arts fields, factual research is a training-ground, or, for the maturer scholar, a subsidiary activity, rather than an end in itself.[2] It is not unusual, especially in fields which have been little cultivated, for some problem or problems of factual research to occupy a worker for many years: sometimes the discovery of one unknown or forgotten fact may lead to researches which last a lifetime. But more commonly, to adapt a metaphor attributed to A. L. Smith, the scholar 'digs into his work' the results of his early researches, and digs into his character, too, the virtues, the qualities and the habits which they have engendered in him, so that his later work bears flower and fruit to which he gives his name and which perhaps

1. Lord Rayleigh, *Sir J. J. Thomson*, Cambridge, 1942.
2. Cf. p. 145, above.

make him famous.[1] One can no more see the results of the early work in the later than one can see the manure in the prize sweet peas, but the one could never have existed without the other. I am old enough now to have past pupils who have done work of distinction, but only they and I are aware how much their fine creative, interpretative work, so highly praised in the learned reviews, owes to the raw articles rejected by those same reviews or tucked away in dark and forgotten corners of them, and the typewritten 'dissertations' which never saw the light of print, and never will.

Let me repeat, then, as emphatically as may be, that research is not, and never can be, limited to fact-grubbing. I have attempted above a comprehensive definition of the work which includes scholarly investigation, appreciation, creative and textual criticism, re-interpretation and a critical treatment of contemporary thought. It also takes in 'not only the pursuit of all these activities oneself, but the encouraging, stimulating and training of others to pursue them, and participation in the activities of bodies devoted to their furtherance'.[2] The A.U.T., in a Report on Research in the Faculty of Arts, makes an admirably liberal and comprehensive survey of the field from which there is space here only to extract brief quotations. It should be read and considered carefully and introspectively by every university teacher: little more would then be heard of the fallacy that research is 'useless'.

1. There is, first, the discovery of new 'facts'. This term ... could be applied to the discovery of new pieces of evidence, for instance an unpublished document or buried archaeological remains. It would also be used when, as a result of this or of the re-examination of evidence already known, the occurrence of a historical event is established, which had not hitherto been known ...

It is undoubtedly important that this sort of work should go on. Much of it is of value, and increased facilities for its publication are, in many directions, needed. But there are serious dangers in over-estimating this aspect of the work. It may easily lead to a

1. Cf. Stuart Hodgson, *Ramsay Muir*, London, 1943, p. 39.
3. Cf. p. 149, above.

false evaluation of facts, which attaches importance to them, not because they really contribute anything to the understanding of the subject, but just because they have been hitherto unknown or neglected ...

2. A much higher degree of originality is shown by the scholar who is able to re-interpret the facts already known, to throw new light on their connexions with each other, their relative import-ance, etc. ... The exact point at which this amounts to a real novelty which ought to be published to the world is a delicate question. It is impossible to over-estimate the value of such work at its best. But it cannot be supplied to order ...

3. An important part of the work of a university teacher should be to keep himself informed of the work that is being done in his subject by other scholars. This requires constant reading and also opportunities for meetings and discussions. Not the least of the benefits of this is the stimulus it provides for the continual re-examination of the existing evidence in order to estimate the value of the new suggestions. A lot of work of this kind can lead to pub-lication in the form of discussions in periodicals and also in the form of reviews of books. A full-scale review can be a real piece of original work, and should be valued accordingly ...

4. It is also desirable for the university teacher to devote some of his time to extending the range of his knowledge of his own sub-ject beyond the particular period or branch of it in which he specializes. This in itself is hardly likely to find expression in published work, but it will have an effect on the quality of his published work in his own specialism, and still more, perhaps, will be expressed in his teaching.

5. He will also find it worth while to acquire some knowledge of other subjects, which may have some bearing on his own, as ancillary to it or closely related to it. The results of this, again, will show themselves indirectly in his research and teaching in his own subject.

6. Finally, there is a suggestion that the university teacher in *some* subjects might regard it as part of his work to keep an eye on current controversies in the outside world to see where they impinge on his own special work.[1]

My only critical comment on this survey is that the six forms of activity which it specifies are of very diverse value. The first two belong to what might be termed 'primary'

1. A.U.T. (Research).

research, representing the scholar's main line of activity and also the normal direction of his progress. A few workers, for special reasons, are justified, as has been said, in confining themselves to factual research. A few others are able to devote their entire lives to criticism, though nearly every critic, at some time or other, discovers factual problems for which a solution has to be sought before he can go farther. But the majority, as they amass experience, graduate from the factual to the critical, or, while directing, or collaborating in, the factual research of their pupils, become predominantly critics themselves. The other four types of activity are both subsidiary and subservient to these and are normally carried on contemporaneously with them. They can also, to a large extent, be carried on in short periods of time during term – in the University Library on free evenings, in the Common Room, during railway journeys, in discussions with colleagues or pupils. Few teachers spend so much time on them, or produce such notable results in them, that they are justified in regarding activity in any or all as absolving them from activity in one or other of the first two. And among themselves the four differ greatly in nature and in importance. Keeping abreast of one's subject is contributing to knowledge only when the results of one's labours are made available to others – as in reviews of books, on the value of which, I fully agree, much more stress should be laid. The same applies to 'keeping an eye on current controversies'. Learning more of one's own subject, on the other hand, and learning about other subjects, are part of the duty of the teacher (including the school teacher) as well as of the researcher, and these least of all can take the place of factual research, though, as the Report rightly remarks, they can subserve it.

A second point which it is desirable to make here, and which is almost as axiomatic as the first, is that research and teaching should go hand in hand. Each is complementary to the other. 'University teaching can neither be divorced from research, nor university research from teaching.'[1] The necessity of considering them separately led me to insist on this at the very outset:

These blend so frequently, and at times so completely, that it is often more accurate to describe them as one single aim which can be regarded from two aspects.[2]

One could hardly be more emphatic than that. The A.U.T. Report says almost exactly the same thing in slightly different language:

Research ... must occupy a large part of the time and attention of the university teacher, if he is to fulfil his obligations as such at all. It is of vital importance, both for its own sake and as a necessary condition of effective teaching at a university level.[3]

Professor A. N. Whitehead, in a striking passage, presents it from another angle:

The two functions of education and research meet together in a university. Do you want your teachers to be imaginative? Then encourage them to research. Do you want your researchers to be imaginative? Then bring them into intellectual sympathy with the young at the most eager, imaginative period of life, when intellects are just entering upon their mature discipline. Make your researchers explain themselves to active minds, plastic and with the world before them; make your young students crown their period of intellectual acquisition by some contact with minds gifted with experience of intellectual adventure. Education is discipline for the adventure of life; research is intellectual adventure; and the universities should be homes of adventure shared in common by young and old.[4]

All this is very true, but one danger must be guarded against which can best be described by a quotation from the opening words of the A.U.T. Report: 'Research in the general sense of the original and independent pursuit of knowledge. ...' That is a well-intended definition, but let us see where, in practice, it is apt to lead us.

1. B.A.C., p. 29.   2. Cf. p. 141, above.   3. A.U.T. (Research).
4. A. N. Whitehead, *The Aim of Education and Other Essays*, London, 1932, pp. 146-7.

'Precisely,' says Professor Deadwood, that well-known academic figure, who always looks slightly shocked when the obnoxious substantive is mentioned. 'Precisely. Research is the original pursuit of knowledge; I pursue knowledge whenever I prepare a lecture; therefore, I perform research and am doing all that is required of me.' That might be thought an exaggeration, but I have heard those very words used, in private and in public, by teachers who are either failing in their own obligations or are attempting to excuse such failures in others. If the contention were a valid one, every school teacher who conscientiously prepares his lessons is engaging in research, and many school-children, in writing essays or attempting to wrest the meaning from a French or Latin unseen, are engaging in research. So, in a sense – a very imperfect sense – they are. But it is not in that sense that the university teacher should view his obligation. His task is not merely to pursue knowledge 'originally and independently'. (How else, by the way, can one pursue anything but 'originally'? And why 'independently'? Does collaboration in research destroy its nature and value?) His task is to attain to the knowledge he pursues, and to diffuse it when it is attained – or alternatively, if it is not attained, to give an account of the pursuit for the benefit of others. Research, that is to say, will begin with pursuit but will end in publication. The act is completed only with diffusion; and although in the most literal sense a certain amount of diffusion can be accomplished viva voce, in lectures and seminars, there is no permanence about this.

One strongly suspects that the man who for twenty years after election to a Chair publishes nothing has nothing to publish. It is surely unthinkable that he should go on delivering lectures, each of which embodies the results of original investigation, for so long a period, and have no desire to communicate these results to a wider audience than he can reach with his voice. To say the least, it hardly inspires one with confidence in their value.

II

I now return to that great unsolved problem of university
life which I have already dealt with at some length – the
problem of the academic person (for brevity, as before, he
may be referred to as a professor) who does no research
worth mentioning after his election to the permanent staff
and shows no intention or desire to do any. If the universities are to fulfil their primary function, this problem
must be solved, and, if the will to solve it is there, no time
will ever be found again like the immediate future. For any
solution, of course, will have reference to new appointments.
The lazy old leopards will never change their spots: they
must be allowed to die out and become relics of an un-
regretted past. It is the future that must be better.

I showed in an earlier chapter that the research in Arts
subjects, both at the old and at the new universities, is
done by a very few people, either genuine scholars of a
mature type or young men who are producing hard in the
hope of getting promotion, and that the vast majority do
practically nothing. I gave statistics illustrating the small
amount of teaching which is demanded of them and pointed
out that in no Faculty are more than a handful of men
overworked with committees. Why, then, is there so little
productiveness? 'The only explanations one can find are
that the staff neither believe in research nor are forced to
do any. Practically every lecturer of any standing – and
every professor who has ever been a lecturer – has a certain
amount of past original work to his credit. But once the
lecturer becomes a professor, or has risen to as high a grade
as he judges himself likely to reach or thinks it worth
while to work for, all such activities come virtually to an
end. That is not cynicism, but a conclusion which will
probably be found inescapable if figures are taken over
any number of years in any one university.'[1]

As preliminaries to remedial action I postulated an

1. Cf. p. 159, above.

education of opinion and a reform of the time-squandering committee system. Before coming to the actual remedies I will discuss the reception of the indictments themselves.

First of all, there was a repetition of the old excuses. A critic in the *Universities Review*, for example, puts the matter bluntly. 'Our cheeks begin to glow. Are we the laziest body of people in the community?' This sounds hopeful. But then, instead of answering 'Yes' and proceeding to ask what is to be done about it, he discovers that 'certain considerations may mitigate our shame'. Just listen:

> Some are obliged to fill vacations with the exhausting work of marking school scripts. Keeping abreast of our subject may take most of our spare time, and many large volumes are put aside for careful scrutiny in the vacation ... [1]

In other words, 'no time'! But, before we examine that excuse, can the critic explain why it is that practically every professor and senior lecturer has a satisfactory, sometimes a quite remarkable, amount of published work to his credit at the time of his election, produced during the very years when he has least time and most needs money, yet often, once he has a position and a comfortable salary secured to him for the rest of his working life, he produces little or nothing more? Everybody knows, and has long known, that this is the case. If it is not, let it be disproved. Let it be explained, for example, why a young man, known over half Europe at thirty-five as the author of two standard works which are still used everywhere, was elected at that age to a Chair and has now reached the age of sixty without having published anything more. Or why another, appointed professor at thirty-eight, on the strength of a small but penetrating book and the unanimous opinions of all the experts that he was the coming man in his field, has utterly failed to justify these prophecies, and devotes himself, when not lecturing or attending meetings, to bee-keeping. Nor are these isolated cases. How many Arts

1. *The Universities Review*, November 1943, p. 35.

professors of twenty years' standing would dare to print in
The Universities Review a list of the contributions to knowledge which they have published during that time? If I am
wrong, any Arts Faculty can prove it by issuing statistics.

However, let us give our critic's excuses serious consideration. First of all, 'the exhausting work of marking
school scripts'. Only a few members of any Arts Faculty
mark school scripts at all, and most of those who do are not
professors. But even if they all did, the scripts period lasts
from about mid-July to mid-August: say four weeks.
Allow three weeks for holiday and relaxation after this
exhausting experience and there is still quite a substantial
amount of vacation left. At Oxbridge the vacations total
twenty-eight weeks yearly; at Redbrick, twenty-two.
That leaves twenty-one and fifteen weeks respectively. How
does the exhausted script-marker use these?

Apparently he takes refuge behind the 'many large
volumes' to which he must devote such 'careful scrutiny'.
But is it so impossible for him to scrutinize them during the
term? Let us try to discover what he does in term-time.
For that purpose I will conjure up Professor Deadwood
and have a talk with him.

'Now, Professor, let us take a working-week as equivalent
to forty-four hours, which gives you five eight-hour days and
nothing after one on Saturdays. How many hours a week do
you lecture?'

'Well, six, as a rule – that is for six periods of three-
quarters of an hour, but I am always glad to see students
in the following quarter of an hour – though few of them
ever come.'

'That leaves thirty-eight. What else do you do at the
University?'

'Oh, there are meetings: they take about two hours a
week on the average. And I have to consult with my staff:
should we call that perhaps two hours more?'

'Well – we might! That will leave thirty-four hours to
account for. I suppose you spend that time on original
research?'

'Well, not exactly. The fact is, I am too tired to do any research during the term. No, there are other things. There is preparation of lectures – at least there was, when I was younger, but nowadays I just give the same lectures year after year. Of course, I add to them or revise them from my reading.'

'So that won't occupy many of the thirty-four hours. Perhaps you use them for reading – keeping abreast of your subject and all that sort of thing?'

'Well, ye-es. That is, I do read, of course. But hardly as much as thirty-four hours a week. Perhaps two hours a day would be a fair average. Not counting Saturdays, of course: I always spend Saturdays in the garden.'

'Right you are, then: that leaves us with twenty-four hours a week unoccupied: rather more than half the total. I wonder how you fill that in!'

So does the Professor. But he can suggest nothing further. Except that, of course, 'a lot of things crop up – letters to answer, don't you know, and students to interview, and what not. The fact is, I don't know where the time gets to.'

But *I* do. It's a strange thing that it should be the laziest people and the hardest-worked people who make that remark, the difference between them being that the hard-worked always seem to be able to make more time if necessary.

This is Professor Deadwood's day in term-time. (I don't know, and I can't imagine, what he does in the vacations.) He has a leisurely breakfast at half-past eight, followed by pipe and paper; reaches the University between ten and half-past; reads his letters and perhaps writes one; saunters into the Common Room for a cup of coffee; calls on a colleague, or the Bursar, or the Clerk to the Senate; returns to his room, glances through the latest issue of a learned review, has a few words with a pupil – and, lo, it's lunch-time. After lunch in the refectory, followed by a chat about the day's news in the Common Room, he gives a lecture at half-past two, and immediately afterwards hurries home lest he should be late for tea. After tea comes the day's exercise (unless it happens to be a day when he has no lecture, in which case he plays golf in the afternoon) and after dinner he spends a couple of hours with a new book on his special subject (or a book from the circulating library on something else), after which, the paper again, a nightcap, and bed at eleven, after a somewhat tiring but thoroughly well-spent day. Certainly the genus professor ought to be celebrated for longevity!

But surely, it will be said, all professors are not like this one? No, not by a long way; but a great many of them are, and the point of my criticism is its being possible. Even were there none, the system would be a bad one. And the system permits worse things than that. It permits a professor to hold his Chair for years on end, just because the Chair is endowed, without having a single pupil and without writing so much as an article or a review. It enables a professor to discourage would-be pupils from reading with him by demanding of them an impossibly high standard or by putting his lectures at hours when they cannot attend. It lauds a professor who turns himself into a caricature of a schoolmaster by teaching hard all the term, engaging in outside activities all the vacations and doing nothing whatsoever to advance knowledge.

And the ironic part of it, let us repeat, is that ten, twenty years ago, these same unproductive professors, then candidates for the Chairs they now hold, were producing useful work, sometimes steadily, sometimes rapidly, until they gained the coveted post which for them has been equivalent to retirement from productiveness altogether.

Another excuse, on which little time need be wasted, is that 'a man may spend many years on a topic before he is ready to publish'.[1] True, he may – and it is a curious coincidence that the professors who sternly deprecate 'rushing into print' and 'premature publication' are those who themselves publish least – but I suspect that he very seldom does. The young and inexperienced lecturer may credit any reverend senior with masses of unpublished work

1. Ibid.

which will be given to an expectant world in his old age, but by the more mature the rare birds of that type are easily recognizable: their names are often to be found at the foot of reviews, minor notices and miscellaneous queries in learned journals; they are well known and well spoken of by the leading scholars in their field; they are always accessible to the younger men; they have always time to spare for anything to do with scholarship. No: that explanation will fit about one per cent of the apparently unproductive and the idea that about eighty per cent of our colleagues are burning the midnight oil in company with unpublished masterpieces is altogether too good to be true.

But now we come to a really bright idea – not in the least a new one but put forward so plausibly by our critic that it must be given careful consideration. For it 'challenges Mr Truscot's principles'!

Some professors and lecturers may feel that their *métier* lies in teaching rather than in original work. They may spend their free periods of the year in collecting material for courses and expend their energies on their pupils and on the practical life of the university during terms.[1]

Now, surely, it is the turn of Mr Truscot's cheeks to glow. What if our poor maligned colleagues are only being true to the inner light and conscientiously following their vocation? How cruel to stigmatize them for neglecting research when they are spending forty-four hours weekly, for thirty weeks, in giving six, eight or ten hours' lectures, and the greater part of their twenty-two weeks of vacation in 'collecting material' for the courses of the ensuing term! One would almost think that, with such a devotion to teaching, they would be happier as masters at Public Schools, where they would be able to teach for thirty periods a week instead of ten and would have so much greater scope for 'practical life' in every shape and form.

For all its plausibility, in short, I find the assumption quite

1. Ibid.

unconvincing. To begin with, I want to know why these people, whose *métier* is teaching and not research, ever entered a sphere in which, as is well known, research is demanded as well as teaching. Some universities even put the demand into their regulations:

It shall be the duty of each Professor:

(*a*) to contribute, so far as in him lies, to the advancement and diffusion of knowledge, especially by the prosecution and promotion of original research;

(*b*) to give instruction in accordance with the curriculum from time to time prescribed by his Faculty and the Senate in the subject committed to his charge ...

Secondly, I want to know how it is that a professor who engaged successfully in research until the date of his appointment to a permanent post discovered that his *métier* lay in teaching only after he had obtained it. To these two questions it will be hard to give a satisfactory answer, and a third one is more disconcerting still. It is generally admitted, in the words of the A.U.T. Report (the italics are mine), that 'research ... must occupy a large part of the time and attention of the university teacher, *if he is to fulfil his obligations at all.*' It follows, therefore, that a university teacher who does no research is not fulfilling his obligations. Should he not, then, leave the university and go into a school? I can see no justification for his remaining at a university.

If the reply made to the third question be that he has such a live, original and inquiring mind that all his preparation, teaching, lecturing and discussions are a true embodiment of the spirit of research, the obvious rejoinder is: 'Then why does he confine his teaching to the limits of his classroom instead of giving it to the world?' And this question brings us to a true assessment of the worth of the excuse which we are considering. In a vast majority of cases the answer is that such a person is not in any sense whatever doing research and the reason that he communicates nothing to the world is that he has little or nothing worth communicating. In a few very exceptional instances there is another reason. I give it in the words of Professor Whitehead:

For some of the most fertile minds composition in writing, or in a form reducible to writing, seems to be an impossibility. In every faculty you will find that some of the most brilliant teachers are not among those who publish. Their originality requires for its expression direct intercourse with their pupils in the form of lectures, or of personal discussion. Such men exercise an immense influence; and yet, after the generation of their pupils has passed away, they sleep among the innumerable unthanked benefactors of humanity.[1]

One of these rare instances was revealed a short time ago. A scholar whom his intimates knew to be of rare ability died, when near retiring age, after having risen to the very top of his profession, but also almost without having published. I withhold his name, because both he and his friends felt keenly the curious inhibition which seemed to prevent him from writing – and the rather pathetic efforts made, since his death, to put together some of his notes for publication have not been particularly successful. But I quote this case to show that I am fully aware of the existence of such an inhibition. It could probably be cured, in most people, if attacked resolutely in youth – but that would mean 'premature publication'! It does not, however, affect our main argument. It is as futile to suppose that our 80 per cent of non-producing staff are haunted by a mysterious inhibition as that they are all hugging epoch-making but unfinished manuscripts.[2] I doubt if one per cent of them falls within each class. In that case, we still have to explain the seventy-eight.

III

Having disposed of the excuses, let us now come to the remedies. Of the four which I proposed:

1. Greater care about new appointments and promotions;
2. Short-term appointments;

1. *The Aim of Education*, pp. 148–9.
2. Professor Whitehead (p. 149) fully recognizes this: 'When all such allowances have been made, one good test for the general efficiency of a faculty is that as a whole it shall be producing in published form its quota of contributions to thought.

3. Annual reports;
4. Reciprocity with other universities, and Sabbatical
    years,

the fourth is the least important, because by itself it would be
of no use at all: the remainder, if adopted, would constitute
a determined attack on the abuse from three sides. But,
maintains the critic in the *Universities Review*, 'this is going
too far'. 'The application of any sort of pressure ... suggested in certain quarters', remarks the A.U.T. meaningly,
'is greatly to be deprecated.'[1] I want now, as regards in
turn principle and practice, to inquire why.

In principle, it will presumably be conceded that the
proposals are reasonable. What is there to be said against
them? It is agreed that the professor has two obligations –
teaching and research. If he spent a whole year on research,
without going once into his classroom, there would be
trouble. Then why should there not be trouble if he spends
a year in teaching (from six to ten hours weekly) without
doing any research? The question to be asked is rather if
remedial action is practicable and advisable. Would the
remedy be worse than the disease?

Admittedly a suitable procedure is not easy to find
because research is a more delicate and a more individual
matter than teaching and absence from the study is less
noticeable than absence from the classroom. But for that
very reason the problem calls more urgently for solution
and if we are in earnest about it we ought not to be content
until a solution is found. One may begin by saying that the
only true, effective and permanent solution is the creation
of a sound tradition. And that can, in time, be done. The
schoolmaster could easily scamp a great deal of his exercise-
marking. The parish priest could omit to say his Mass or
Office in church if nobody was present. The nurse often
performs duties which she could omit without anyone's
being the wiser. Our trouble, as university professors, is
that we have allowed teaching to absorb our energies till
we have no longer any conscience about research. We have

1. *The Universities Review*, November 1943, p. 35.

now to develop a conscience; and it is for the decades of its development, not for all time, that we have to legislate.

The objections which have been raised to my remedies have concentrated, as I expected they would, on the second and third. As to the first, the critics assume that the maximum care about appointments is already taken. My view is that it is not. But about that no argument is possible. We have to consider the arguments against appointing professors and lecturers for not more than ten years at a time and making their reappointment as conditional upon their research during each period as upon their teaching. The objections which have been raised to that proposal are as follows:

1. *Intangibility of the evidence.* That difficulty one can fully understand. Not only is it impossible, maintain some, to define and delimit research, but, even were it possible, it is undesirable. One critic, for example, writes to me of the need for keeping "research" free of set rules purporting to define it'. Another correspondent, however, supplies a working definition which would take us a part of the way:

> If a man is so strongly moved by a problem as to apply himself to it without reserve until he has resolved (so far as in him lies) its difficulties and perplexities, he is doing research.

Let us face the facts. How many professors and lecturers in any Faculty of Arts would even claim that they were doing that during (let us say) the past academic session? Is it not rather a quibble to object to the applying of 'set rules' to define what hardly exists?

Another aspect of this problem is that (to quote once more the correspondent last referred to) 'it is easy to apply original thought to gain results which are largely negative in character'. An exercise of this kind, if conscientiously and ably performed, will have been well worth while as a discipline for the researcher, and probably, if the negative results are published, from an objective point of view as well. But how is one to assess the ten years' work of a professor, who, for all his concentrated labour, has practically no results to show? Will he not be dismissed, and some facile investigator, doing statistical work which any hack under direction, could accomplish, be commended and given his place?

Certainly not. To start with, even the briefest account by the professor of the work he has attempted to do could be checked by an expert in the field and any doubts cleared up by correspondence or interview. Deception would be next to impossible. Then, if assessment of this kind were not effective, how would researchers who get no results fare in their applications for professorships? Are they turned down in favour of facile fact-grubbers? No professor would maintain that, save in an exceptional case, such a thing is possible. An external expert, in private correspondence with a committee, is absolutely frank. 'This man', he will say, 'has achieved very little so far, but he is on the right lines and you will be quite safe in taking him.' Or 'of these two people, the first has done work which is satisfactory as to bulk and attractive in presentation, but not strikingly original; the second has contributed only a couple of papers to the *English Historical Review,* but each one opens up a new line of thought and I can see from his letter of application that he is developing these energetically and on the right lines.' Why cannot referees write in the same way of men who already hold their Chairs? There seems no essential difference between pre-election and post-election procedure.

As a matter of fact, the same difficulty may arise at a still earlier stage. In June 1934, an able young graduate was awarded a travelling fellowship with which he went to Rome to search for a document which he proposed to transcribe and edit for his M.A. It took him three months to trace the document, and, when he had studied it carefully, and copied a large part of it, which took six months more, he discovered that the work was leading him in a different direction from that which he had been given to expect, and, further, that the competent editing of it demanded qualifications which he did not possess. Having spent several weeks in learning Italian before starting work in Rome, he had by now consumed nearly half the time which he could give to his M.A. work, without apparently having achieved any result whatever. What was to be done? He came home for consultation with his Professor, who accepted the evidence which he produced of a session's research; in the second session he began work in a related field which he hopes one day to resume. Though he wrote no 'thesis', and showed up nothing which could conceivably be published, there was never any question of his not being awarded the degree. Presumably one can be as fair to a professor as to a candidate for the M.A.

2. *Impracticability of terminating appointments.* 'How can you possibly get rid of a man at fifty-five? Provided the terms of his appointment are clear, I see no kind of difficulty. He is appointed for five years at, let us say, thirty-five; then for five years more till forty-five; and finally for two successive periods of ten years till sixty-five, the usual compulsory retiring age. Of course he could have a magnificently lazy time in his last decade, but that we must allow him if, after twenty years of productivity, he were capable of laziness at all. The thing to be avoided at all costs is his settling down to a routine of ten hours' work a week in term and nothing in vacation before he is forty. Now if at forty and forty-five the external experts who had reported upon his work at thirty-five were still favourable, he would have a clear and peaceful run each time. But if at fifty-five they, or their successors, reported that his activity had come to an end, and he had no extenuating circumstances to plead, his appointment would automatically terminate according to the agreement. The only reason we find this difficult to envisage is because our rule has always been life appointment for the lazy and the industrious alike – and generally at the same salary.

In practice, actual dismissal would very seldom occur. Once a few examples had been made, and candidates for permanent posts knew that research was expected, and would be demanded, of them, they would either seek other fields of usefulness or do their job. If they grew tired of research, and gave it up, they would feather their nests in advance of the expiration of their decade, or take an earlier opportunity of flying elsewhere. After all, there are a good many other openings than a university for a man or woman with a First Class Honours degree and long experience of teaching and handling undergraduates, even if he or she is in the fifties.

3. *Dignity of the Professor.* Some of the younger people have sounded quite alarmed and I have heard them discussing with great concern if five-year appointments are likely to come in the near future. The older men view the prospect with commendable serenity. Being 'safely seated', as one of them, a well-known scholar, put it to me, they have nothing to fear; no regulation that may be made is likely to be retrospective. So they speak their minds freely. 'You won't catch me', remarked the same scholar, 'submitting my record in research to a bunch of my colleagues, even though they were dignified with the name of "committee".'

No external experts, of course, or anything but a formal motion, would be necessary where so distinguished a professor was concerned, nor need a Research Committee ever do more than send forward such a motion where (as would soon generally happen) the report of the professor himself testified unmistakably to his fulfilment of the statutory requirements. But why is there loss of dignity in submitting one's record of research to a committee for the purpose of a reappointment, and yet no loss of dignity in not only submitting a record, but soliciting and presenting testimonials, together with specimens of one's published work, for the purpose of a first appointment – to say nothing of the humiliating experience of waiting upon such a committee in person! Has one, between thirty-five and forty, grown so much more important that what one was only too glad to do then is a humiliation now? Is it not rather that the permanent member of a staff has come to look upon immunity from criticism as a right and resents any attempt to take it away? If not, why do senior men present themselves for doctorates of letters, a procedure which involves submission of published or unpublished work to a committee? One never hears the suggestion that there is any loss of dignity in that.

4. *Risk of the production of inferior work.* Any pressure, says the A.U.T., 'could only result in increasing the quantity of publication at the expense of its quality'. 'There is reason to think that many young scholars have suffered in their wider understanding of their subject by the necessity that they feel to produce something in publishable form in order to qualify for appointments.'

The last sentence has strictly no relation to what is being proposed. If young scholars have so suffered, that concerns the period before their appointment and is due to the unwise procedure adopted by the committee of selection. No committee should require any large amount of published work from a young scholar. Evidence that serious research work is being done, with a view to ultimate publication, can be given and tested in other ways. In my own special line I could pronounce on anyone's claim to be doing original research without his having published so much as an article.

The same applies to work submitted for reappointment. The specialist referee will not be deceived. Naturally, as a man grows older, more published work is expected of him, but each case would be considered on its merits, and the idea that a volume of work actually published should be demanded within any period does not come from me: I should decisively reject it. My view is that publication must be the goal of research; and, if a man dies and leaves work adjudged by experts to be worthy of publication, it should be published, as the discharge of an honourable obligation, by his University.

This does not mean that inferior work never *would* be produced, but it does mean that it *need* not. There would always be professors trying to make sure of reappointment by publishing early in each period, and the quality of their production might suffer. At the same time, the reception

of such work by the critics would probably deter a serious
man from doing this too often; while, with the majority, the
alternative to inferior work from them would be no work
at all. And, of the two, inferior work, if of publishable
quality, is surely preferable.

Everything depends here, in the last resort, on the policy
and the standards of the individual Faculty, and this, in its
turn, upon its conception of research and the degree of its
determination to get it.

IV

I close this chapter by reiterating the hope that the proposals I have put forward will be given serious and unprejudiced consideration.

The A.U.T. seems hardly to realize the seriousness of the
position. 'The risk of a few idle professors', says its Report,
'would be a lesser evil than the certainty of a flood of inferior published work done to order.' That sentence is
unsatisfactory because it begs the question: it is not certain
that a flood of inferior work would be published; nor is it
necessary that it should be; nor would it, in any case, be
'done to order'. But principally it is unsatisfactory because
it misstates the case. There is no 'risk' of 'a few' idle professors. There is the *fact* that a *large number* of idle professors
are ruining the traditions of their calling.

In its Science Report the A.U.T. lays it down that 'every
member (of a Department), including the Professor, should
be able to give at least half the working week to research'.[1]
Supposing it were possible for all members of the Arts staff
to have half the working week for research, does the A.U.T.
for a moment suppose that they would use it for that
purpose?

Not on your life; but there would be a tremendous improvement in the standard of the Arts staffs' front gardens!

1. A U.T. (Research): Science, par. 15.

CHAPTER FIVE

The University and its Region

THIS chapter sets out to treat at greater length a subject which was touched upon very briefly in an earlier chapter – the relations which can, and should, exist between a university and the region in which it lies. A subject which, as it were, intersects this – the contacts of a general kind which it is possible to make between universities and schools – will be considered only incidentally,[1] and treatment of another – the future of adult education – can be satisfactorily undertaken only when developments now proceeding become assessable. What is said about this last, therefore, must be taken as no more than tentative.

I

It must be emphasized at the outset that the chief business of a university is not, and can never be, the service of a region – still less the creation of numerous contacts, whether social or educational, with a region. The aims of a university must be, primarily, the pursuit, and secondarily, the dissemination, of knowledge. Those two aims should be at once its soul and its inspiration; they should lie at the heart of its activities and be the source of its life; the others, however attractive they sound – and, to anyone with a passion for education, are – lie upon its perimeter. Universities were not founded to spread thin layers of beneficent influence over the country; and, if they are content to devote their main energies to a merely peripheral development, they will rot at the centre and in due time cease to be in any true sense universities at all. If they allow abuses, such as that described in the last chapter, to grow unchecked, they will find themselves devoid of motive power, and their peripheral, as well as their central, activities will suffer. 'We

1. Cf. p. 240, above.

sometimes feel', one of our leading Vice-Chancellors has said, 'the risk that the universities may be too much in contact with affairs. Many things are necessary for the making of a university. But the most important thing of all is a good staff dedicated to its job. If a university has that, all else will come in due season. The centre of the university's influence *and service* is always the great teacher, the man whose passion it is to know, to teach and always himself to be learning.'[1]

In its Report on University Developments the A.U.T. made the following enumeration of the functions of a university: (*a*) the free pursuit of knowledge; (*b*) the dissemination of knowledge; (*c*) the formation of young people as individuals; (*d*) the study of social problems.[2] That is unexceptionable; but an early draft report, which met with considerable criticism, began in this way:

In the modern world the universities necessarily take a central position, and their responsibilities grow. With the greater complexity of society, its growing technical needs, there is an ever increasing demand for experts in the spheres of science, business, administration, social services. If this demand is not met, there will be a relative impoverishment in our national efficiency and equipment, and we shall be unequal to the tasks set by a modern society. What seems a truism in time of war may easily be forgotten, or obscured by deliberate interest, in times of peace. It is for the universities both to make society more conscious of this demand, and to supply it.

But the universities are central in another sense. Modern society imposes problems of citizenship as serious as those of technical efficiency. Many of the most gifted of our youth pass through the universities; many of those who will later take leading positions in our society there pass from childhood to the age of responsibility. It is essentially the universities who have the task of training them. It is there that the foundations of an enlightened and cultured

1. From a broadcast by Sir Hector Hetherington in the B.B.C. African service, December 1943. Quoted by permission.

2. A.U.T., May 1944, par. 3, pp. 52–3. The definitions are longer than these, but I think I have been faithful to their spirit in abbreviating them.

democracy should be laid. This was the traditional achievement of Oxford and Cambridge before the twentieth century, when culture and social leadership were confined to a small class. With the immense increase in the number of those called on to fill posts of responsibility in modern society, the universities have to meet the need of educating great numbers of students in social responsibility and culture; they must be, more fully than before, schools of citizenship as well as academies of learning.[1]

Now that is dangerous doctrine – not because it advocates a single thing which ought not to be done if and as more fundamental duties allow, but because the whole idea which it presents of the university is out of focus. I am sure we ought to regard with suspicion the demand that the university should continually be thinking of 'society', teaching citizenship, stimulating the social consciousness, mingling with people of all classes and occupations, supplying experts to local industries, taking part in local activities, and the like. The National Union of Students, at its 1944 congress, discussed university reform 'as a social problem of national and international significance'. It laid down, as a 'fundamental' premiss of all its arguments, that 'the universities should be of maximum service to the community'.[2] The Association for Education in Citizenship holds that the aims of the universities should be to give a general education, promoting an understanding of nature and society, a functional or technical (i.e., vocational) education and a moral or social education. Well, the university can find time and opportunity to do some of these things, and to the extent that it can, it should. But they must always come second to its fundamental task; and, the better it does that, the better, in the long run, it will do everything else.

To the university in a large city, for example, the citizens should, as I have suggested, turn continually for guidance when some great political or international issue fills their minds. But if its professors are not men who have learned

1. A.U.T., April 1943, Cf. D. G. James, 'New Notions about Universities', *The Universities Review*, November 1943, pp. 10–13.
2. T.E.S., 12 February 1944.

through disciplined thought and study to view life whole, they will turn to them in vain. The university should seek to influence the surrounding schools from which most of its students come; but, if it is not itself wholly and sincerely devoted to the pursuit of knowledge, any influence it may have will at best be evanescent and ephemeral – at worst, definitely harmful. The same principle holds good of the influence which the university exerts on the region, and on the world outside it, by means of its graduates. If, during the three or four short years which they have spent in close contact with its teachers, they have become imbued with the spirit that informs true scholarship, which is so much more than learning, they will in their turn imbue others with it too. If they have not, they will pass on knowledge, and nothing else.

The university, then, should be a regional power-house, but it must be sure about the source and nature of its power. Its motto must be 'First things first'; and to that motto it must always be true, however strong may be the temptation or the pressure to disregard it. All that follows must be read in the light of that principle.

II

Even in a country no larger than our own it is well that regional characteristics and interests should be preserved, and it is to be hoped that determined resistance will meet the efforts made from time to time to supplant them all by a drab national uniformity. Our universities, well placed as they are, form excellent centres for regional development. Leaving aside Scotland, where the heaviest task is that which confronts the University of Aberdeen, and Wales, the four constituent colleges of whose single University are suitably spaced, we find that, with but little adjustment, the twelve Universities and five University Colleges of England will find the regions which they should serve at their doors.

The two Lancashire and the two Yorkshire universities

serve regions which, though small in area, contain large populations. Manchester and Liverpool would partition Cheshire, Liverpool taking the larger portion to compensate for the work which would fall to Manchester in North Lancashire and probably Westmorland. Hull has a natural region in the East Riding of Yorkshire, and Leeds a great responsibility in the rest of that large county, save that Sheffield would operate to the south of Huddersfield and Wakefield, as well as in Derbyshire. Durham, which already has a college at Newcastle, would take care of Northumberland, Cumberland, and County Durham, with most of the North Riding, the remainder falling to Hull. The future interests of the north-west would probably be better served if Durham could establish a college at Carlisle.

In the Midlands a very wide area is served by the University of Birmingham, which, having also to cater for so large a city, might reasonably be relieved by Oxford. If the whole of Berkshire were assigned to Reading, Oxford, besides Oxfordshire and Buckinghamshire, could take North Wiltshire and most of Gloucestershire, Bristol providing for that part of Gloucestershire south of Stroud as well as for Somerset. To Berkshire, Reading would add North Hampshire and East Wiltshire. South Wiltshire, with Dorset and South Hampshire, would fall to Southampton. Exeter, as a full University (perhaps with some of its Faculties at Plymouth or Truro), would be, as to a great extent it is to-day, the academic centre for Devon and Cornwall.

London, numerically the largest of our Universities, would have to cater for the vast population of London County, as well as for Surrey, Sussex, Kent, Middlesex, South Hertfordshire and Essex as far as a line drawn from Bishops Stortford to Colchester. Though communications are easy, some small measure of devolution, in extra-mural work at least, might not be impossible here. An almost equally extensive task falls to Cambridge. The University of Nottingham and the University College of Leicester, besides attending to the counties in which they are situated, could easily share the entire county of Lincolnshire, but that would still leave Cambridge with Cambridgeshire, the Isle of Ely, Bedfordshire, Huntingdonshire, North Essex, Suffolk and Norfolk. If an increasing university population brought a demand for more University Colleges, an excellent choice would be either Norwich or Ipswich, or both. A College at Ipswich could relieve London of its portion of Essex, as far as Brentwood and Southend.

With such an apportionment drawn up and agreed upon by an Academic Council representing all the Universities and University Colleges of the country, regional activities would be organized upon a scale as yet unapproached. It may be asked if Oxford and Cambridge, after their centuries of hegemony over the entire country, would willingly resign themselves to the role of regional universities like the rest. They would still, of course, draw their undergraduates from all parts, for so long as the quality of their work was high enough and their historical and social prestige powerful enough to enable them to do so. But London and Durham Universities already do this, not to mention certain Schools of outstanding brilliance elsewhere. Oxford and Cambridge would be asked only to recognize their responsibilities towards the regions of which they are the geographical centres, to relinquish the extra-territorial centres they now hold to the Universities in whose constituencies these lie,[1] and to take part in a co-ordinated extra-mural scheme embracing the entire country.

Both these Universities have in fact already done much good work locally. Oxford has long had an extra-mural committee covering work in Oxfordshire, Berkshire, and Buckinghamshire, a great part of which is carried on by three full-time tutors resident in the districts which they serve. The last report available of the Oxford Extra-mural Delegacy relates to the most difficult period of the War, yet it can show a total of 97 courses held at 52 centres, an increase of 34 courses and 8 centres over the year preceding.

1. Cf. p. 249, above.

Cambridge works similarly, with four resident tutors, in Cambridgeshire, the Isle of Ely, Northamptonshire, Bedfordshire, Essex and Norfolk. Both Universities maintain close collaboration with the Workers' Educational Association.

To these results, achieved in face of transport difficulties, shortage of man-power and other impediments incident to total war, has to be added the work accomplished in the various departments of education for the Forces, which is of amazing volume and is omitted here only because it does not immediately concern our present theme. There is every reason, therefore, to believe that Oxford and Cambridge will collaborate willingly in regional education, and in some respects will even lead the way. Yet they must not be content to rely, as they have done to a great extent in the past, on the services of young and unknown tutors, of graduates of foreign universities, and of graduates of their own who are working in universities in other parts of the country. One can look down a list of Oxford and Cambridge Extension Courses without seeing the name of a professor or a resident lecturer from either University: only rarely is there the name of a resident don who is an acknowledged authority in his field. Occasionally a meeting, or a series of meetings, is held at the University, and then a professor will deliver an opening address while other professors will give some of the lectures. But that is not good enough. While the professors' main duty is their primary job, those of them who can lecture well should occasionally find time to go out into the region. The leading Oxford historians should be heard at Cheltenham and Swindon, the heads of the Cambridge schools of English, French and German at Bedford and Norwich as often as the corresponding professors in the North and Midlands can be heard in the great industrial towns of their constituencies. And that is not to say that even they are heard in such places as often as they might be. There is a lot of ground to be covered everywhere.

III

Taking now the city and the constituency in turn, we
need only repeat what has already been said about the
influence of the university on the city. Lord Simon, who,
as Chairman of the Council of Manchester University,
knows more about this than most people, suggests that
'civic universities' – why not 'all universities'? – ought
to 'study the special problems of the regions in which
they are situated, and make themselves centres of active
thought on the history, geography, language, archaeology,
geology, climate, agriculture, industry, local government and planning of their "home" area'.[1] The American
Universities, he says, are doing this effectively: Wisconsin
University has a committee on regional study with twenty
standing sub-committees; Purdue 'brings 50,000 persons
from the State on to the Campus for different forms of
discussion and study every year'; Minneapolis (presumably the University of Minnesota is meant) 'has a
fine building on the Campus for extra-mural work,
constantly filled by all sorts of regional conferences'.[2]
The regions served by the American Universities are, of
course, much larger than ours, and there is a good deal that
can be said on University Extension in the United States by
one who has lived and taught in that country which would
not be obvious to a visitor. Nevertheless the United States
points us a way here which we shall do well to follow –
perhaps, in some respects, more intelligently.

I am much less interested, however, in courses on Brewing and Aeronautics than in the position which the universities, old and new, should hold in the cities where they
have made their homes. At one time the University of
Oxbridge – or, at any rate, the undergraduate portion of
that society – was conscious of the existence of a town of the
same name only to despise it. That hotel and lodging-

1. Simon, p. 17.   2. Simon, p. 18.

house keepers, grocers, stationers, booksellers and suchlike persons should establish themselves there to batten on the University was perfectly natural, but that the University should have any contact with them that was avoidable seemed mere quixotism. That attitude, of course, has now entirely gone: town-and-gown controversies are things of the past; novels in which wicked undergraduates seduce the daughters of publicans are no longer written; and Oxbridge dons serve terms as Mayors of Oxbridge to the satisfaction of all. Redbrick dons (if the transference of the noun can be permitted) have not done more – in fact, considering how many of them are Drabtown men, one would like to see them elected more frequently to the Drabtown City Council.

It is the more important that the modern universities should live in close association with the cities which are their homes because so few of these cities have anything approaching a cultural tradition. The admiration with which we all regard that great provincial centre of musical activity, the Hallé Orchestra, is symptomatic of the rarity of such a tradition elsewhere. It would create a wild shock if one were to suggest that Wigan might become a Mecca of musicians, Derby a centre of interest in painting, Crewe the meeting-place of a famous group of literary critics, Reading a manufactory of Biblical scholars as well as of biscuits, and so on. Yet all these towns are within easy reach of academic influences, and either they, or others not vastly different from them, have all the potentialities enumerated. Not that I want the universities to start by thinking in terms of special interests: their duty to their home towns is rather to serve as centres of knowledge and thought. To the university the city should come for information, unbiased by prejudice, and sufficiently full and varied to enable individuals to make decisions for themselves on matters of moment. On the university the city should depend for help in forming right habits of thought on political, social and international issues, and, I hasten to add, on religious issues as well. As I have already made clear, a very important part of these contacts is their personal aspect. At present, with two or three exceptions, the professors at Redbrick are completely unknown in Drabtown; so, too, except to a small group of public men, is the Vice-Chancellor. That is all wrong. A leading professor should be better known than a leading City Councillor. Men should flock to the University to hear him pronounce on a current issue as they would flock to the pictures on a Saturday, or to a political meeting at election-time. If the universities had the right men, and used them as they should, the Vice-Chancellor should be as well-known a figure in Drabtown as the Lord Mayor and the Bishop, while the dozen or so most gifted and public-spirited professors should be among its best-known citizens – men of whom the city is proud and whom it would grieve to lose. Who would care in Drabtown to-day if Redbrick's Professor of International Politics accepted a Chair in the United States? Who, in fact, even knows anything of him beyond his name?

(Once more, let it not be supposed that this is a plea that professors should talk more and think less – that they should desert the study for the platform. On the contrary, unless they live a life seen by none they will wield no influence when they are heard by all. It is the months of the year which they spend in gathering power that give them the power in the days and weeks that remain.)

Such was the general plan which I laid down above for the impact of the university upon the city. Professor Bonamy Dobrée has worked independently along similar lines in *The Universities and Regional Life,* a lecture delivered at King's College, Newcastle-upon-Tyne, in April 1943. He asks that the university premises should include 'some inviting buildings, well designed, well decorated, common to ourselves and the public'.

There they will gather to rub shoulders with staff and students, to inquire with intelligent curiosity what they are all engaged in and why; to tell them of their own needs and to relight their vision. There will be good club-rooms, a library reading-room, possibly a dining-hall; and through them will flow infinite discussions on the issues of the day – on whether the church should pronounce upon politics, on the proposed regional power scheme, on the ideas of justice or freedom, on cultural relations with other countries, on new developments in painting, on whatever hopes and passions stir the time.[1]

Professor Dobrée asks boldly for many things which I had dared only to imagine as belonging to the future – 'a People's Repertory Theatre, working under the direction of the university, playing weekly the best drama of every time and clime'; 'a public concert-room, where experiments in music, as well as the old masterpieces, will from time to time be heard, for the university will be eager to foster new life in the arts. In the same way the university picture gallery will always contain recent works lent by the best living painters, sculptors and architects, more especially of those who hail from the region'; a cinema theatre, 'for here, in the film, is the greatest cultural organ ever discovered, more important to-day than printing'.[2] For a University Cinema Theatre, open to a public to be defined on a later page, I should like to make a plea of special urgency. This, more than anything else, we who stand for intellectual life and culture actually owe to the public. For it was we (or our fathers – which, as the wolf said to the lamb, is the same thing) who allowed this great potential instrument of culture to be captured by commercial interests and put to base uses. It might, from the first, have become, as to a large extent the radio has become, an educational institution of a high order. The British Film Society has of recent years been created to do what little it can to atone for the non-establishment, a generation ago, of a British Cinema Corporation. Vested interests may now make a B.C.C., working in close collaboration with the B.B.C., impossible; but surely it is the universities' duty, at the very least, to supplement the efforts of the British Film Society by having a University Cinema Theatre in their

1. Dobrée, pp. 16–17.   2. Op. cit., p. 17.

own cities, and, ultimately, in the chief centres of their regions as well. 'Unless the universities as such', says Professor Dobrée, 'interest themselves actively in the film, they are losing one of the greatest cultural opportunities ever presented them'.[1]

And what of the radio? Here, for a moment, we must go farther than the region, in order to suggest that the B.B.C., which is so assiduous in broadcasting to schools, should also plan courses for undergraduates and persons of under-graduate type. Redbrick, as we have said, gets all too few of the distinguished speakers who go so readily to Oxbridge, but, through the medium of the microphone, it might have of the very best. Discussion groups can be arranged as easily in universities as anywhere. It is a thousand pities that these possibilities were not explored during the demobilization period, when the overflowing of our lecture-rooms led to a time-wasting duplication of lectures.

But there is also an important part for the B.B.C. to play in the universities' regional life. The universities, and espe-cially their Extra-mural Departments, should be closely linked up with its extra-mural organization: at present they have only the flimsiest of connections with it. One obvious form which collaboration might take (especially during the years in which university numbers will be increasing and teachers hard pressed) is that of experiments with the substi-tution of broadcasts for lectures in the chief extra-mural centres. Other forms of mutual aid will readily suggest them-selves and here little experimenting is necessary. On the one side the universities can organize more discussion groups for the broadcasts which the B.B.C. already gives and use all their local machinery to encourage and stimulate serious listening. On the other hand, the B.B.C. should make much greater use of the universities' personnel. It is astonishing, but perfectly true, that there should be members of university teaching staffs – young, middle-aged and old – who are excellent lecturers in the technical sense of the word,

1. Op. cit. p. 17.

yet have never been invited to give so much as a ten-minute broadcast. Nor does the assistance which the universities would give the B.B.C. end here. Through their extra-mural organization, their lecturers, teachers and administrative officers come into continual contact with young men and women of great promise who are forceful speakers (though not necessarily in the B.B.C. accent!) and could be utilized at the microphone with much greater effect than many of the speakers employed at present. So low is the present standard of radio-speaking that a good deal of money might advantageously be spent on its improvement, and no agency could more profitably be used for this task than the universities.

IV

But already we have passed the city limits and entered the wider university constituency generally described as its 'region'. Little that falls to be said under this heading can be applied to all these constituencies: practice must vary according to situation, composition and size. But it can at least be said that in all, without exception, links should be forged with every type of person and institution – with boys and girls at school, with their teachers, with professional people and associations, with artisans and tradesmen, with men and women living in retirement or for other reasons enjoying ample leisure. Besides taking such particular measures as those now to be described, each university should establish, in some form or other, an organization which would serve as a vast 'Extension Society', building up nuclei of people interested in its extra-mural activities and perhaps appointing local correspondents who would keep interest alive and create more. These key men and women would be given a very special place in the university's life and would be invited frequently to social and business meetings held in the university buildings.

Let us now look at some representative forms of a university's regional activity.

1. *Schools*. Much of the contact that it is so desirable to establish between university and schools can best be made departmentally. Though it affects only a part of the school, a departmental bond (e.g., an informal visit made by the Professor of Latin to the Classical staff and to the Latin classes) is stronger than a more general one (e.g., an address or a lecture given by any professor to the whole school), and it also has the advantage of influencing the abler pupils, many of whom, in due course, will go to a university – as a rule, let us hope, to the university of their own region. General contacts, on the other hand, touch a far larger number of pupils, and their repercussions are often felt in homes and in the community as a whole. Within the city, an obvious opportunity can be taken by inviting large parties from the schools for lectures, or series of lectures – either parties of senior scholars for talks of a general kind or parties of boys and girls studying one particular subject for talks on that subject. The organizers of the well-known series of lectures for children given at the Royal Institution in London utilize a season of the year – the Christmas holidays – when time is apt to hang heavily on young hands, and all the civic universities might do something for children during that period. Similar lectures could be organized in any large centre outside the town or city which is the university's home; in smaller places, the only practicable procedure is for Mahomet to go to the mountain – if only once in every three, four or five years. If these visits can be made to coincide with Open Days, or Parents' Evenings, so much the better.

2. *School teachers*. Contacts of the departmental kind here are occasionally made through professional bodies – e.g., local branches of the Classical Association, the Historical Association, or the Modern Language Association – of which both school and university staffs are members. This is a particularly valuable thing, because the two parties meet on equal terms, and with the best will in the world it is difficult for a middle-aged professor to walk into the Staff Room of a Grammar School at the mid-morning

break and be completely at his ease. The wise professor will welcome such occasions as these meetings and use them as a jumping-off point for making the teachers' acquaintance. Another obvious means of contact is the University Training College or Department of Education. A third is through such a general extension scheme as has just been described. There is no better local correspondent than a teacher: he is in touch with pupils past and present, and, through them, with their homes. A real and living interest shown by a large body of teachers in University Extension work may get it almost anywhere.

Another method of establishing relations with teachers is through refresher courses, which I have suggested that the universities ought to organize, chiefly, though not entirely, for their own graduates.[1] A special invitation to any such course might be sent to teachers who are not graduates of Redbrick but live or work in the region. A related method is to invite the teachers' associations, or their local branches, to hold their conferences and other meetings at the University, social meetings, to which the appropriate sections of the University staff would be invited, being among them. None of these opportunities, perhaps, will occur very often, but they should all be seized whenever they do.

3. *Workers.* Under this comprehensive heading would come the activities in which the universities collaborate with the Workers' Educational Association, and various other aspects of adult education, which it is relevant here to treat only in so far as they affect the universities. The story has often been told[2] of how, in 1875, some twenty years after F. D. Maurice and his friends had founded the Working Men's College in London, Cambridge University, with its Extension lectures, entered the field of adult education closely followed, in turn, by London and Oxford. These lectures, being unsubsidized, had to be somewhat expensive, and they were, and to a large extent are still, attended

1. Cf. p. 242, above.
2. Recently it has been outlined once again, by the British Association Committee on Post-war University Education: B.A.C., pp. 30–3.

chiefly by the middle classes. The Workers' Educational Association, founded in 1903, did a great deal for adult education farther down the social scale, and, four years later, the formation, at Oxford, of the first Tutorial Classes Joint Committee initiated that collaboration between the W.E.A. and the universities which has given such great results and will yet give greater. At the apex of the movement, in which all the English universities now collaborate, come the three-year Tutorial Classes, organized by the W.E.A. and conducted by university tutors: these, and classes of allied type, were attended, in the year before the War began, by some 15,000 students. Shorter courses, some of university type, occupied another 42,000.[1] So much instruction has been given during the War to the Forces and the Women's Services that we may safely predict an immense accession of students for these classes when times are once more normal. It is also probable that more classes will be demanded of a type which can best be given by the universities, and that there will be a considerable flow of students from these classes into the full-time courses of the universities. Until more is known of the nature and extent of this demand, of the part which will be played by local authorities in meeting it, and of the amount of public money which will be available for this purpose to each of the parties concerned, it is impossible to discuss it in great detail. A few general principles, however, may be laid down.

One is that the instruction given by the universities should be largely non-vocational. This is especially true of Arts subjects. What university teachers can do for working people above everything else is to initiate them into the habits of disciplined thought which they themselves have formed and which govern all their activities. (Once more this makes it clear how important it is that the universities

1. In his Presidential Address for 1943 to the W.E.A. Educational Conference (*Education; The Task Before Us*, London, 1943, pp. 8–9), Professor R. H. Tawney gives the total numbers in 1942–3 as 72,950. He predicted that by 1948 they would be 'well over 100,000'.

should be sound and healthy at the centre.) Beneath the content of the lectures and classes in English, History, Psychology, Art, and so on, are the qualities which the teacher has gradually developed, and which the worker often admires and desires to develop for himself: the ability to think clearly, to examine thoroughly, to judge dispassionately, to pronounce impartially, to stand for what is good, to show contempt for what is bad, to keep an open mind about what is uncertain – above all, to develop, feed, and sustain a passion for knowledge and to remember that, however much one may learn, it is of small volume beside all of which one is ignorant. The great achievement of the union between scholars and workers has been the following and nurturing of this ideal, and each party has benefited from the union.

Next, there is the question of tutors. These have always been provided by the universities, and it seems likely that, once the demand for them becomes greater than in the past, more efficient arrangements will be made for their training. For, while the full-time tutor must always have a university background and be in essentials of an academic type, he needs special qualifications for as specialized a type of student as any other.

The feeling is growing that, especially in rural areas – and it is in such areas that the greatest progress has still to be made and is the most difficult to make – the tutor should be resident in the area in which he lectures. The Oxford Extra-mural Delegacy writes quite decisively:

The experience gained by the Delegacy over many years has convinced them that it is mainly by the influence of such tutors that a solid foundation is laid for the development of Adult Education in an area. Not only are they able to teach both Tutorial and other Classes but by being constantly available and giving their whole minds to the work they become known and trusted. They receive appeals from many quarters, and by responding to them strengthen the idea that education is an integral part of well-ordered life. Whilst the results achieved in the sparsely populated villages of the countryside may take longer to

become obvious than in the towns, yet even in the relatively short
time for which two of the tutors have been engaged there is
evidence of the value of their efforts.[1]

There has been some discussion of late as to whether the
universities should hold evening courses leading to degree
examinations, so that adolescents and adults employed in
commerce and industry should qualify for degrees in their
spare time. There is much to be said on both sides of this
question, but for myself, having seen something of it at first
hand, I am on the whole opposed to it. In all probability
it will become unnecessary, since a wider avenue from shop,
office and factory to university is likely to be opened in the
near future for those who can prove their ability to tread it.
Part-time degree classes are, of course, quite another
matter. If compulsory part-time education up to eighteen
is to be given more time, as before long it surely must, than
the meagre day a week at present assigned to it, and if to
this are to be superadded facilities for further part-time
education, it should become quite practicable to institute
degree courses within a part-time framework, using days
and hours when the students are not fatigued, as they must
be in the evening. A colleague of mine who used to teach
young business men in a large Midland city for two hours
on one evening weekly tells me that, through representations made by the Education Committee to the large firm
which employed most of the men who came to him, one
hour in the middle of the day was substituted for one of the
evening hours. 'Without exaggeration,' he says, 'we got
through three times as much work at midday as in the
evening.' The same will be true of part-time day degree
courses as contrasted with evening courses.

The British Association Committee predicted that, when
the world had settled down once more to peace, a new set-up
in adult education would bring the local authorities more
fully into the picture than they have been in the past. This,
the Committee believes, is entirely to the good. Much of

1. University of Oxford. Delegacy for Extra-mural studies. Report for
the year ending 30 September 1943, pp. 7–8.

the adult education which has been administered and provided by the W.E.A. and the universities is not, even in the broadest sense, of university type, and is very similar to education which those authorities themselves provide. 'There seems to be no reason why it should not become the statutory duty of the local education authorities to provide this kind of education for all who cannot obtain it otherwise.' If Parliament assigns them this duty, they would enter, as third parties, into the partnership already in existence and the Committee suggests that they might function as 'Joint Committees of local education authorities, one for each of eight or ten English regions, and one for Wales',[1] or alternatively that special authorities, financed by the Treasury, might be set up to organize non-vocational education below the university level, each of the three parties, and other voluntary organizations, to be represented on them.

There is still another way in which the universities can collaborate in the provision of education for adult workers. If in due course their residential facilities are increased in the way that has been suggested on all sides they will have many new hostels, halls or colleges, which will be unoccupied for short periods at Christmas and Easter as well as for three full months in the summer. Sometimes these will be needed for their own refresher courses, but, when free, they could often be used for adult education courses – or, if pleasantly situated, for holiday settlements at which occasional lectures, concerts and cinema shows would be given and men and women could spend their leisure in an environment of tranquillity, taste and culture. To have permanently available from thirty to forty of such buildings, each with accommodation for about 200 people, will be of very great assistance to whatever body is responsible for adult education courses. This consideration need not in any way prejudge the question of whole-time residential colleges for adult education, for much of the instruction (e.g.,

1. B.A.C., p. 32.

pre-university courses) would be given for longer periods than the length of a vacation, and some of it, at least, would have to be residential if it was to be effective. For these institutions country houses might be purchased as they come into the market: those familiar with life at the Bonar Law College at Ashridge will appreciate the great advantages of this solution. The British Association Committee on Post-War University Education has calculated the total annual cost per place of such residential education, at 1938 prices, to be £125: 20,000 places per annum would therefore cost £2,500,000, 'or an addition of about 6d. in the pound to the pre-war cost of the national system of education to public funds.' This estimate does not include the maintenance allowance which would have to be paid to the worker's family while he was not earning. But, on the other side, some of the accommodation for short courses could certainly be provided in university hostels during vacations, which would bring down the capital costs. And, secondly, the estimate is made on a basis of accommodation in each college being provided for only 150 men or 100 women. For several reasons, it seems much better that they should be co-educational, and it should surely be possible to have from 200 to 250 in each, with a corresponding economy in organization.

So much has been said of education for the working classes that it may be feared the more leisured have been forgotten. They have, however, been left to the end of this survey only because they present less of a problem. This class comprises a large portion of the community which has in the past enjoyed Secondary, and often Higher, education, has a fairly wide range of interests, can adapt itself to whatever facilities may be provided for it and is able to make some financial contribution to their cost. It includes men and women who have retired from business or professional life or who are physically either permanently or temporarily incapacitated through disability or illness; men and women who are doing either part-time or full-time work of a kind which enables them to attend courses of instruction in the evenings; and women of no occupation (living, for example, in hotels or boarding-houses) or occupied mainly with domestic duties in their homes. This may not seem a very extensive class, but it is remarkable how large and constant an audience it can provide for lectures almost anywhere.

It is this class which, for seventy years, through good days and bad, has provided audiences for the Oxford, Cambridge and London University Extension Lectures. One Cambridge centre recently celebrated the seventieth anniversary of its foundation: during this period it had held courses without a single session's break in either in the two world wars, and in the session 1943–4 it mustered an average attendance per lecture of just under 100. Distinguished though this record is, it is only an outstanding example of an interest of which the level is extremely high. Let it be recorded that despite air-raids, the blackout, transport difficulties, war duties, absences on National Service and all kinds of other hindrances, the last war-time report of the Cambridge Board of Extra-mural Studies listed twenty-two centres which had average attendances of over fifty people for lectures, and sixteen more of between forty and fifty. If, after seventy years, in the midst of a world war, such lecture-courses as the universities could provide still drew such audiences, it seems clear that, far from coming to an end, they may competently embark upon a new period of development.

There are a number of reasons for their success. One is that these three Universities – and some of the others are following them here – have been careful to employ lecturers who, though not always noted specialists, are invariably strong in technique. Another is that the energetic organization of the University has been ably seconded by a strong local committee – and the enthusiasm of some of these committees, or often of some one person who is the soul of the local Extension Society, has to be seen to be believed. A third is that the lectures, as a rule, are not mere entertainment, but provide real intellectual food. They vary in subject a good deal according to current interests: nowadays, for example, they turn mainly on international politics, foreign history, post-war planning and reconstruction, modern art and literature and contemporary views and interpretations of art and literature of the past. Each lecture is followed by a discussion class – and the weary lecturer need not suppose that he will be allowed to evade the class, however small may be the attendance for it. Weekly papers are written by a few; and for the fewer still who wish to take it there is an examination.

These details are given of set purpose, because in our concern for one type of worker we are apt to forget another, and too little is known of this highly educative activity which has weathered so many crises, and, notwithstanding the counter-attractions of cinema and radio, is still going strong. It should not only be continued by the Universities which at present carry it on but be incorporated by the combined Universities and University Colleges of the country as a part of their regional organization. This would mean the rupture, or the partial rupture, of the relations between the oldest of our universities and a few centres which lie within the regions of others, but the creation of new centres everywhere would more than outweigh this, and the well-tried experience of the past would give new life to the future.

This survey of possible developments in the regional work of the universities has ranged over a wide field and it remains to add that not all the suggestions it makes are intended to be put into force tomorrow. It is not forgotten that they would entail considerable expense: all the universities would need to expand their extra-mural departments and to increase their administrative and clerical staffs; some of them would have to create departments of adult education; others would erect special buildings for classes and large meetings (including social meetings) or might even establish outposts ('University

Houses') in outlying parts of their constituencies. And this expense would fall just at the time when large demands are beginning to be made upon the country for educational expansion and other forms of reconstruction which are even more necessary than some of these. Obviously there must be precedence according to urgency of need and the main lines of the 1944 Education Act must be got into working order before all else. But that is no reason why we should not proceed with regional planning even before the plans can be put into action. The first thing is always the vision.

The following pages describe

other recent

Penguin and Pelican

publications

A NEW PELICAN

*

OUR LANGUAGE

Simeon Potter

A227

It is the purpose of this book to present a clear and up-to-date picture of the English language as it is spoken and written in all its amazing variety and complexity. Dr Potter, who has written these chapters specially for the Pelican series, is a university teacher of wide experience and a well-known authority on the history of English. He believes that more people to-day are interested in speech than ever before and that a new spirit of linguistic enterprise and adventure is astir. All of us, both British and Americans, are becoming more conscious of our mother tongue as something living and changing and amenable to our corporate will. The story of our language, to be sure, is one of gain and loss. Its peculiar structure and its superabundant vocabulary are the outcome of long centuries of growth. To-day English is both strong and rich but, even at its best, it is far from perfect. Is it beyond the wit of man to remedy manifest deficiencies in its inherited mechanism? Can we make the English language of to-morrow yet more effective as a means of communication? These, and scores of other similar questions, will readily occur to the intelligent reader of this book.

One shilling and sixpence

LITERATURE

*

EARLY VICTORIAN NOVELISTS

Lord David Cecil

A 190

Lord David Cecil's study of the seven outstanding novelists of the nineteenth century is generally regarded not only as a major work of literary criticism but also as a brilliant piece of English prose. The novelists are: Dickens, Thackeray, Charlotte and Emily Brontë, George Eliot, Trollope and Mrs Gaskell.

A BOOK OF ENGLISH ESSAYS*

Edited by W. E. Williams

A 99

A selection from the works of Bacon, Addison, Lamb, Hazlitt, Hilaire Belloc, J. B. Priestley, V. S. Pritchett and many other great English essayists from the sixteenth century to the present day. A new and enlarged edition is now available.

ENGLISH LETTERS OF
THE EIGHTEENTH CENTURY (A 163)

and

ENGLISH LETTERS OF
THE NINETEENTH CENTURY (A 164)

Edited by James Aitken

These two volumes contain a selection of letters written by such people as Horace Walpole, Addison, William Blake, Lord Byron, Nelson, Dickens, Disraeli, Keats – in all thirty-six famous men and women whose letters reflect vividly many different aspects of the life of their time.

One shilling and sixpence each   * *Two shillings and sixpence*

HISTORY

*

JUSTINIAN AND HIS AGE*

P. N. Ure

A217

The life and achievements of the great sixth-century ruler who revived in Byzantium something of the military and cultural glories of departed Rome. The book includes a number of extracts from contemporary accounts.

THE GREEKS

H. D. F. Kitto

A220

A description and discussion of the civilization of classical Greece up to the time of Alexander. The author has tried to write something like a biography and a character-sketch of the Greek people. His theme is not what they did, but what they were; in particular, what were the habits of mind and way of life that made their civilization and culture what it was.

MEDIEVAL PEOPLE*

Eileen Power

A19

An illustrated history of the Middle Ages, presented through descriptions of the daily life of various ordinary people, chosen because they represent different aspects of social life. This is the second Pelican edition.

One shilling and sixpence   * *Two shillings*

THE PENGUIN POETS

*

THE PENGUIN BOOK OF
CONTEMPORARY VERSE (D12) *

Edited by Kenneth Allott

An anthology containing 127 poems by sixty-one modern poets from W. B. Yeats to Sidney Keyes.

THE CENTURIES' POETRY

Edited by D. Kilham Roberts

A comprehensive anthology in five volumes:

1 CHAUCER TO SHAKESPEARE (D6) – in preparation
2 DONNE TO DRYDEN (D7)
3 POPE TO KEATS (D8)
4 HOOD TO HARDY (D9)
5 BRIDGES TO THE PRESENT DAY (D10)

A BOOK OF ENGLISH POETRY (D5) *

Edited by G. B. Harrison

An anthology selected from the works of sixty-one English poets from Chaucer to Rossetti.

SELECTIONS FROM INDIVIDUAL POETS

WORDSWORTH (D2) – Edited by W. E. Williams
ROBERT BURNS (D3) – Edited by H. W. Meikle and
  W. Beattie
T. S. ELIOT (D4) – Selected by himself
D. H. LAWRENCE (D11) – Edited by W. E. Williams
JOHN DONNE (D13) – Edited by John Hayward
ALEXANDER POPE (D14) – Edited by Douglas Grant
C. DAY LEWIS (D17) – Selected by himself

Selections from the poetry of *John Milton, Edith Sitwell* and *Gerard Manley Hopkins* are in preparation

One shilling and sixpence each   ∗*Two shillings and sixpence*

THE PELICAN
HISTORY OF ENGLAND

*

While each volume is complete in itself, this whole series has been planned to provide an intelligent and consecutive guide to the development of English society in all its aspects. Of the eight volumes, four are already available:

TUDOR ENGLAND† – *S. T. Bindoff, Reader in Modern History at University College, London*

ENGLAND IN THE EIGHTEENTH CENTURY** – *Dr. J. H. Plumb, of Christ's College, Cambridge*

ENGLAND IN THE NINETEENTH CENTURY (1815–1914)* – *David Thomson, of Sidney Sussex College, Cambridge*

ENGLAND IN THE LATE MIDDLE AGES† – *A. R. Myers, Lecturer at Liverpool University*

**One shilling and sixpence*   ** *Two shillings*   † *Two shillings and sixpence*

The others, which will follow as soon as possible, are:

ROMAN BRITAIN – *Professor Ian Richmond, King's College, Newcastle-on-Tyne*

THE BEGINNINGS OF ENGLISH SOCIETY (from the Anglo-Saxon Invasion). – *Dorothy Whitelock, Fellow of St Hilda's College, Oxford*

ENGLISH SOCIETY IN THE EARLY MIDDLE AGES – *Doris Stenton, Lecturer at Reading University*

ENGLAND IN THE SEVENTEENTH CENTURY – *Maurice Ashley, M.A.*

THE PENGUIN CLASSICS

A LIBRARY OF NEW TRANSLATIONS

EDITED BY E. V. RIEU

*

VOLUMES NOW AVAILABLE

One shilling and sixpence except where otherwise stated